MW00649927

BRIDGES
OF
BATTLE

BRIDGES
OF
BATTLE

**Famous Battlefield Actions at
Bridges and River Crossings**

DONALD FEATHERSTONE

ARMS AND
ARMOUR

Arms and Armour
An Imprint of the Cassell Group
Wellington House, 125 Strand, London WC2R 0BB

First published 1998

British Library Cataloguing-in-Publication Data:
a catalogue record for this book is available from
the British Library

ISBN 1-85409-449-1

Distributed in the USA by Sterling Publishing Co. Inc.,
387 Park Avenue South, New York, NY 10016-8810.

Designed and edited by DAG Publications Ltd.
Designed by David Gibbons; layout by Anthony A. Evans;
edited by John Gilbert.

Printed and bound in Great Britain
by Creative Print and Design (Wales).

The author is grateful to
The Institution of Royal Engineers, Chatham, for
permission to quote from *The Military Engineer in India*
by Lieutenant-Colonel E. C. W. Sandes.

Jacket Illustration
The Bridge at Arnhem by David Shepherd.

Publisher's Note
For the sake of clarity, and the avoidance of
excessive numbers of inverted commas in the text,
quoted passages are distinguished by being set
in seriffed type like this...
in contrast to the author's narrative, which is
set in sans serif like this.

CONTENTS

INTRODUCTION

Throughout history, the physical features of the landscape have provided the setting for many wars and battles, and have often played an influential role in the course and outcome of the fighting. As stage plays are enlivened by their scenery and backcloth, battles, unrivalled for drama and spectacle, are acted out in natural arenas and amphitheatres, the backdrop formed by the landscape, the scenery by man-made buildings, roads and bridges. Because of the human propensity for violence, many of the best-known names in history, in this timeless tale of conflict, are those of sites that mark the scene of a notable victory, a significant defeat, or a famous last-stand.

Among such memorable encounters are those that have featured rivers and the bridges thrown across them to enable armies to get to grips with each other. One of the most famous early examples, in 508BC, was Horatius Cocles' heroic holding of the bridge over the Tiber against the invading Etruscans. Subsequent military history is milestoned by actions that bear the names of the places where they occurred or the rivers they spanned, given prominence by the clamour and carnage of war, immortalised by the courage of the men who fought and died there: Stamford Bridge, Stirling, Bothwell, Arcola and Lodi, Concord, the Coa and Sorauren, the Beresina, Antietam, Eben Emael, Arnhem, Remagen...

This book provides detailed descriptions, often first-hand, of major or minor battles fought on and around bridges, both in attack and defence. On countless occasions, the essential mobility of armies has been impeded by the bottleneck represented by a bridge. Defended or undefended, they create hindrance and delay to the progress or junction of advancing forces; and time is invariably an all-important element.

Commanders throughout history have worked out plans of campaign in the knowledge that rivers and bridges tend to confer an advantage on the smaller defending force. Yet defensive tactics alone are not enough. Military history has long taught that the passive defence of a river line, i.e. a bridge, never prevails against an enterprising enemy.

Since the beginnings of warfare, fording a river has been dependent either on gaining possession of an existing bridge or by extemporising a means of crossing the river, at some advantageous point, with whatever materials are to hand. To attack a bridge resolutely defended is usually a costly undertaking and it is only when surprise can be achieved and the defence momentarily paralysed, that the passage of a river can be gained in that way without great loss.

7

Having said that, the argument that the enforced relationship between attacker and defender is unvarying, and that battles for bridges are overwhelmingly similar in pattern, is refuted on every page of this book.

Donald Featherstone
Southampton, 1998

1. RIVERS AND BRIDGES

The defence of a position or area depends to a large extent on the shape and formation of the surrounding countryside. Physical features such as rivers offer defensive lines which have been turned to advantage by every great military commander of history. The measure of protection afforded by a river depends on its breadth and depth, the state of the bottom, the height and nature of its banks, the volume of water, the changes of course, the speed of its currents. It may be directly accessible or difficult to approach, perhaps lined by marshes or flanked by gorges.

A decisive factor in determining the defensive opportunities offered by a river is, of course, whether it is spanned by a bridge. Such a structure has to be considered in terms of width, length, position (proximity to villages or buildings) and construction (i.e. strong enough for the passage of cavalry, guns and, in later times, wheeled and tracked vehicles).

The tactical use of a river depends upon whether it runs parallel to the direction of the intended attack, or across it. In the former case, where it tends to follow a valley, a river may not confer great defensive strength. Lateral communication by road (and rail) will probably be good, enabling attacking forces to be moved quickly from one point to another to effect a crossing.

A river, as a barrier in defence, is most formidable when limited in extent and swelled by a considerable volume of water. Passage across an unfordable river requires the attacker to gain possession of a permanent bridge or build such a bridge – often under fire – at an advantageous point. To cross a bridge that is resolutely defended is usually a costly business, as proved in almost every historical example given in these pages.

Before airpower and airborne troops revolutionised the techniques of warfare, military operations on and around bridges tended to follow a similar pattern, allowances having to be made for the potency and capability of weapons – ranging from bows-and-arrows and arbalests to hand-held muskets and rifles, and artillery.

In attacking a bridge, artillery fire would be concentrated on the defenders' positions, and infantry advanced, where possible, under any available natural or man-made cover. Buildings in the vicinity would need to be taken before the attack could proceed. If the approach to the bridge was through fairly open country, the foremost attacking troops, on reaching the river, would take advantage of any cover or lie down and maintain as heavy fire as possible against the defenders. When supports arrived, or it was considered that sufficient men were available for the final assault, the attackers would close up and charge forward over the bridge, attempting to force a passage with the bayonet. If successful, the main body, now on the enemy's side of the river, would hold the entrance to the bridge, while newly arriving supports spread out and moved forward to eliminate the defenders. Finally, the entire force would advance to secure the objective and its approaches.

So much for the theory. Reality is provided by a contemporary writer on the attacking of bridges during the relief of Lucknow in 1857 (Illustrated London News, 1897):

The advance was sounded, and Outram placed himself at the head of the first, or Neill's brigade, while Havelock followed in front of the second. It was not many minutes before the fight began in deadly earnest. In spite of a tremendous fire from guns in front, and from houses and walls on either side, Neill's war-tried Fusiliers, stoutly aided by the men of the 64th and 84th Foot, by Maude's battery, and part of the 5th Fusiliers, ere long drove the enemy from a succession of gardens and walled enclosures which blocked the approach to the Chârbagh bridge.

As the column neared the bridge a halt was sounded by Havelock's orders. The bridge itself was defended on the Lucknow side by a battery of five guns, light and heavy, nearly hidden by a strong breastwork, on each side of which rose lofty houses held by a crowd of musketeers. For many long minutes the troops had to find what shelter they could from the hail of lead and iron that beat upon them, while Maude's guns kept up an answering fire upon the batteries in his front. Outram was struck by a bullet which pierced his arm; 'but he only smiled,' says Colonel Maude, 'and asked one of us to tie his handkerchief tightly above the wound'. Several times during the halt Maude 'turned to the calm, cool, grim general, and asked him to allow us to advance, as we could not possibly do any good by halting there. He agreed with me, but did not like to take the responsibility of ordering us to go on. At last Havelock sent the welcome order to advance.' At a word from Neill the Madras Fusiliers with a dozen or so of the 84th, covered by the fire from Maude's guns, rushed on with a cheer towards the bridge through a storm of grape-shot, and, before the enemy had time to reload, carried the breastwork, bayonetting the gunners and spiking the guns. At the same moment Outram emerged at the head of the 5th Fusiliers from the walled gardens which he had cleared of the foe. The 78th were left to hold the bridge with the adjacent houses until all the troops and baggage had passed.

Meanwhile the rest of the column marched quietly forward along the northern bank of the canal, hindered only by the dead weight of the heavy guns, which stuck fast at any part of the road where the mud lay

10

deepest. Avoiding the certain dangers of the direct road to the Residency, Havelock finally struck off from the canal into a road which led northwards past the Sikandrabagh towards the line of palaces about the Kaiser Bagh, or King's Garden. Here on that afternoon the crowning struggle of an eventful day began. A fire of grape and musketry, under which, as Havelock said, 'nothing could live', mowed down scores of brave men as they rushed across a narrow bridge that led to the shelter of some deserted buildings near the Chatar Manzil and the palace of Farid Baksh.

Defending a bridge, as the scene at Lucknow proves, might also prove a fierce business, although the defenders could disperse and bring concentrated fire to bear on the head of an attacking force as it narrowed to crowd over the causeway and outlet.

If the bridge connected portions of a village, buildings and walls on the side of the river approached by the enemy would be occupied, both as a defence and to prevent the attackers obtaining cover as they advanced. If a defending force was not large enough to be distributed on the near side, it would try to level all cover on that bank before withdrawing to the far side. The main consideration when defending a bridge was to concentrate as much fire as possible, both artillery and musketry, upon the actual bridge and the ground in front of it.

In the event of a retreat having to be conducted over a bridge, the main body would aim to cross and take up a position on the far side, throwing out a fighting line along the river bank on both sides of the bridge. The rear-party, who meanwhile had been holding the opening to the bridge, would gradually give way, run quickly across and take up position behind the main body to form a new firing-line to hold back the advancing enemy.

All very well at a time when ground forces alone were locked in combat. Leaping through time, this principle was rendered impossible on 11 May 1940, when German glider-borne and parachute troops took out nearby Fort Eben Emael by storm, preventing its guns from commanding the adjacent bridge across the Albert Canal, over which the Germans were allowed to pour unchecked.

TACTICS OF DEFENCE AND OFFENCE

Late Victorian military writers evidently competed in putting pen to paper on the subject of tactics. Thus, modern military historians have at their disposal the following books by qualified writers, all offering varied accounts and advice on tactics in warfare since the beginnings of history.

Lieutenant-Colonel L. C. Clery was Professor of Tactics at the Royal Military College, Sandhurst, and the lectures he delivered to offcers training at the college were collected in his book, Minor Tactics, first published in 1874 (revised fifth edition 1880).

Clery's Minor Tactics was followed in 1882 by the publication of General Sir Edward Hamley's The Operations of War. This became the definitive textbook not only for the British army and was also widely circulated in the United States, France, Germany and other European countries. And the following year saw the appearance of A Summary of Tactics by H. F. Morgan, modestly claiming to be 'Late Captain 28th Regiment'.

Stressing the importance of rivers and their bridges in warfare through the ages, each of these books considers those aspects exhaustively, providing descriptions of real-life occasions when they sometimes played passing parts, but often major roles upon which the outcome of the battle depended. Consequently, this book has gained a deep insight on its subject from these sometimes lengthy verbatim quotations, taken from the three books named, and no apologies are asked for their frequent inclusion.

On the highly relevant subjects of rivers and bridges, all three books provide exhaustive information on their role in warfare since the beginning of military history, and this chapter considers their findings.

Throughout the tortuous course of military history soldiers have been trained, or learned from hard experience how to tackle bridges, how to defend, attack and, if need be, retreat over them. Lieutenant-Colonel Clery lectured and wrote as follows on the subject of defending bridges:

The most advantageous position for the defence of a bridge is usually in rear of it. Circumstances, as before mentioned, may require it to be defended from the enemy's side, but the attendant disadvantages of such a position have been stated. Sometimes a part of a force is pushed forward beyond the bridge when buildings or other cover exists that offers special advantages for retarding the enemy. The danger of holding this advanced position is that, if forced, the defenders may have some difficulty in withdrawing across the bridge, or may be followed so closely by the enemy that the latter may gain the passage. This occurred at Ebersburg, in 1809, where an Austrian detachment, occupying some houses beyond the bridge, prolonged the defence until the French, forcing them, pressed so closely in pursuit over the bridge that its destruction, prepared beforehand, was prevented and the passage seized. Yet if the bridge connects parts of a town or village, the houses on the further side may be so advantageously occupied, both to delay the enemy and deprive him of a good offensive position against the defenders, that they cannot be disregarded. But in this case care should be taken to provide for the withdrawal of the troops so posted, without compromising the further defence of the bridge. At Wavre the Prussians at first held the houses on the enemy's side, but, driven from these, the defence was so vigorously continued from the near bank that all the French efforts to carry the passage failed. Should the force be small, it had better be concentrated from the outset in a position in rear of the bridge, and the further bank abandoned. Thus, in the defence of Tauber Bischofsheim, in 1866, the Prussians at first did not attempt to defend the houses beyond the bridge, from the smallness of the force at hand, but when sufficiently reinforced they pushed forward troops, to occupy them.

The character of the ground on both banks materially influences the manner of the defence. Bridges are usually associated with a village or town, where the river either borders its outskirts or divides it into parts. A bridge in the centre of a village rests its defence so much on the houses adjoining, that it becomes one of the phases in the defence of the village, and there is little choice about positions. When the river skirts the village and the latter is on the defender's bank, then the defence will still be organised close to the bridge and river bank, every use being made of the adjoining buildings. But when the village is entirely on the enemy's side, and the ground on the near bank comparatively open, the position of the defenders must be removed to some distance from the bridge, else they will suffer heavily from the enemy, while he remains under cover. Similarly, if no houses exist in the vicinity, and should the country on the further bank be undulating, wooded, or otherwise afford cover, the defence must be retired from the bridge, and it is only when the country is very open beyond that the defence will be organised near it. The course of the river itself will sometimes considerably affect the facilities for defence. When bending towards the enemy on both sides of the bridge, it offers greatest advantages to the defenders. The efforts of the defence would be directed to sweeping with fire all the approaches, and then concentrating this fire on the bridge itself. When a close defence is attempted, this fire is maintained by both infantry and artillery, the former lining the bank and occupying the houses if there are any. At the action of Wavre, the bridge over the Dyle, near the village of Bierge, was defended by two companies lining the banks and occupying a mill on the defender's side, supported by a battalion, with a battery in action on the slope in rear. This combined fire swept the approaches with such effect that repeated attempts of the French, led by Gérard and Grouchy in person, failed to force the passage.

When a position has to be taken up at some distance, the fire will be more particularly directed to preventing the enemy from debouching from the bridge. Artillery fire will aid powerfully in achieving this. At the action of Tauber Bischofsheim, in 1866, the Austrians concentrated a heavy artillery fire on the bridge at a distance of 1,200 yards, and made the passage so impossible while it lasted that part of the Prussian infantry, who had gained a footing on the further bank, could only have their ammunition replenished by its being carried through the river which was with difficulty fordable. An artillery fire that sweeps the approaches or commands the outlet is an indispensable requisite to a vigorous defence.

A position of this kind retired to some distance requires the force employed to be considerable. Its general disposition will be similar to that for a mountain defile. Should the force be small a distant position would be unsuitable from its general weakness, and in such a case a close defence must be undertaken.

Writing a decade later, former Captain H. F. Morgan was more succinct but equally to the point:

If the defenders can select their position for defence, they would choose the side farthest from the enemy. A position of this description in rear of a bridge has the same advantages as those in the defence of the outlet from the defile, and which have already been detailed. A great deal, however, will depend on the nature of the surrounding country. If the bridge connects portions of a village, the houses and fences on the side nearest the enemy should be occupied, not only as a defence, but to prevent the attacking force from obtaining cover from them. When the defending force is not strong enough to be distributed on the near side, all cover that can be secured by the attackers should be levelled. Again, if the bridge is in the rear of a village, the defence must be organised on the enemy's side. The main consideration in the defence of the bridge itself is to concentrate as much fire as possible (both of artillery and infantry) upon it and the ground in its front. This can be better effected when the river bends towards the enemy on both sides of the bridge.

Captain Morgan also brought an optimistic air of simplicity to the procedure for attacking a bridge:

In attacking a bridge, the artillery fire should be concentrated on the defenders' position, and the infantry advance (as much as possible) under cover in extended order. If any detached houses are occupied for the defence, they can either be attacked or passed by, leaving a detachment to hold the defenders in check. If, however, many buildings are defended on the near side, they must be taken before any attack can be made on the bridge. In a fairly open country, the fighting line, on reaching the river, will lie down (taking advantage of any cover), and keep up a rapid fire on the enemy. The supports, on nearing the bridge, close on the supports opposite to it, and, assisted by the main body, charge and force the passage with the bayonet. This gained, and the main body having crossed the bridge, the supports extend from the centre, leaving the main body to hold the outlet of the bridge until the fire of the old fight-

14

ing line is clouded by the new skirmishers. Then the new supports will be furnished by the main body, and the old fighting line form up in rear of the main body.

In the continuation of his lecture on 'Defence of Bridges', Colonel Clery, too, considered offensive tactics:

The attack of a bridge, defended in this manner by modern fire-arms, would appear to be an undertaking very difficult of success. And considering the heavy loss always incurred, even with the old weapons, and the frequent failures encountered, the enterprise must be regarded as of the most formidable. Hitherto the principle of attack has been first to subdue more or less the fire of the defenders by artillery and light troops and then to assault the bridge itself with a strong column of infantry formed on a front equal to the width of the passage. The assaulting column was advanced as much as possible under cover, yet even this did not save it from very heavy loss. Yet it cannot be hoped that the enemy will renounce the defence without an engagement at close quarters, but the fire of the attacking force must have effectually reduced that opposed to it before an assault can be attempted with much hope of success. It is now, therefore, more than ever necessary to subdue the enemy's fire before the bridge can be attacked by infantry. When the ground is open on the assailant's side this work will mainly fall on the artillery. When cover admits of the approach of infantry it will be pushed forward to line the banks or occupy any shelter afforded, and co-operate by its fire with the artillery. The assailants have the advantage that, unless the ground be very unfavourable, they should be able to concentrate a superior artillery fire against that immediately defending the bridge. And should this fire prevail, the strong arm of the defence is thereby paralysed. Yet disadvantages of position will often occur to neutralise superiority of armament. At Ebersburg, Masséna's artillery had little effect against the Austrian guns, from the relatively commanding position of the latter.

The assault, once entered on, should be prosecuted with the utmost resolution and rapidity. Hesitation or half measures are likely to entail quite as much loss as a vigorous onslaught, with the almost foregone certainty of failure. Should the assault be successful it must be rapidly supported, and the energetic action of all three arms will usually be required to prevent the enemy's reserves from overwhelming the leading troops and throwing them back again into the defile.

Writing some forty years later, at a time when the world was engaged in a mammoth conflict doubtless far beyond the wildest conceptions of Colonel Clery or Captain Morgan, Canadian officer Lieutenant-Colonel D. P. Pap-

15

ineau submitted his Notes on Training (1915). With hindsight, his teachings might be seen as reflecting reasons for the appalling casualty lists of that stage of World War One:

1. Advancing. The fighting line, on reaching the margin of the river or the beginning on the defile, will (when the flanks cannot be gained) lie down and cover themselves, keeping up a brisk fire upon the enemy. The supports, on approaching the bridge (or defile), will close upon that part of a support which may be opposite to it, and, supported by the main body, charge and force the passage with the bayonet; this point gained, and the main body having crossed the bridge, the supports will gradually extend from their centre, the main body maintaining possession of the bridge, the old fighting line will keep up their fire until masked in succession by the new line; when the new line has completed its extension the main body will send out fresh supports, and the old fighting line will assemble in rear of the main body. The whole will then move forward according to the original formation.

Colonel Papineau's textbook likewise gives advice on retiring over a bridge, which is also considered by Captain Morgan, although Colonel Clery scorns even to mention the subject! Here is the Canadian officer's view:

2. Retiring. In retiring, the main body will first pass, and take post at the bridgehead, or the outlet of the defile, immediately detaching parties to both flanks to line the river, in extended order. The supports will close upon each other opposite the bridge, and, in compact order, halt in front of it until the fighting line is withdrawn; in order that this may be effected without unnecessary delay, the fighting line should incline towards the bridge when at some distance from it, they should run briskly over it, and form in rear of the main body. The supports will then cross, and in like manner joining the main body, the whole will be prepared to defend the bridge or to retire, as may be ordered. The new fighting line will recommence firing as soon as its front is clear; and if the retreat is to be continued, supports will be again thrown out between them and the main body.

And here, bearing certain similarities, is the earlier advice of Captain Morgan:

In retiring over a bridge, the main body first crosses, and takes up a position on the other side, throwing out a fighting line on both sides along the river bank. The supports close on each other, and hold the opening of the bridge until the fighting line have safely crossed. This they (the fighting line) do by gradually inclining towards the bridge,

16

and, when near it, running quickly over, forming up in rear of the main body. The supports then cross, and take up a position in rear. The new fighting line opens fire as soon as its front is clear.

From a later age, and dealing with a somewhat different problem, is this passage from Guerrilla Warfare, a small book published in 1941. The author, 'Yank' Levy, was a colourful character who learned his 'trade' in the Spanish Civil War (1936–9) and who seems to have believed that bridges were simply for blowing up!

Whenever there are bridges or culverts which cross rivers or streams, you have an excellent opportunity of doing some long-distance exploding. The water, of course, must have a fairly good current. Find some good cover about one hundred yards from the bridge. Float a piece of wood down stream from there, timing the period it takes to reach the bridge. Then make a tiny raft, and float that down, timing it too. Then you can make another raft on which you will place some sticks of dynamite or gelignite, together with a few pounds of blasting or lifting powder, with a time fuse coiled inside a can. As you have timed the current – the length of time it takes to float your raft down to the bridge – you can cut your fuse to match, so that, when the raft passes under the bridge, up she goes. This is only effective when the bridge under-surface is near the water.

RIVERS

Clery now considers the question of river crossings in a wider context, with particular emphasis on the Napoleonic campaigns:

A riverline, as a barrier in defence, is only formidable when its extent is limited and the volume of its water considerable.

   To deny the passage of a river to an enemy he must be opposed in force wherever he presents himself. If the river line be long, great latitude is allowed him in selecting his point for crossing. And if he is enabled, as he usually will be, to conceal this point until the eve of the operation, his opponent may not then be in a position to impede it. For to resist successfully, the defender must be in force at, or within reach of, the point selected; and strength at one point necessarily entails, where the front is extended, weakness at some other. If, therefore, the defender concentrates at certain points, others must be left unguarded, and if he disseminates his force along the whole line he becomes weak everywhere. In the first case the assailant has only to surprise a point weakly held; to effect his purpose in the second he should succeed wherever he presents himself.

But considerations both strategical and tactical fix on certain localities in every river line as those most vulnerable to the side holding it. These the defender should be able to discern, and by them his dispositions should be regulated. To distinguish them it is only necessary to reverse the situation, as those most suitable for forcing the passage are clearly those most menacing to the defence.

The success of the defence mainly depends on preventing the enemy from gaining a footing with even a portion of his force on the defender's bank. For under cover of this party the remainder will cross in comparative security, and usually in much less time, from the opportunity afforded them of constructing a bridge. But if this first party be successfully opposed the attempt is for the time defeated, and its renewal later on at the same point should not succeed. For the defenders will have had time to be reinforced, whereas the assailants cannot return in greater strength, as it is not to be supposed that they would have previously neglected to use all the means for crossing at their disposal; and to be able to construct a bridge under the enemy's fire from the opposite bank cannot be calculated on as a probability. This was very cleverly proved in the Archduke Charles's attempt to force the passage of the Aar in his campaign in Switzerland (early 19th century).

It follows, therefore, that to oppose the crossing it is as a rule necessary to prevent the enemy from establishing a covering party on the defender's bank; also, that in achieving this the attempt is thereby more than half defeated.

But the numbers of the first party the assailant can send across can never be great, as the means of transport in the locality will usually be limited, and the assembling of an unusual amount would alarm the enemy and so defeat the project. Hence it is not always necessary for success that the defender's main body should be present where the passage is attempted. For a force equal to any the enemy has the means of sending across at one time should defeat his effort at landing, or at least of permanently establishing himself on that bank.

But the enemy once committed to such an enterprise will make strenuous efforts to support the party first sent across, and the position of that party would, if defeated, become so desperate that its own efforts in defence will usually be very resolute. Thus in the secondary passage of the Linth in 1799 some 600 French thrown over to the further bank were suddenly isolated by the breaking of the bridge of Grynau. They were attacked by three Russian battalions but so vigorous was their defence, aided by the fire of troops from the opposite bank, that they defeated the enemy with great loss.

It will be necessary therefore for the defenders to be prepared to deal not only with the first force the enemy passes over, but with the reinforcements he will use every effort to make speedily follow. For this purpose, in addition to holding the points likely to be assailed with a force able to make head against that the enemy first sends across, it will be necessary to concentrate within reach at some central position in rear, a force adequate to securing whatever point is attacked. For on the defender's power to assemble at this point in greater numbers than the enemy, depends his ability to defeat the crossing. In the defence of the Linth in 1799 Hotze broke up his corps into posts along the length of the river, and kept only two battalions concentrated at Kaltenbrun. Soult, crossing at Bilten, seized with his first troops the village of Schoenis. Hotze moved up at once with his two battalions, and after some very obstinate fighting drove the French out of the village. But in the meantime the boats had recrossed and landed strong reinforcements to the French, while Hotze's reinforcements came in slowly and by driblets from the neighbouring posts. The French now attacked the Austrians in superior numbers, completely defeated them, and secured the passage.

The general principle of defence may therefore be said to lie in watching the river throughout its length with advanced posts, guarding in force certain points most suitable for a passage, and concentrating, in one or more central positions in rear, the main body. If a division (two brigades) of 10,000 men be required to hold a river line of ten miles, and if the brigades be posted five miles apart, and happen to be about equidistant from the centre, then 10,000 men can be collected on the centre within an hour, 5,000 at any point of the line within an hour, and the latter can be reinforced with the remaining 5,000 within two hours.

The breadth of the river, inasmuch as it affects the time taken in throwing a bridge and the number of bridges the enemy has the means of simultaneously constructing, will materially influence the defender's power of assembling his force sufficiently rapidly to dispute the passage. Napoleon's two passages of the Danube in 1809 form an instructive contrast on this head. In the first he possessed but a single bridge, and commenced crossing from the island of Lobau on the evening of the 20th. He began the battle of Essling the following day with 23,000 men, increased during the afternoon up to 30,000. By the following morning (22nd) 60,000 men in all had crossed. In his second crossing his preparations were so elaborated that he was able to construct simultaneously four bridges from Lobau to the left bank, each calculated to be completed within two hours, while one bridge made in a single piece was fixed in twenty minutes. The first covering party was embarked at 9 o'clock at night, and by daybreak the following morning 70,000 men were drawn up in line of battle on the opposite bank. But such extensive preparations as these are usually impossible, both from the time they require and the warning they give the enemy.

19

It will sometimes happen that the defence of a river line is not made to rest on denying the passage to the enemy. For circumstances may render it more conducive to defeating its projects that the passage itself be surrendered or but feebly disputed, and a position for defence be taken up at some distance. This might occur where the points easy of passage were too numerous to guard, and a strong-position existed on the defender's bank which the enemy after crossing dare not pass by. Such was Kaunitz's position behind the Sambre in 1794, from which he defeated three attempts in succession of the French to pass the river. A similar position was Lee's at Fredericksburg, in 1862, defending the line of the Rappahannock against Hooker.

The following is from E. B. Hamley's Operations of War:

In 1862, Burnside threw the Federal army on the right bank of the Rappahannock, at Fredericksburg, almost without opposition, covered by his powerful artillery. Lee observed the passage from his position on the opposite heights, and received the Federals, when they advanced to attack him, with so destructive a fire that they were driven in rout over the river.

Clery now continues:

Such a course might be pursued too, when the point chosen by the enemy had too many disadvantages for defence. This was the case with Bertrand at Wartemburg in 1813, in holding the passage of the Elbe against Blücher. Or it may happen that the enemy, after crossing, was confined to a single line of advance on which some strong position for defence lay to bar his progress. Such was the position of Feldkirch, closing the road from Chur to Landeck and Bregenz, in which an inferior force of Austrians completely paralysed Masséna after his passage of the Upper Rhine in 1799. Notwithstanding the seeming advantages such an obstacle should afford, military history teaches us that the passive defence of a river line never prevails against an enterprising enemy. The latter, screened in all his movements and preparations, ends by eluding the vigilance of his opponent, and, presenting himself at some point but weakly guarded, throws his force across and fixes himself on the other bank before a sufficient force can be assembled to overwhelm him. The most that can be hoped in a passive system of defence is to delay the crossing and sometimes to make it very costly.

An active defence is that which promises most chance of success. When the defenders hold a bridgehead or other fortified post on the river, the power it gives them of issuing to attack the enemy while

20

engaged in the passage, or to cut off its communications should he effect it, makes such a position very menacing. Of this kind was Bellegarde's position on the Mincio in 1800. He held the bridgehead of Borghetto, and had his main body massed in rear about Villafranca. Brune, to force the river, allowed two of his divisions to become entangled in an attempt at crossing at Pozzolo below Bellegarde's left, while the two others and the reserve were drawn towards Monzambano on his right. Issuing from Borghetto, Bellegarde might have concentrated the mass of his force between the two fractions of the enemy, with a choice of acting against either; and he appears to have been justly censured for allowing such a favourable opportunity to escape him.

Forcing the passage of an unfordable river is effected either by gaining possession of one of its permanent bridges, or extemporising a means of crossing at some advantageous point.

To attack a bridge resolutely defended is usually a costly undertaking, as proved at Lodi, Ebersburg, Landshut; and always of doubtful success, as at Arcola, Wavre, the Coa. It is only when it can be surprised and the defence thereby for the moment paralysed, that the passage of a river can be gained in that way without great loss. Masséna forced the Adige in 1805 by a well-organised *coup de main* on the bridge of Verona, and in a similar way the French forced the Zamega in 1809 at the bridge of Amarante. In both cases the loss was inconsiderable.

To construct a temporary bridge when the enemy is at hand to oppose it, the conditions must be unusually favourable to the assailants, and when he holds the opposite bank and can disturb the operation by his fire, the attempt can rarely, and should never, succeed. Instances will occur where a broken bridge may be made passable even under the fire of the enemy, as was the bridge over the Danube at Elchingen by Ney, and that over the Saal below Kissingen in 1866 by the Prussians; but these instances can only be quoted as exceptional. Napoleon's efforts to repair the broken arch of the bridge at Borghetto over the Mincio, in 1796, were rendered fruitless by the fire of the enemy until a party of French, fording the river, chased the former from the opposite bank.

The usual mode of throwing a force across a river the enemy undertakes to defend is to extemporise a means of passing at some point that has been left comparatively unguarded. The intention to cross at this point must be concealed to the last, and then the enemy must be alarmed along the whole length of his line by feints of passing at other points. In the meantime the main body has been secretly concentrated at the true point of crossing, and the whole passed over to the further bank before the enemy can assemble an equivalent force to oppose it. This is in effect to surprise the passage.

21

The actual crossing is effected either by a fixed bridge, a flying bridge, or by boats. Rapidity in accumulating troops of all arms on the opposite bank being one of the essentials to success, it is always sought to construct as quickly as may be a bridge by which cavalry and artillery can pass. But means for this are not always at hand. Boats, when possible supplemented by a flying bridge, must then do the work. In Soult's passage of the Linth, in 1799, all the means for crossing at his disposal consisted of eight boats; with six of these he carried over his infantry, and of the two largest he made a flying bridge. But this mode of crossing is dangerous through delay, for delay in such operations too often means failure.

The locality for crossing we have seen to be dependent on the enemy's dispositions for defence, but strategical considerations often further influence its selection. For the advantages to be derived from forcing the passage may vary according as it is effected on the enemy's centre, or on one flank rather than another. And this may determine the adoption of a point that, as regards local advantages, would not be the most favourable. So materially may such considerations weigh, that the certainty of success at one point may be surrendered, and the risk of failure at another accepted, from the results it is hoped to achieve in case of success. Thus in forcing the passage of the Mincio, in 1800, Brune determined to pass his main body at Monzambano, on the Austrian right. The enemy's attention was to be attracted by a secondary passage at the same time at Molina di Volta, on the left. The principal passage was at the last moment deferred for twenty-four hours through incompleteness of the preparations. The secondary passage in the meantime succeeded, two bridges were constructed, and two-fifths of the whole force established on the other bank. Yet so strongly did Brune hold to passing his main body on the enemy's right flank that he withdrew during the night half the force that had passed at Molina, and commenced anew the work of crossing at Monzambano the following morning. Similarly, in Moreau's passage of the Rhine in 1800, Napoleon strongly urged that the whole force should be thrown over where eventually only one division crossed; but Moreau's cautious disposition made him forego the advantages for which Napoleon would have gladly accepted the risk.

The locality being fixed, tactical considerations alone determine the actual point of crossing. When a bend of the river indents the assailant's bank, a convergent artillery fire may be brought to bear on the other. Of such account is a fire of this kind in protecting the crossing, that this configuration of ground is carefully sought for. The assailant's bank should command the other, and both should be favourable for embarking and disembarking. The approaches to the river side should be sufficiently open to allow of guns and carriages moving freely, and sound enough to bear them. In the French passage of the Rhine at Reichlingen, in 1800, it was found on cutting a ramp when the bridge was completed, that the ground on the other bank, which appeared of sound turf, was in fact so marshy that guns or carriages could not be moved over it. In the passage of the Linth a similar impediment obliged planks to be laid down for about 600 yards to get the boats to the river side, and the noise made by the carriages in moving over them prematurely alarmed the enemy.

A tributary stream whose confluence is close by, affords material assistance. In it the boats and other appliances can be collected in concealment, and floated down to the main river with little labour when required. In Moreau's passage of the Rhine, in 1796, a canal connecting that river with the Ill enabled all the materials to be collected secretly at Strasbourg. This canal being unserviceable the following year when the French were again engaged in forcing the passage, the same point was no longer suitable for crossing. The stream of Schwachat concealed Napoleon's preparations for the first bridge at Ebersdorf, and the different canals in the island of Lobau rendered him similar important service in his second passage of the Danube.

Wooded islands, where the river is wide, also aid in the work of crossing. They break the length of the bridge, and thereby give it more stability. The labour of construction is shortened by allowing of the first part to be commenced at both ends at once. An advanced point is gained, whence a closer fire can be brought against the defenders; and an island often serves to shelter the preparations for throwing the bridge. The islands of the Danube did much to facilitate its passage by Napoleon in 1809, as did those of the Rhine the passage of Moreau in 1796 and 1797.

On the further bank it is of extreme importance that some point should exist that would form a support to the first troops sent across. For on their power to maintain themselves against the enemy's attacks will depend the construction of the bridge, and therefore the success of the undertaking. A small wood, a village, a house, or an embankment afford valuable aid in this way. No position should exist from which the enemy's guns could, under cover, play on the bridge, for their effect would be to rapidly destroy the pontoons. Finally, the ground in the neighbourhood should admit of free space for the remainder of the force to form for action, according as it crosses. But it will seldom happen that all these favourable conditions are found united. It may even be necessary to select a point where some of the most essential are conspicuously absent, and being therefore considered safe, has been left unguarded by the enemy. Such was the point of Reichlingen, where Moreau's right crossed the Rhine in 1800.

When it is determined to pass a river, the near bank should be cleared of all the enemy's advanced posts. For it is now assumed that his main body is already on the further bank. Should he hold a bridgehead on the near side of the river, this point must be observed in sufficient force to prevent his issuing to attack the troops engaged in the passage.

Everything necessary for the actual crossing should be carefully and secretly prepared beforehand, so that nothing may be wanting when the moment arrives to delay the work. Faulty materials, which time did not admit of improving, contributed to the destruction on Napoleon's first bridge over the Danube, in 1809, and faulty preparations entailed the failure of the Archduke Charles's fine combination in the passage of the Aar.

The conveyance to the point of crossing of the materials required should be provided for with great care, and the operation itself accurately timed. For as everything tending to reveal the intended movement should be guarded against, all appliances to be used should be kept to the last moment out of sight. The locality of the passage should be carefully reconnoitred, and the bed of the river itself, when possible, sounded. The minutest details cannot be disregarded, for the success of the operation will, as a rule, depend on its being entered on with all the suddenness, and executed with all the rapidity, of a surprise.

The troops to be employed will be secretly collected close at hand, but their assembly should be deferred as long as possible to avoid arousing the suspicions of the enemy. Accurately timing such operations, if the force be large, is however a work of great delicacy, and its execution subject to all kinds of accidents. Yet a hitch in any part is apt to react fatally on the whole, as simultaneous co-operation being essential, partial action will prematurely disclose what is intended. Notwithstanding extreme efforts at precision in conveying orders for the French passage of the Mincio, in 1800; an error in calculating distance, coupled with the bad state of the roads, so delayed the arrival of the troops that the crossing had at the last moment to be deferred for twenty-four hours. On the other hand, the movements of the Austrian troops for the passage of the Aar, in 1799, were so well timed that the Archduke collected 50,000 men close to the point of passage, without the enemy on the opposite bank having the least suspicion of their presence.

The crossing must be protected by as strong a force of artillery as can be got into position, to clear the enemy's bank of troops occupying it, and silence any artillery with which he could trouble the construction of the bridge. The positions for the guns will be previously chosen, but they will not be occupied until immediately preceding the crossing.

It has been said that a covering party should be established on the opposite bank, before the construction of the bridge is attempted. This precaution is indispensable, and should never be omitted. The guns in position will do much to drive off the enemy where the country is open, but where even slight cover exists, good infantry will hold their ground against artillery alone, and when their fire would command the bridge, it becomes impossible to construct it. The strength of the covering party will depend on that of the enemy's posts on the spot, and on his power of rapidly assembling reinforcements. For this party should be able not only to drive off the troops first met with, but also to make head, until reinforced, against any further force the enemy may be able to gather. Thus in Masséna's passage of the Limat, it was known that some 2,500 of the enemy were encamped near the point of crossing. So great exertions were made to procure boats of the country from a distance, to enable the French to pass 600 men at once, as to attempt it with fewer numbers would probably lead to failure. In his second passage of the Danube the Emperor's preparations secured the passage at once of 1,500 men to cover the construction of each bridge.

But it sometimes happens that conveyance for a covering party cannot be obtained. To remedy this, a body of infantry trained as swimmers have often been used with great success.

Moreau, held in check by Kray on the Danube in 1800, determined to force a passage below Ulm. But he had neither pontoon equipage nor boats, and all the permanent bridges had been broken by the enemy. It was ascertained that those at Blindheim and Gremheim were easiest to repair, so having collected all the materials necessary for restoring them, Lecourbe made a false attack on Dillingen to attract the enemy to that point.

On the following morning he drove off the posts on the opposite bank with his guns, and 80 men swam across at Blindheim, two small boats carrying their clothes and arms. They immediately overpowered the enemy's post and took two guns. Some gunners at once crossed on ladders laid between standing pillars of the bridge, and worked the guns against the enemy. The bridge was rapidly made temporarily passable, and, more infantry crossing, the passage was secured. In a similar way the passage of the Douro at Tordesillas was seized by the French in 1812, and Wellington's position on the river completely turned. Soult's covering party in the passage of the Linth was composed of a body of 150 trained swimmers. After driving in the enemy's posts, the covering party should seek to strengthen itself against a counter attack. Some natural feature may exist to aid it, such as the small wood covering the French passage of the Danube near Essling, or the embankment that saved Dupont at Molina di Volta on the Mincio. For in most cases it must expect to be vigorously attacked before the bridge can be established. To hold its ground until sufficiently reinforced to attempt an attack itself is the first duty of a covering party. It should never be tempted into premature efforts to dislodge the enemy from a position he has taken up in the neighbourhood until sufficient troops have passed over to render the passage of the remainder secure. In Napoleon's attempt to surprise the passage of the Danube at Nussdorf in 1809, the covering party successfully gained a footing in the Schwartze Laken. But advancing in pursuit of the enemy's picquets instead of protecting the crossing of reinforcements, it was over-whelmed before it could be supported, and the passage of the river lost. Similarly, on the Narew, in 1806, the secondary crossing at Modlin was lost through the covering party pursuing the enemy's posts instead of establishing itself in the village it was in possession of.

While the bridge is being constructed the boats should continue to carry infantry across, and as soon as it is completed some cavalry and guns would be at once moved over to their support. The ground on the other bank will alone determine in what proportion either arm would be of use, but the combined action of the three will generally be required to deal with the force the enemy will have assembled. At the passage of the Rhine at Reichlingen the covering party was a good deal harassed by the enemy's cavalry, until the completion of the bridge enabled some squadrons to cross. The timely arrival of two squadrons who had filed one by one over the partly restored bridge at Blindheim decided a very obstinate engagement in favour of the French.

It has been said that while the real passage is being conducted, the enemy's attention should be attracted to other points of the river. This will usually be effected by secondary crossings simultaneously under-taken at some distance from the main one. This distance must not be too great, else the enemy may afford to neglect them; and it must not be too small, else they will not achieve their object of attracting him far enough from the main point. The points must be chosen with care, and the attempt made with an appearance of force, to give it as much as possible an air of probability; otherwise the enemy will see through the ruse and be warned to look for danger elsewhere rather than deceived into supposing it at hand. A secondary crossing may be either confined to a feint or converted into an actual passage, as the force the enemy is met in, and the general situation determine. Masséna, defeated in his attempt to force the passage of the Upper Rhine at Flasch, left a part of his force to maintain a false attack at that point, and rapidly moved the remainder down the river to Azmoos, where a secondary crossing had been in the meantime effected.

The principal and secondary crossings should be closely combined, if not actually simultaneous. For a delay in one may enable the enemy to concentrate against the other and overwhelm it. When Brune in forcing the passage of the Mincio allowed the secondary crossing at Pozzolo to precede by twenty-four hours the principal one, he exposed it to the weight of an attack by the whole Austrian army, in which Dupont's division suffered heavy loss to little purpose and barely escaped a disaster. A good instance of a skilful commander being completely deceived by a secondary crossing was that of the Archduke Charles on the Adige in 1805, when that river was forced by Masséna. The Archduke had his main body at St Gregorio, his right at Verona, his left at Legnano. Masséna concentrated his army about Zevio, opposite the Archduke's centre. He determined to force the bridge at Verona, and at the same time make a feint at Bocca-Civetta. The latter penetrated to Cologna and alarmed the Archduke's camp. Supposing the true point of crossing to be on this side, and the attack on Verona a feint, the Archduke slightly reinforced the latter and moved his main body against the former. Before he discovered his error Masséna had carried the bridge of Verona, defeated his right wing, and secured the passage.

Secondary crossings are sometimes made with a view to more rapidly throwing the whole force across, or to aid the principal one by moving down the opposite bank. MacMahon's passage of the Ticino at Turbigo was a movement of this kind made to favour the main passage at San Martino. But such detachments must be made in sufficient force lest they be intercepted and themselves overwhelmed. Lecourbe's passage of the Rhine at Reichlingen was accompanied by a secondary one at Paradis. But the latter was only composed of two battalions and four guns. Having gained the other bank, it was attacked by three regiments of infantry and two of cavalry, and nothing but the sudden arrival of a detachment from the main body, which had in the meantime crossed, saved it from destruction. Attempting to pass by a number of points should be avoided, unless they are so close that the different columns could afford each other mutual support.

The ensuing passages come from Hamley's book:

A river offers as an obstacle conditions peculiar to itself. The defenders can deploy, so as to bring an overwhelming convergent fire, both of small-arms and artillery, to bear on the columns crossing the bridge, and these, as they successively pass the obstacle, must still deploy under fire. The detachments of the defensive army along the course of the stream will generally have good communications with each other; for as the banks of a river, especially one that is navigable, are generally fertile and populous, good roads often follow its course on both banks. Hence the defenders need not, as in mountain passes, fear the unexpected appearance of an enemy on their flanks or rear.

On the other hand, as it is easier to throw bridges in a rich populous territory than to make roads over rugged and desolate mountains, the good passages over all but the largest rivers will generally be far more numerous than over a corresponding extent of mountain-range. Thus, there are six passages on practicable roads over the Ticino in 36 miles, from Turbigo to Pavia; while in the whole extent of the western face of the Italian Alps there is but one good road (fit to supply such an army as that of Napoleon III in 1859), that of the Mont Cenis. And the more numerous the practicable avenues, the greater the difficulties of the defence; for either some must be left unguarded, or the army must be spread on an extended front.

When an army approaches a river defended by the enemy, its first object will be to drive all the hostile troops then in its front to the further side, and to extend a cordon of posts and vedettes along the stream within the limits of possible operations. For, having possession of one bank, it can manoeuvre unknown to the enemy; and as the enemy's movements will also be screened, it will be better (instead of forming a theory of his doings, which will very likely be false) to follow a sound plan – that is, one which will enable the army to cross with least risk, and at the same time with the most effective strategical result, whether by turning the flank or breaking the front of the defensive line. There are two features of the case of special significance – namely, that a river is generally winding, and that the higher bank is sometimes on one side, sometimes on the other. The object of an assailant will be to pass part of his troops at some point where he possesses the commanding bank, for he can thus, with comparative impunity, drive the defenders from the other shore, and bring his forces, and materials for passing, undiscovered to the spot. And if at that place the river also winds inward, indenting his front, he will, by disposing his troops round the bend, command and enclose the angle of the other bank. For instance, in the campaign of 1813, Napoleon wished to pass the Elbe near the village of Priesnitz. The conditions were favourable, for the French bank commanded the other, and the bend of the river there indented the French front. Three hundred men were thrown over in the night, and established themselves on the further side. They were attacked, in the morning, by superior forces, with artillery; but the French, bringing 100 guns to bear from their own side, forced the enemy to retreat. During the following night nearly 3,000 men crossed, and a work was constructed capable of holding two divisions; whereupon the enemy retired altogether. The conditions may be so favourable as to enable large masses to pass even in face of an assembled army. In 1809, Napoleon, after entering Vienna, and guarding all the bridges of the Danube up to Passau, wished to cross and attack the army of the

Archduke Charles, then opposite Vienna, on the left bank. First, the Emperor seized the large island of Lobau, and connected it with the right bank by a long bridge. Then he accumulated on the island the means of crossing, together with a force of more than 20,000 men. The arm of the river is 120 yards wide, and makes a favourable bend; and by seizing the two villages of Aspern and Essling a space would be enclosed and secured capable of holding a considerable force. On 20 May bridges were thrown, two divisions crossed, and Aspern and Essling were seized. The Austrians, who had assembled on a height twelve miles up the river, came on in line of battle, and a desperate struggle ensued, chiefly for the possession of the villages. But the rein-forcements to the French from the right bank came too slowly to main-tain the battle; and the part of the army that had crossed – numbering, when first attacked, 30,000, afterwards, 60,000, against 90,000 Austri-ans – was compelled to repass the branch of the stream to the isle of Lobau.

When the most important passages on the main line of operation present conditions specially favourable to the assailant, it will be diffi-cult and hazardous to oppose the passage. 'So important,' said Giulay, the Austrian general, 'the enemy, whom it is impossible to observe from the left bank, can mask his movements and bring all his forces suddenly on any point before our troops can be warned and concentrated.' And he had a precedent to justify his opinion, for in 1796, the Austrians being on the defensive from Peschiera to Mantua, Napoleon broke their front by crossing at Valeggio.

Yet the Mincio possessed otherwise great advantages for defence, being a short line, secure on the flanks, and having two issues over it secured by Austrian fortresses. It may be assumed, then, that when the assailant's bank decidedly commands the other throughout its length, or at the points where the roads forming the line of operation cross, the river is unsuitable for a defensive line.

But it must be observed that the mere command of one bank over the other will not be promptly effectual unless the opposing troops are unable to obtain shelter from the assailant's fire. It will naturally often happen that villages and towns are situated on one or both sides of a bridge. In this case, even if the assailant's bank has a moderate com-mand, the buildings on the other side may, for a time be defensible. At the battle of La Rothière, in 1814, the French right rested on the bridge of Dienville, on the Aube – and the Austrians sought to turn that flank by sending a corps along the other bank. The Austrian bank com-manded the other by about 30 feet, rising abruptly to a plateau less than 50 yards from the bridge which was 50 yards long and 5 yards wide. But at 20 or 30 yards from its extremity on the French side was a substantial church, proof against field-artillery, backed and flanked by the houses of the place. This was occupied so successfully that the Austrians were unable to pass the bridge throughout the battle, or even to drive over the river a French detachment on the left bank.

When the defender sees that the passage cannot be opposed, his usual course will be to take a position in the neighbourhood of the bridge; and the assailant, after passing, cannot manoeuvre to turn this position, for by so doing he would uncover the bridge, the sole link in that part of his line of operation. He must therefore make a direct attack on the position, which will almost certainly be on commanding ground.

If, therefore, circumstances are so favourable as to enable an army to pass a river in the presence of the enemy, it must generally advance afterwards to attack that enemy in a strong position. But, in the great majority of cases, circumstances are unfavourable to an open passage. An army, however superior, seeking to force its way over a bridge, against an enemy posted on the higher bank, would certainly experience heavy loss. Thus, in 1810, Craufurd with the Light Division was driven over the Coa by a greatly superior force under Ney; but when the French attempted to pass the bridge, the British troops lining the high bank destroyed the head of every column till the unavailing carnage caused the French to desist. And if the banks were on equal command, still the task would be too formidable for an equal army; for the only point at which an attacking column could advance being known – namely, the bridge – provision could always be made for bringing an overwhelming fire to bear on it. And if buildings, woods, or dykes, near the bridge, afford a shelter for the defender's infantry, the passage, in face of their fire, will be still more impracticable; indeed, such advantages will, as at Dienville, frequently balance the superiority conferred by the commanding bank. It may be inferred, therefore, that the points where a passage can be forced are comparatively few: and we may draw, for future use, the conclusion, that, in the majority of cases, to attempt to pass an unfordable river at a known point, in the presence of a prepared enemy, demands a great superiority of force – especially in artillery.

For this reason commanders generally seek to gain a footing on the opposite bank by manoeuvring.

Having obtained command of the whole or a large portion of one bank, the assailant will show the heads of his columns, and make preparations as if to cross, at many points; while the real bridge will be constructed, or seized, and the first troops thrown across, elsewhere. Unless the defender's bank confers a very extensive and commanding view, he will be doubtful which column will make the real attempt – all must therefore be opposed; meanwhile, covered by the high or wooded banks, the assailant's troops will be moving towards the real point. In general, a bridge of some kind, fixed or flying, must be thrown; and it will be a manifest gain to possess some creek or tributary stream where the materials of the bridge may be prepared unseen, and floated to the point of passage. If time allows, the means for throwing great numbers across at once may be prepared. In his second passage of the Danube, Napoleon placed 70,000 men, with artillery and cavalry, on the further bank in a single night. In 1704 the French had a flying bridge on the Rhine (that is, a bridge or raft passing from bank to bank by means of an anchorage up the stream), by which 500 infantry and 140 cavalry crossed at each trip. But, in all cases, success will in great measure depend on the ability of the assailant to augment his force on the opposite bank faster than the defender can bring troops to that point from other parts of the river, and from the reserves.

Although it is essential to an advance of the army, after passing, that the assailant should possess the bridge of a great road on the line of operation, yet it is not necessary that the first troops should pass at a great road. On the contrary, if secrecy is an object, a point of passage will be more likely to be found unguarded elsewhere; all that is essential for the passage of the first detachment is that the ground on both banks should admit of the manoeuvring of troops of all arms. And it will be a great advantage to find, unguarded or weakly guarded, on the opposite bank, some easily defensible point, such as a village, a church, farm buildings, or a small wood. For as the necessary preliminary to throwing a bridge is to establish a party on the other bank, so some defensible point will enable the first troops to hold their ground, and to protect the construction of the bridge, or the completion of other modes of sending the rest of the troops across, such as the passage by boats or rafts. The seizure of the Portuguese seminary on the further bank of the Douro by Wellington's advanced-guard is a well-known example. Even when a permanent bridge is mastered, it will be necessary to throw other bridges at convenient spots near it, so as to concentrate on the other bank faster than the enemy; and throughout the operation feints should be persisted in at other points, to confuse and deceive the opposing general.

A force, then, being thrown across sufficient to deal with any that the defender can assemble at that point, it may advance along the bank and assail in flank or rear the defenders of some important neighbouring point, while at the same time, a force makes a direct attack from the other bank on the same bridge. This is the usual method of gaining a footing – and it may be executed either between the extremities of the enemy's line, or beyond one extremity – that is to say, either by breaking his front or turning his flank. The expediency of preferring either of these methods to the other must depend in great measure on the dispositions of the defender. For he must conduct the defence in one of two ways: either he must guard only the passages on the direct line of operation – in which case his front, too compact to be broken, may be turned; or he will guard all the passages by which the assailant can possibly seek to pass – in which case his front, thus dangerously extended, should be broken.

And finally, the views of Victorian officer H. F. Morgan, from his book A Summary of Tactics: 'How is the defence of a river conducted?':

The most important point is to prevent the assailants effecting a lodgement on the defender's side of the river, for under cover of this party the remainder could cross easily, and with security. The first force that crosses is small, and the easier crushed; but should the assailants effect a landing, and push over reinforcements, it is essential the defenders should have troops ready to oppose them. Thus the general principle of defence is to watch the length of river with advanced posts, guarding, in force vulnerable points (such as fords, etc), and concentrating the main body in one or two central positions. If the river is broad, it adds to the difficulty of throwing a bridge across it, or of crossing it by boats. On the other hand, if narrow, and with a good defensive position on the defender's side, it will often be advisable to offer a feeble defence to the crossing, and devote all the defender's energy to making a determined resistance at the strong tactical position on the assailant's line of route. A passive defence has only the advantage of delaying the assailant, and making his crossing a costly one. Thus it is of little use, and an active defence is therefore essential.

If the defenders hold a bridgehead, or other fortified post, they have the means of attacking the enemy during the passage, and of cutting his communications subsequently, should he effect it.

This was the case on the Mincio, in 1800, where Bellegarde held the bridgehead of Borghetto.

What preliminary measures should be adopted before attempting to cross a defended river?
The first object is to select a suitable locality for crossing.

Strategical considerations will sometimes influence the choice, but if not, tactical considerations usually determine the actual point.

To attack a bridge resolutely defended would be too costly, therefore a bend of the river, indented towards the assailant, with firm ground on both sides, and a commanding bank, is usually sought for.

32

With such a formation a convergent fire of artillery can be brought to bear on the defenders; and by having the approaches open and sound, guns and carriages can move freely and quickly.

A village, wood, or cover of some sort, where the covering party (first moved across) could shelter themselves and successfully hold their ground till reinforcements arrive, as was shown in the crossing of the Douro in 1809, is also most essential; and if there are tributary streams or islands near at hand, they would be useful.

The point of crossing being chosen, the next measure is to collect under cover everything necessary for doing so. Boats should be searched for, sound materials for bridges collected, troops and guns massed behind some height near at hand, and parties detached to make feints on other spots. Choose the position for the batteries to cover the movement, but do not post the guns till the last moment.

The preliminaries being arranged, how ought the attempted crossing be proceeded with?
All being in readiness, and everything being accurately timed, open fire on the opposite bank, to clear it of troops and silence the defender's Artillery. Push over with the greatest celerity as strong a covering party as possible, who, after effecting a lodgement, should lose no time in strengthening their position against counter attack. On this all depends, therefore they should take advantage of any natural shelter, and obstinately contest the ground till reinforced. In the meanwhile, the assailants, by boats or other means (swimming has been resorted to, and arms, etc, conveyed on a small raft), push over reinforcements while the bridges are being constructed. Sometimes the parties detached to make feints at other points of the river find they can cross unopposed, and, by turning the defender's flank, materially assist the assailants. In that case, if strong enough to act independently, they might risk it; but care must be taken that they are not overpowered and annihilated before they could recross the river or effect a junction on the defender's side.

2. THE ANCIENT WORLD

The first bridge to be publicly recognised in the annals of military history was that over the Tiber where, in 508BC, a brave Roman – Horatius Cocles – saved Rome from the invading Etruscans. But before that date, in 1288BC, the very first recorded account of a battle, in which Pharaoh Ramses II of Egypt defeated the Hittites, includes picture-reliefs showing the king of the Hittites being pulled, feet-first, from the swirling waters in which he drowned when attempting to cross a river without waiting for a bridge to be built.

Horatius and the Sublician Bridge over the Tiber, 508BC

In his book The History of Rome, Book II, the Roman historian Livy (Titus Livius, 59BC–AD17) tells the story of Horatius:

Some parts of the city seemed secured by the walls, others by the River Tiber. The Sublician bridge well-nigh afforded a passage to the enemy, had there not been one man, Horatius Cocles (fortunately Rome had on that day such a defender) who, happening to be posted on guard at the bridge, when he saw the Janiculum taken by a sudden assault and the enemy pouring down thence at full speed, and that his own party, in terror and confusion were abandoning their arms and ranks, laying hold of them one by one, standing in their way and appealing to the faith of gods and men, he declared that their flight would avail them nothing if they deserted their post; if they passed the bridge, there would soon be more of the enemy in the Palatium and Capitol than in the Janiculum. For that reason he charged them to demolish the bridge, by sword, by fire, or by any other means whatever; declaring that he would stand the shock of the enemy as far as could be done by one man. He then advanced to the first entrance of the bridge, and being easily distinguished among those who showed their backs in retreating, faced about to engage the foe hand to hand, and by his surprising bravery he terrified the enemy. Two indeed remained with him from a sense of shame: Sp. Lartius and T. Herminius, men eminent for their birth, and renowned for their gallant exploits. With them he for a short time stood the first storm of the danger, and the severest brunt of the battle. But as they who demolished the bridge called upon them to retire, he obliged them also to withdraw to a place of safety on a small portion of the bridge that was still left. Then casting his stern eyes towards the officers of the Etruscans in a threatening manner, he now challenged them singly, and then reproached them, slaves of haughty tyrants who, regardless of their own freedom, came to oppress the liberty of others. They hesitated for a time, looking round one at the other, to begin the fight: shame then put the army in motion, and a shout being raised, they hurled weapons from all sides at their single adversary; and when they all stuck in his upraised shield, and he with no less obstinacy kept possession of the bridge, they endeavoured to thrust him down from it by one push, when the crash of the falling bridge was heard, and at the same time a shout of the Romans raised for joy at having completed their purpose, checked their ardour with sudden panic. Then said Cocles: 'Holy Father Tiber, I pray thee, receive these arms, and this thy soldier, in thy propitious stream.' Armed as he was, he leaped into the Tiber, and amid showers of darts, swam across safe to his party, having dared an act which is likely to obtain with posterity more fame than credit. The state was grateful for such valour; a statue was erected to him in the comitium, and as much land given to him as he could plough in one day. The zeal of private individuals was also conspicuous among his public honours. For amid the great scarcity, each contributed something, according to his supply depriving himself of his own support.

In another version of the legend, Horatius defended the bridge unaided and was drowned in the Tiber.

Persian invasion of Greece, 481–480BC

In revenge for his father Darius' defeat by the Greeks at Marathon in 490BC, the Persian Emperor Xerxes spent four years assembling an invasion army and preparing to march to march from Asia into Europe. Two long floating bridges of boats, each a mile in length and some distance apart, were constructed, one by the Egyptians and the other by the Phoenicians, across the Hellespont. They had only just been completed when a violent storm carried them away, smashing the boats into shattered timber. The chronicler Herodotus, an Ionian born in the city of Halicarnassus, who became known as 'the father of history', writes:

Xerxes was very angry and gave orders that the Hellespont should receive 300 lashes and have a pair of fetters thrown into it. He also ordered that the men responsible for the bridge-building should have their heads cut off. This unseemly order was carried out, and other engineers were appointed to start the work afresh.

This time, the cables connecting the boats were made of double thickness so that the bridges held firm. Herodotus continues:

35

Then, Xerxes poured wine into the sea out of a golden goblet and, with his face turned to the rising sun, prayed that no chance might prevent him from conquering Europe. Then he flung the cup into the Hellespont and the crossing began.

Xerxes had gathered together possibly the largest army the world had ever seen to date, between 180,000 and 200,000 men with 800 triremes, far larger than any the Greeks could muster. The Persian despot, sitting on a marble throne set up on the bluffs, watched his army going across. It was an awesome sight as it rolled down from the Asian hills and swarmed along the shores; it seemed as though the entire world had assembled to destroy Greece.

'There was not a nation in all Asia that Xerxes did not take with against the Greeks,' comments Herodotus. He goes on to describe the Medes and Persians, distinguished by their soft round hats; camel-borne Arabs; Bactrians from Afghanistan; troops from Thrace wearing fox-skin headgear; the tall pointed leather caps of the axe-bearing Scythians from Russia contrasting oddly with the leopard-skins of the Ethiopians and the cotton-clad Indians, carrying cane bows-and-arrows. And he concludes:

But of all the troops, the Persians were the best and most magnificently equipped. Every man glittered with gold and they were accompanied by carriages, full of their women and servants, all elaborately fitted out, with special food brought along for them on camels and mules.

It is said that the crossing occupied seven days and nights without a break, and on the far shore Xerxes held a grand review when they had all assembled. Turning to Demaratus, a renegade Spartan in his retinue, Xerxes asked: 'Tell me, will the Greeks dare to lift a hand against me?' Demaratus replied: 'My lord, the Spartans will not under any circumstances accept terms which would mean slavery; they will fight you even if the rest of Greece submits. Fighting singly, the Spartans are as good as any, but fighting together they are the best soldiers in the world.' It is reported that Xerxes appeared unmoved.

Perhaps he should have taken more note because, in the campaign of Thermopylae and Salamis in 480BC and a string of other battles extending over a number of years until 448BC, and despite Athens being occupied, the Greeks totally routed the invaders.

Alexander the Great crosses the River Jaxartes, 328BC

The Macedonians, whose kingdom lay to the north of Greece were a warlike race of Greek stock and traditions but lacking their characteristic culture. Philip II, who unified the Macedonians, had spent some years as a hostage in Thebes and had learned much from the Theban general Epaminondas. On his return, he improved upon the Theban phalanx, increasing its mobility by thinning its ranks to sixteen men and by lengthening their pikes (sarissa) to as much as 24 feet so that the weapons of men as far back as the fifth rank projected beyond the soldiers of the front rank. To cope with this two-handed weapon, the shield was reduced in size and strapped to the left arm, leaving the hand free. With these exceptions, the arms and equipment of the Macedonian peasant-soldier were not very different from those of the regular Greek hoplite. The usual ratio of cavalry to infantry in most Greek states was about one to twelve or one to sixteen, but Philip, trusting in the riding qualities of his 'farmers', employed a higher proportion of about one to seven.

Inevitably, Macedonia eventually came into conflict with the other Greek states, and at the battle of Chaeronea in 338BC Philip defeated a combination of Athenians and Thebans. Although this victory gave him control of Greece, Philip never achieved his dream of uniting the Greek city-states for an attack on Persia. Philip was murdered in 336BC and his splendid army came under control of his son Alexander, a man destined while still young to become one of the greatest generals ever known.

By breaking the phalanx into smaller units, Alexander turned it into a spear-hedged mobile base rather than a juggernaut of moving spear-points. But the real striking force of the Macedonians lay in the shock power of their heavy cavalry charging at speed in formation. They were formed of eight squadrons – the Companions on the right wing and Thessalians on the left, both supported and strengthened by light cavalry and light infantry. Alexander also devised a new class of highly trained foot-soldier – the hypaspists – who were a cross between the heavy pikemen of the phalanx and the light-armed peltasts. They wore armour and carried a shorter spear, thus forming a link between the phalanx and the cavalry.

In battle the Macedonian phalanxes advanced in echelon so that the right division struck the enemy first and 'fixed' him. Then the Companions, often under Alexander himself, attacked the enemy's left, supported by the hypaspists. If the enemy attempted to outflank the left of the Macedonian phalanx, the Thessalian right flank was there to provide a flexible hinge between the fast-moving cavalry and the relatively slow hoplites. Flanks and rear were protected by the peltasts of the light infantry, drawn up in a line approximately eight men deep behind the phalanx, and psiloi (servants and foragers for the heavy infantry) formed a skirmish line in front; they were armed with bows, javelins, darts and slings. Besides being a base of manoeuvre for the shock action of the cavalry, the heavy infantry phalanx was a highly mobile formation, capable of attacking at the run while retaining formation so as to hit the disordered enemy ranks before they could recover from the impact of the early cavalry attack.

Alexander the Great was a military genius, capable of adjusting his tactics and formations to suit prevailing conditions. His tactical skill in mountain warfare and against irregular forces was of the highest order.

The crossing of the River Jaxartes was outstanding if only because no such advanced conception of artillery tactics was seen again until the last stages of the Roman Empire. Alexander and his Macedonians used cavalry as their main arm of battle, but relied greatly on their war engines, which, reduced to parts, could be carried on the soldiers' backs in areas inaccessible to pack animals. It is estimated that there were about 4,000 Scythian light horsemen in this action, and that the Macedonian force consisted of some 2,000 light infantry, 1,000 heavy infantry (possibly a chiliarchia or taxis of 1,024 men, ranged in a phalanx with a 64-man frontage), and three cavalry hipparchies (one of which was the famous Companions), each consisting of 512 horsemen.

The well-trained and disciplined Macedonians were all first-class troops, with the Companions forming an élite body. The Scythians, although irregulars, were natural warriors, and formidable horse archers (as at Carrhae in 53BC, Pharaspa in 36BC and even up to the Crusades of the twelfth century).

In the three years since the battle of Arbela (331BC), Alexander's campaigns had taken him to the Hindu Kush in modern Afghanistan, where his frostbitten soldiers laboriously made their way over a pass to descend on to desert steppes. At last they reached the River Jaxartes (also known as Syr Darya, the River of the Sands) where Cyrus the Great had been defeated and slain by the Scythians. On the far side of the muddy river, swollen by rains, appeared increasing numbers of these dreaded barbarians, who were armed with long swords and strangely curved bows, and whose long braided hair and baggy trousers matched the appearance of their shaggy horses. They jeered at the Macedonians while keeping up a dropping fire of arrows that irritated Alexander's troops but caused few casualties.

The difficult river crossing had to be made, for to retreat south would invite the assembled Scythians to cross the river and harass Alexander's men unmercifully. For three days Macedonian engineers laboured to build 12,000 small wooden rafts and floats made from leather tents stuffed with hay. Others set up a series of gastraphetes (large mechanical crossbows), which Alexander ordered not to be fired until the hour of the crossing. (The concept of covering fire with crossbows was centuries in advance of its time.) Then, with the rafts positioned in readiness and his troops lined up, Alexander gave the order to loose the barrage of crossbow javelins. The heavy missiles flashing across the water astonished the Scythians with their range and caused consternation by virtue of the ease with which they penetrated wicker shields and leather body armour. The barbarian horsemen promptly scattered away from the river bank and Alexander ordered the first rafts into the water. The Roman historian Arrian (Flavius Arrianus) later recorded the event:

Seeing the Scythians confused by the discharge of his missiles, Alexander ordered trumpets to sound and keep on sounding. He led the first wave of the crossings. After the leading archers, javelin throwers and slingers had got to land, he ordered them to advance and harass the Scythians with missiles, to keep the horse archers from charging the first ranks of the infantry phalanx stepping out of the water, until all the cavalry had got across.

The enemy horsemen, braving the fire of the mechanical crossbows, tried to halt the crossing while the main Macedonian force was still on the water, but their firepower was matched by that of Alexander's light troops, and soon the Macedonian army was formed up in battle array on the north bank of the river. Aware of the tactics of the Scythians and similar light cavalry nomads encountered in the Balkans and in central Asia, Alexander knew that they had to be brought to battle and prevented from following their usual practice of circling groups at a respectable distance, harassing them with archery fire and then overwhelming any small bunches separated from the main body. When attacked in force, these elusive mounted archers could vanish like a mirage, releasing showers of arrows over their shoulders as they went.

Alexander, therefore, sent forward a greatly outnumbered cavalry force which, as he anticipated, soon came under fire from encircling horse archers. Next he sent out a skirmish line of about 2,000 light infantry (those who had served as a screen during the river crossing), which advanced in crescent formation with orders to engage but not to attack the Scythians who stood between them and the surrounded Macedonian cavalry. To the rear of the light infantry and hidden by them were two outlying cavalry squadrons (hipparchies) and farther back in the centre, close to the river bank and out of sight, were the Companion cavalry. Behind them the infantry phalanx formed up at the river's edge.

The fire from the light infantry screen diverted the Scythians' attention from the Macedonian cavalry vanguard, but they continued to circle that force while sending groups of mounted archers to range up and down the slowly advancing Macedonian skirmish line. They made numerous attempts to drive back the light archers and javelin throwers, but found them to be as elusive as they were themselves.

At the trumpet call, the two flank columns of Macedonian cavalry charged through their own skirmish line to trap several thousand surprised Scythians in the area between the cavalry vanguard and the light infantry screen; at the same time the surrounded cavalry counter-charged to the rear. The central column of the Companion hipparchy, closely followed by the phalanx, then charged into the centre of the milling mass of confused barbarian horsemen. Suddenly the Scythians, who a few moments before had been part of an encircling force, found themselves completely surrounded. It is recorded that of the 4,000 or so involved, at least 1,000 were killed, including a known chief, and several hundred captured in the swirling dusty battle that followed. Macedonian losses were greater than this, but they had won a decisive moral victory.

3. THE MIDDLE AGES

Stamford Bridge, 25 September 1066

Stamford Bridge lies eight miles east of York on the A166 road, and the main action occurred just south of that road on what is now private property, Battle Flats Farm. Part of the site has been occupied by caravans, and on the eastern (left) bank of the River Derwent the ground rises fairly steeply to what is now Danes Well Garage. In 1066 the actual bridge was about 400 yards upstream from the present bridge, and about twenty yards below the modern cut in the river.

Background to the battle
Edward the Confessor, king of England, died on 5 January 1066. By immediately electing Harold Godwinson, Earl of Wessex, to ascend the throne, the Witan or Great Council set in train great problems concerning the succession to the English throne.

Five separate claimants existed: Edgar Atheling, from the ancient royal house, a boy to whom the Witan were not then prepared to entrust the throne; Sweyn, king of Denmark; Harald Hardrada, king of Norway; William, Duke of Normandy; and Harold, Earl of Wessex.

Arising from this, in 1066 three distinct invasions of England occurred: in May, by Harold's troublesome brother Tostig, who opposed Harold's accession; in September, by Harald Hardrada; and from 2 September to 14 October, by William of Normandy.

Tostig's attempt was a hopeless failure; after raiding the Isle of Wight, his force was destroyed in Lincolnshire by Edwin, Earl of Mercia. Tostig sailed with a few surviving ships to join the king of Scotland, later contacting Harald Hardrada.

Harald Hardrada's invasion
Aware of the danger, King Harold mustered the southern fyrd and kept the fleet in southern waters until forced to disband on 8 September. Almost immediately, Harold heard that Hardrada, accompanied by Tostig, had sailed via the Orkneys, up the River Ouse, to disembark at Riccall, ten miles south of the town of York. Before then, landing from 200 longships, they attacked sites including Cleveland, Scarborough and Holderness, and on 20 September defeated in battle at Fulford, the forces of Edwin, Earl of Mercia, and his brother Morcar, Earl of Northumberland.

Although minor, Fulford was a battle of some importance because if the earls had remained on the defensive until Harold arrived, it is unlikely that they would have been defeated; the lost levies would have greatly strength-ened Harold at Hastings and, under the missing Edwin and Morcar, could possibly have brought about a Norman defeat.

Subsequently, Hardrada's army pitched camp at Stamford Bridge, some twelve miles from the Norsemen's base at Riccall, probably arriving there on 24 September where, in an unprepared state, they were surprised by Harold on the following day, who had marched at least 180 miles in less than a week, possibly only four days.

The Norse army consisted of Norwegians, Flemings, Scots and even some English; perhaps two-thirds of their total strength (say 5,000 men) had marched from Riccall to negotiate with local leaders. It is difficult to assess how well matched numerically the opposing armies were, but it is likely that the English had the initial advantage, because it was late in the day before the Norse commander, Eyestein Orre, and reinforcements from Riccall joined the fray. Harold had pushed his house-carls up the straight Roman road to the north, calling out the shire levies as they made their hur-ried way through their areas. Undoubtedly it was a rapidly assembled loose army of ill-assorted warriors and it is highly creditable that they should, despite fatigue, have defeated one of the best collections of fighting men in Europe, under an almost legendary leader.

Course of the battle
Harold's force arrived unseen by the Norsemen, marching through Gate Hemsley village where the ground rose so that they were out of sight until they topped the ridge, when the sun's glint off their armour and the waving banners shocked the unprepared enemy. The Norsemen had put out patrols and outposts on the west side of the Derwent, but the bulk of their army were reclining lazily on both banks, their mail tunics lying on the grass beside them. Halting, Harold formed up his army on the west bank, just short of today's caravan site, his right astride the present A166 road. The outposts were ordered to resist Harold's advance on the west bank, giving time for mail to be donned and three horsemen to ride off to Ricall warn Eyestein Orre to bring the rest of the army to Stamford Bridge as fast as possible.

There are no reliable accounts of the battle available, but it would appear to have followed a fairly predictable course, with the narrow foot-bridge (some 300–500 yards upstream from the present road bridge) play-ing a sufficiently notable part to give the battle its name. The ground sloped fairly gently down to the river, which was about 40 feet wide, with slippery but not steep banks. While the outposts momentarily halted Harold's advance, those of the main body who had hastily donned their mail tunics rushed across the bridge to form a defensive line about 300 yards long and 100 yards in advance of the river-line; their second line on the east bank was positioned about 200 yards back from the little bridge. Very narrow and the only link between the two formations, the bridge allowed only one man at a time to cross, so that reinforcement or withdrawal from one bank to the other was a hazardous business. Sheer weight of numbers quickly forced the west-bank Norsemen back to the river, some managing to reach the far bank by way of the bridge; others, weighed down by armour and equipment, perished in the water which, for the same reason, prevented Harold's men from pouring across.

The berserker on the bridge
Their advance across the bridge was initially prevented by a brawny Viking who, wielding an axe, positioned himself at the western end of the bridge and held it single-handedly for a while, loudly taunting his Saxon enemies to move him. Man after man took up his challenge in this gladiatorial-style battle, with a reputed fifty Saxons falling to his bloodstained axe until his feat of arms came to an inglorious end. A local man, with some knowledge of the river and its facilities, pushed a swill-tub into the water and, concealed by overhanging willows, paddled unseen until under the planking of the bridge-floor, immediately beneath the fighting-mad berserker. Through a gap in the planking he thrust his spear upwards into the Viking's groin, bringing him crashing to the ground with a piercing scream. The Saxons flooded across the now undefended bridge, pushing the solo defender's body into the river below.

House-carls versus Vikings
Quickly forming into a battle-line, Harold's army faced the continuous line of shields presented by Hardrada's force, drawn up shoulder to shoulder, perhaps in a hollow triangle with its apex showing a relatively narrow front. It was this shield-wall that had to be smashed by the Saxons who, now they were across the river and on the enemy's side of it, had no escape route except through the river's swirling waters. At once both sides became locked in combat, known to have been on Battle Flats, a level piece of ground some 50 feet above the river and 200 yards north of the little bridge. It was around early afternoon and it is said that the relentless and continuous fighting lasted until dusk, as the outnumbered Norsemen doggedly stood their ground, reluctantly falling back literally inch by inch, with men pushing to the front to take the place of fallen comrades and gaps immediately closed, all in the face of hacking, slashing axes and swords, backed by slings and javelins. Hardrada himself was brought to the ground by a Saxon missile, perhaps well-aimed, perhaps random, and as happens when a brave and inspiring leader falls, the morale and courage of his followers began to crumble. Despite the arrival of reinforcements from Riccall and Tostig's taking over command with frenzied

43

efforts to rally the Norsemen, the shield-wall began to crumble as the new arrivals realised that their exhausting march had brought them to their doom. Tostig and Eyestein Orre fell, and the shattered Norsemen fled before a pursuit lasting all the way to Riccall, where the survivors embarked in twenty-four longboats, remnants of the last Scandinavian army ever to trouble the shores of England.

It was a decisive but costly victory; the house-carls and levies had taken heavy losses, and Harold, feasting in York to celebrate the success, heard with heavy heart that William of Normandy had landed at Pevensey. Without delay, the exhausted Saxons were formed up and began the march back to the south, covering almost 260 miles in twelve days, to face the Normans at Hastings.

The village of Stamford Bridge, on the busy A166, can still offer tangible memories of the battle, such as the rough-hewn memorial stone on the village-green fifty yards back from the bridge, bearing an inscription in both Norwegian and English:

> THE BATTLE OF STAMFORD BRIDGE WAS FOUGHT IN
> THIS NEIGHBOURHOOD ON SEPTEMBER 25, 1066

The top of the slope up to Battle Flats (marked on the map and with a local field bearing the name) on the road to Barmby-on-the-Marsh, has houses covering it, but behind their gardens lies the flat ground where the Viking shield-wall stood. The site of the original bridge is precisely indicated by the nearby weir, with rocks that almost certainly supported the wooden piers. Alongside the last building, a garage, overlooking the river, lies about twenty feet on a terrace some ten feet above the water. From it can be seen, within about 200 yards, the site of the old bridge, the weir and the caravan site.

Orewin Bridge, 1282

In early fourteenth-century England a coherent military practice evolved which entailed the use, within a single tactical scheme, of the distinctive power of archery, the defensive solidarity of dismounted men-at-arms and, when necessary, the offensive power of mounted troops. King Edward I had comprehended what was already apparent: first, the virtues of archery in attack to break up a defensive infantry formation and, second, its power in defence when based on an array of dismounted knights and men-at-arms.

A beginning was made during the Welsh Wars, at Orewin Bridge in 1282, against the men of Prince Llewelyn, who prepared to stand their ground in a defensive position. The English advanced against them, archers interposed with cavalry – the arrows inflicting sufficient loss on the Welsh troops to cause them to lose their cohesion and fall into comparative disarray, so that the cavalry were able to ride them down.

Stirling Bridge, 11 September 1297

Following a series of disasters to the rulers of Scotland, including the deaths by accident and sickness of two who might have been expected to ascend the throne, in 1292 Edward I of England judged John Balliol to be king of Scotland. As intended, he was a 'vassal king' expected to comply with Edward's wishes, and by 1295 the Scots had concluded a treaty with France; Edward marched north and sacked Berwick while Warenne, Earl of Surrey, defeated the Scottish nobles at Dunbar. Balliol sued for peace and Edward occupied Scotland, appointing Warenne as Governor and Hugh de Cressingham as Treasurer.

The colourful account of the battle of Stirling Bridge which follows comes from a popular series, British Battles on Land and Sea by James Grant (London, 1877).

Amid incessant turmoil, petty strife, and marauding, this state of matters only remained two years, when a body of Scots were again in arms. This time their leader was William Wallace, a man neither rich nor noble, but the second son of Sir Malcolm Wallace, of Ellerslie, near Paisley. He is said by his detractors to have come of Norman blood; but even were it so, the lapse of 230 years and nearly six generations must have made him Scot enough to resent the oppression of his country. His father, his elder brother, and many of his kinsmen, had been slain in skirmishes with the enemy. His wife and family had been burned with his house at Lanark, and from that time he devoted himself to the cause of vengeance and freedom. Distinguished for bravery and hardihood in an age when all men were hardy and brave, the fond admiration of his countrymen has endued him with attributes of strength and beauty equalled only by the demigods of Homer; but, however, his many achievements prove that he must have been no ordinary man. Scotland owed little then as ever to her unpatriotic and infamous nobility; and in this case it was to one of the people she was to owe all her future existence.

Among the many victories he won, that at Stirling Bridge, on 13 September 1297, is alike the most splendid and remarkable. Edward I was then warring with France, but he had remitted to John de Warenne, Earl of Surrey and Sussex, and to Hugh Cressingham (whom we have already named), a military ecclesiastic, his Lieutenant and Treasurer, or Justiciary, in Scotland, full power to repress all resistance; and for this purpose an army of 50,000 infantry and a great body of horse, under their orders, marched through the south Lowlands in quest of Wallace, who was then besieging Dundee with all the men that he and his friends, Graham, Ramsay and Murray, could muster – only 10,000 in all. Yet, quitting Dundee, they crossed the Tay and marched with all speed to dispute with the English the passage of the Forth, by which they alone could penetrate into the more northern parts of the kingdom.

The bridge across the Forth near Stirling was of timber, and stood at Kildean, where some remains of the stone pillars which supported the woodwork are still visible, exactly half a mile above the present ancient bridge. It is described as having been so narrow that only two persons could pass along it abreast, yet the English leaders absurdly proposed to make 50,000 foot and all their horse undergo the tedious operation of passing it in the face of an enemy. Walter de Hemingford, Canon of Gisborough, in Yorkshire, and author of a *History of England* from 1066 to 1308, records that a Scottish traitor named Sir Richard Lunday (Lundin?), who served the Earl of Surrey, strenuously opposed this measure, and pointed out a ford at no great distance where sixty men could have crossed the stream abreast; but no regard was paid to his suggestions, and the sequel proved how headstrong was the folly of the English leaders. To increase their troubles, they had in their army certain Scottish barons of the Baliol faction, on whom, with their followers, they could little rely in case of disaster. Notwithstanding all his force, Surrey was by no means anxious to encounter Wallace, whose success in past encounters had won him a formidable name; he wished to avoid a general action, all the more so that he knew that he was about to be superseded in his post by Brian Fitzalan, and consequently was less zealous in the cause of the king their master.

Seeking therefore to temporise, he dispatched two Dominican friars to Wallace, whose force was then encamped near Cambuskenneth Abbey, on the hill so well known as the Abbey Craig; thus both armies were within perfect view of each other, and only separated by the river, which there winds like a silver snake between the green and fertile meadows. The request of the friars was brief – that Wallace and his followers should lay down their arms and submit. 'Return to your friends,' said he, 'and tell them we come here with no peaceful intent, but ready for battle, determined to avenge our wrongs and to set our country free. Let your masters come and attack us; we are ready to meet them beard to beard.' Enraged by this reply, many of the English knights now clamoured to be led on. Then it was that the active traitor Lunday said to Surrey, 'Give me but five hundred horse and a few foot, and I shall turn the enemy's flank by the ford, while you, my Lord Earl, may pass the bridge in safety.' Still Surrey hesitated, on which Hugh Cressingham exclaimed, passionately, 'Why do we thus protract the war, and waste the king's treasure? Let us fight, it is our bounden duty.' Surrey, contrary to his own judgment, yielded; and by dawn of day the English began to cross the bridge, and Wallace heard the tidings with joy. Slow was this process; when the sun rose they were still defiling across, and were permitted to do so without interruption till eleven o'clock, by which time one-half of Surrey's army was over the river, and gradually forming in order of battle, while the Scots looked quietly on from the gentle slope above it.

When one-half of the Englishmen were over, Wallace began to advance, having previously sent a strong detachment to hold the ford already referred to. The moment the Scots began to move, Sir Marmaduke Twenge, a gallant knight, belonging to the North Riding of Yorkshire, who, together with Cressingham, led the vanguard of horse, displayed the royal standard amid loud cries of 'For God and St George of England!' and at the head of the heavily mailed horse, made a furious charge up the slope upon the Scottish infantry, who received the shock upon their levelled spears, while their archers kept shooting fast and surely from the rear, and caused the English forces to waver and recoil upon each other.

Led on by Wallace, Sir John Grahame of Dundaff, Ramsay of Dalhousie, and others, the Scots made a furious downhill charge towards the bridge; while in the meantime a masterly movement was executed by another body, who by a quick detour got in between it and those who had already crossed the river, completely cutting off their retreat. All became immediate confusion, and the little discipline then known was entirely lost. Wallace, as soon as he saw the movement for intercepting their retreat achieved, pressed on with greater fury; and the half-formed columns of the English on the north of the river began at once to give way, and thousands of their heavy-armed cavalry were hurled into the river and drowned. Surrey, who witnessed this scene from the opposite bank, sought to retrieve the fortune of the day by sending across, at a moment when the bridge was open, a strong reinforcement at full speed, with his own banner; but unable to form amid the recoiling masses of their own infantry, they only added to the confusion and slaughter, being assailed on every side by Scottish spearmen. At this terrible moment the bridge parted, a disaster of which there are several versions; but this catastrophe, together with the passage of the river by a body of Scots at the ford, whence they fell on Surrey's own rear, decided the victory. An incredible number of English were drowned in attempting to cross the stream. There perished the nephew of Sir Marmaduke Twenge, a young knight; greatly beloved by his soldiers; while his uncle cut his way across the bridge before it fell, and escaped. On being advised at first to throw himself into the river, he replied, 'It shall never be said of me that I voluntarily drowned myself. God forbid that such dishonour should ever fall on any Englishman!'

The traitor Scottish barons who served in Surrey's ranks – one of whom was the Earl of Lennox – now threw off the mask, and, with their followers, joined in the pursuit, when the flight became, as usual in those days, a mere scene of barbarous slaughter:

No quarter was given. The country for miles round was covered with the bodies of the English soldiers; 20,000 men are believed to have fallen in the battle and the flight. Among these was Cressingham, a man so detested by the Scots that they mangled his dead body, and are said to have torn the skin from the limbs. The loss of the Scots was trifling; and the only man of note among them that fell was Sir Andrew Moray.

Surrey, after making one brave attempt to rally his soldiers in the Torwood, on being assailed by Wallace, again resumed his flight, and rode on the spur to Berwick, and thence sent to his master news of his terrible defeat.

Scottish historians assert that the bridge had been sawn through by order of Wallace, and that on a certain trumpet being sounded a man beneath it drew out a wedge and let the whole fabric fall. On the other hand, an English chronicler says it was broken down by Surrey to secure his retreat. The present burgh seal of Stirling seems to commemorate this victory. It represents the old wooden bridge, in the centre of which is a crucifix. At the south end are soldiers with English bows attempting to pass, on the northern are others with Scottish spears; and the legend around it is *Hic armis Bruti, Scoti stant hic cruce tuti*, a plain allusion to the safety of church and state resulting from the valour and victory of Sir William Wallace, who by this event also won the castle of Stirling, where he supped that night with his companions. The Scots now regarded him as the deliverer of their country, and crowded to his standard. He was chosen protector of the kingdom, an office which he executed with fidelity and dignity, though not without exciting the malignity of those who have so generally been Scotland's curse, her nobility; and as warfare had brought a famine on the land, and a pestilence too – 'produced by the exhalations from the putrid carcasses that lay rotting on the ground, aggravated by the deficient and unhealthy food of the people' – he marched his army into England, that he might subsist it in the northern counties, and send food to the famishing people at home.

By the result of this single battle the English were entirely driven out of Scotland, save at Roxburgh and Berwick, and in the castles of which two gallant garrisons maintained a stubborn resistance, till they were relieved by Surrey when, in January 1298, he entered Scotland for that purpose.

Boroughbridge, 1322

Innumerable sites of minor historical importance remain completely anony-mous, both to passers-by and usually to those residing in the area. The town of Boroughbridge on the A1 in North Yorkshire is no exception, despite the violence that occurred there, with two leading English noblemen losing their lives, one by subsequent execution. It happened in the year 1322, when a powerful group of English barons set themselves up in oppo-sition to the weak and corrupt government of King Edward II. Led by Edward's uncle, the Earl of Lancaster, they began a civil war with Lan-caster, raising and leading an army of rebels in the north and eventually coming to grips with Edward,who had marched from the south and pushed them back to the river Ure. Here, Sir Andrew Hacla, Edward's warden of Carlisle Castle, marched from the Pennines to meet them at Borough-bridge, the only bridge across the river for a stretch of five miles.

Lancaster's cavalry attempted to force a nearby ford but were repulsed as Hacla's archers and spearmen at the bridge held off the lords Clifford and Hereford, who nearly broke through, until Hereford was killed by a man concealed beneath the bridge. Clifford was also wounded and Lancaster, many of whose men had deserted after his abortive attack on the ford, called it a day and bivouacked on his side of the bridge. Next morning, Hacla's men forced their way across and, after driving Lancaster and some of his officers into the church, captured the rebel leader. He was taken to Pontefract, tried by Edward and summarily executed.

A new bridge was built in 1557 on the site of the old one and from it today the entire area of the action can be seen, though it requires a great deal of imagination to people the site with fighting men and the noise of battle. The ford at which Lancaster was repulsed can be reached by walk-ing half a mile along the footpath on the northern bank of the river; it can be seen that the river flowed through a marsh below the ford and would have been difficult to cross. It is also possible to get a further idea of the strength of the bridge by gazing from it down into the deep cutting it crosses.

The Bridge at Lussac, 1369

In 1340, while in Brabant with his mother, the young Black Prince met a man destined to become his dearest and most influential comrade for the rest of his life. Sir John Chandos was a youthful knight, some ten years older than the prince, who had shown great courage and ability in recent campaigns, displaying all the talents of a good soldier allied to the firm and inspiring presence that marked a founder-knight of the Order of the Garter. He stood out among many other famous men of his time, being continu-ously mentioned in the history of medieval warfare, ably advising and encouraging the prince at the battle of Poitiers in 1356. His death on the bridge at Lussac in 1369, when he was 49 years of age, inspired a colourful account in Froissart's Chronicles.

The historian and poet Jean (Jehan) Froissart, born in Valenciennes, Hainault, in 1337, was a contemporary of both the Black Prince and Sir John Chandos. Living at a time when the turbulent history of Europe was being played against a backcloth of great castles and tall cathedrals, when armoured knights on huge war-horses pounded the ground, and chivalry was in the air, Froissart gloried in this life, entranced by its brilliant pictures and heroic deeds. He sang of it in poetic ballads and wrote a history, the famous Chronicles, dealing with events from 1326 to 1400, providing a most vivid account of the superstitions and romance of that medieval warring world. It is from Froissart's writings that we get accounts of the Hundred Years War, with its picturesque battles of Crécy and Poitiers, and so much else faithful to the spirit and pageantry of those days, although his sympathies were invariably with the lordly knights rather than the humble peasant.

Here is Froissart's account of the death of Sir John Chandos:

Sir John Chandos, being seneschal of Poitou, was seriously afflicted with the loss of St Salvin: he was continually devising means to retake it, whether by assault or by escalade was perfectly indifferent to him, so that he could gain it. He made many nightly ambuscades, but none succeeded; for Sir Louis, who commanded in it, was very watchful, as he knew the capture of it had highly angered Sir John Chandos. It happened that, on the night preceding the eve of the new year (1370), Sir John Chandos, who resided in the city of Poitiers, had sent out his summons to the barons and knights of Poitou to come to him as secretly as they could, for he was going on an expedition. The Poitevins would not refuse him anything, being much beloved by them: they obeyed his summons, and came to Poitiers. Sir Guiscard d'Angle, Sir Louis de Harcourt, the lords de Pons, de Partenay, de Pinane, de Tannaybouton, Sir Geoffry d'Argenton, Sir Maubrun de Linières, Lord Thomas Percy, Sir Baldwin de Franville, Sir Richard de Pontchardon, came thither, with many others. When they were all assembled, they were full three hundred lances.

They left Poitiers in the night, and no one, except the principal lords, knew whither they were going. The English, however, had scaling-ladders and everything they might have occasion for with them. They marched to St Salvin; and, when there arrived, were told what was intended; upon which they all dismounted, and, giving the horses to their valets, the English descended into the ditch. It was then about midnight. They were in this situation, and would very shortly have succeeded in their expedition, when they heard the guard of the fort wind his horn. The reason was this. That very night Carnet le Breton had come from la Roche-Posay, with forty lances, to St Salvin, to request Sir Louis de St Julien to accompany him in an expedition to Poitou: he therefore awakened the guard and those within the fort. The English, who were on the opposite side, ignorant of the intentions of this body of Frenchmen wanting to enter the fort, thought they had been seen by the guard, or that spies had given information of their arrival to the garrison. They immediately left the ditch, and said 'Let us away; for this night we have been disappointed in our scheme.' They mounted their horses, and advanced in a body to Chauvigny on the river Creuse, two short leagues distant. When all were arrived there, the Poitevins asked Sir John Chandos if he wished them to remain with him: he answered, 'No, you may return in God's name: I will today stay in this town.' The Poitevins departed, and with them some English knights; in all, about two hundred lances.

Sir John Chandos entered an hotel, and ordered a fire to be lighted. Lord Thomas Percy, seneschal of La Rochelle, and his men, remained with him. Lord Thomas asked Sir John Chandos if he intended staying there that day; 'Yes,' replied Sir John, 'why do you ask?' 'Because, sir, if you be determined not to go further, I shall beg of you to give me leave to make an excursion, to see if I shall meet with any adventure.'

'In the name of God, go then,' replied Sir John. At these words, Lord Thomas Percy set out, attended by about thirty lances. Sir John Chandos remained with his own people. Lord Thomas crossed the bridge of Chauvigny, taking the longest road to Poitiers, having left Sir John Chandos quite low-spirited for having failed in his intended attack on St Salvin. He continued in the kitchen of the hotel, warming himself at a straw fire which his herald was making for him, conversing at the same time with his people, who very readily passed their jokes in hopes of curing him of his melancholy. After he had remained some time, and was preparing to take a little rest, and while he was asking if it were yet day, a man entered the hotel, and came before him, saying, 'My lord, I bring you news.' 'What is it?' asked Sir John. 'My lord, the French have taken the field.' 'How dost thou know this?' 'My lord, I set out from St Salvin with them.' 'And what road have they taken?' 'My lord, that I cannot say for a certainty; but it seemed to me they followed the road to Poitiers.' 'And who are these French?' 'My lord, they are Sir Louis de St Julien and Carnet le Breton, with their companies.' 'Well, it is indifferent to me,' replied Sir John. 'I have not any inclination to exert myself this day; they may be met with without my interference.' He remained a considerable time very thoughtful; after having well considered, he added: 'Notwithstanding what I have just said, I think I shall do right to mount my horse; for at all events I must return to Poitiers, and it will

51

be soon day.' 'It is well judged,' replied the knights who were with him. Sir John ordered everything to be got ready, and his knights having done the same, they mounted and set off, taking the road to Poitiers, following the course of the river. The French might be about a good league before them on this same road, intending to cross the river at the bridge of Lussac. The English suspected this from perceiving the tracks of the horses, and said among themselves, 'Either the French or Lord Thomas Percy are just before us.' Shortly after this conversation, day appeared; for in the early part of January the mornings begin to be soon light. The French might be about a league from the bridge of Lussac, when they perceived Lord Thomas Percy and his men on the other side of the river. Lord Thomas had before seen them, and had set off full gallop to gain the bridge. They said, 'There are the French: they are more in number than we are; let us hasten to take advantage of the bridge.' When Sir Louis and Carnet saw the English on the opposite side of the river, they also made haste to gain the bridge: however, the English arrived first, and were masters of it. They all dismounted, and drew themselves up to defend and guard it. The French likewise dismounted on their arrival, and giving their horses for the servants to lead them to the rear, took their lances, and advanced in good order, to attack the English and win the bridge. The English stood firm, although they were so few in comparison with the enemy. Whilst the French and Bretons were considering the most advantageous manner to begin the onset, Sir John Chandos arrived with his company, his banner displayed and flying in the wind. This was borne by a valiant man-at-arms, called James Allen, and was a pile gules on a field argent. They might be about forty lances, who eagerly hastened to meet the French. As the English arrived at a small hillock, about three furlongs from the bridge, the French servants, who were between this hillock and the bridge, saw them, and, being much frightened, said, 'Come away: let us save ourselves and our horses.' They therefore ran off, leaving their masters to shift as well as they could. When Sir John Chandos, with displayed banner, was come up to the French, whom he thought very lightly of, he began from horseback to rail at them, saying: 'Do you hear, Frenchmen! you are mischievous men-at-arms; you make incursions day and night at your pleasure; you take towns and castles in Poitou, of which I am seneschal. You ransom poor people without my leave, as if the country were your own; but, by God, it is not. Sir Louis, Sir Louis, you and Carnet are too much the masters. It is upwards of a year and a half that I have been endeavouring to meet you. Now, thanks to God, I do so, and will tell you my mind. We will now try which of us is the strongest in this country. It has been often told me, that you were very desirous of seeing me; you have now that pleasure. I am John Chandos: look at me well; and, if God please, we will now put to the proof your great deeds of arms which are so renowned.' With such words as these did Sir John Chandos greet them: he would not have wished to have been anywhere else, so eager was he to fight with them.

Sir Louis and Carnet kept themselves in a close body, as if they were willing to engage. Lord Thomas Percy and the English on the other side of the bridge knew nothing of what had passed, for the bridge was very high in the middle, which prevented them from seeing over it. During this scoffing of Sir John Chandos, a Breton drew his sword, and could not resist from beginning the battle: he struck an English squire, named Simkin Dodenhale, and beat him so much about the breast with his sword that he knocked him off his horse on the ground. Sir John Chandos, who heard the noise behind him, turned round, and saw his squire on the ground and persons beating him. This enraged him more than before: he said to his men, 'Sirs, what are you about? How suffer you this man to be slain? Dismount, dismount.' And at the instant he was on foot, as were all his company. Simkin was rescued, and the battle began.

Sir John Chandos, who was a strong and bold knight, and cool in all his undertakings, had his banner advanced before him, surrounded by his men, with the scutcheon above his arms. He himself was dressed in a large robe which fell to the ground, blazoned with his arms on white sarcenet, argent, a pile gules; one on his breast, and the other on his back; so that he appeared resolved on some adventurous undertaking; and in this state, with sword in hand, he advanced on foot towards the enemy.

This morning there had been a hoar-frost, which had made the ground slippery; so that as he marched he entangled his legs with his robe, which was of the longest, and made a stumble; during which time a squire, called James de St Martin (a strong expert man), made a thrust at him with his lance, which hit him in the face, below the eye, between the nose and forehead. Sir John Chandos did not see the aim of the stroke, for he had lost the eye on that side five years ago, on the heaths of Bordeaux, at the chase of a stag: what added to this misfortune, Sir John had not put down his vizor, so that in stumbling he bore upon the lance, and helped it to enter into him. The lance, which had been struck from a strong arm, hit him so severely that it entered as far as the brain, and then the squire drew it back to him again.

The great pain was too much for Sir John, so he fell to the ground, and turned twice over in great agony, like one who had received his death-wound. Indeed, since the blow, he never uttered a word. His people, on seeing this mishap, were like madmen. His uncle, Sir Edward Clifford, hastily advanced, and striding over the body (for the French

53

were endeavouring to get possession of it), defended it most valiantly, and gave such well-directed blows with his sword that none dared to approach him. Two other knights, namely Sir John Chambo and Sir Bertrand de Cassilies, were like men distracted at seeing their master lie thus on the ground.

The Bretons, who were more numerous than the English, were much rejoiced when they saw their chief thus prostrate, and greatly hoped he was mortally wounded. They therefore advanced, crying out, 'By God, my lords of England, you will all stay with us, for you cannot now escape.' The English performed wonderful feats of arms, as well to extricate themselves from the danger they were in as to revenge their commander, Sir John Chandos, whom they saw in so piteous a state. A squire attached to Sir John marked out this James de St Martin, who had given the blow; he fell upon him in such a rage, and struck him with his lance as he was flying, that he ran him through both his thighs, and then withdrew his lance: however, in spite of this, James de St Martin continued the fight. Now if Lord Thomas Percy, who had first arrived at the bridge, had imagined anything of what was going forwards, Sir John Chandos's men would have been considerably reinforced; but it was otherwise decreed: for not hearing anything of the Bretons since he had seen them advancing in a large body towards the bridge, he thought they might have retreated; so that Lord Thomas and his men continued their march, keeping the road to Poitiers, ignorant of what was passing.

Though the English fought so bravely at the bridge of Lussac, in the end they could not withstand the force of the Bretons and French, but were defeated, and the greater part made prisoners. Sir Edward Clifford stood firm, and would not quit the body of his nephew. If the French had their horses, they would have gone off with honour, and have carried with them good prisoners; but, as I have before said, their servants had gone away with them. Those of the English also had retreated, and quitted the scene of battle. They remained therefore in bad plight, which sorely vexed them, and said among themselves, 'This is a bad piece of business: the field is our own, and yet we cannot return through the fault of our servants. It is not proper for us who are armed and fatigued to march through this country on foot, which is quite against us; and we are upwards of six leagues from the nearest of any of our fortresses. We have, besides, our wounded and slain, whom we cannot leave behind.' As they were in this situation, not knowing what to do, and had sent off two or three of the Bretons, disarmed, to hunt after and endeavour to find their servants, they perceived advancing towards them Sir Guiscard d'Angle, Sir Louis de Harcourt, the Lords de Partenay, de Tannaybouton, d'Argenton, de Pinane, Sir James de Surgères, and several others. They were full two hundred lances, and were seeking for the French; for they had received information that they were out on an excursion, and were then following the traces of their horses. They came forwards, therefore, with displayed banners fluttering in the wind, and marching in a disorderly manner.

The moment the Bretons and French saw them they knew them for their enemies, the barons and knights of Poitou. They therefore said to the English: 'You see that body of men coming to your assistance: we know we cannot withstand them; therefore', calling each by his name, 'you are our prisoners; but we give you your liberty, on condition that you take care to keep us company; and we surrender ourselves to you, for we have it more at heart to give ourselves up to you than to those who are coming.' They answered, 'God's will be done.' The English thus obtained their liberty. The Poitevins soon arrived, with their lances in their rests, shouting their war-cries; but the Bretons and French, retreating on one side, said, 'Holla! stop, my lords; we are prisoners already.' The English testified to the truth of this by adding, 'It is so; they belong to us.' Carnet was prisoner to Sir Bertram de Cassilies, and Sir Louis de St Julien to Sir John Chandos: there was not one who had not his master.

These barons and knights of Poitou were struck with grief when they saw their seneschal, Sir John Chandos, lying in so doleful a way and not able to speak. They began grievously to lament his loss saying, 'Flower of knighthood! Oh, Sir John Chandos! Cursed be the forging of that lance which wounded thee, and which has thus endangered thy life.' Those who were around the body most tenderly bewailed him, which he heard, and answered with groans, but could not articulate a word. They wrung their hands, and tore their hair, uttering cries and complaints, more especially those who belonged to his household.

Sir John Chandos was disarmed very gently by his own servants, laid upon shields and targets, and carried at a foot's pace to Morthemer, the nearest fort to the place where they were. The other barons and knights returned to Poitiers, carrying with them their prisoners. I heard that James Martin, he who had wounded Sir John Chandos, suffered so much from his wounds that he died at Poitiers. That gallant knight only survived one day and night. God have mercy on his soul! For never since a hundred years did there exist among the English one more courteous, nor fuller of every virtue and good quality than him.

When the prince, princess, Earls of Cambridge and Pembroke, and the other English knights in Guienne heard of this event, they were completely disconcerted, and said they had now lost everything on both sides of the sea. Sir John was sincerely regretted by his friends of each sex; and some lords of France bewailed his loss. Thus it happens through life. The English loved him for all the excellent qualities he was possessed of. The French hated him because they were afraid of him.

Not but that I have heard him at the time regretted by renowned knights in France; for they said it was a great pity he was slain, and that, if he could have been taken prisoner, he was so wise and full of devices, he would have found some means of establishing a peace between France and England; and was so much beloved by the king of England and his court, that they would have believed what he should have said in preference to all others. Thus were the French and English great losers by his death, for never have I heard otherwise; but the English the most, for by his valour and prudence Guienne might have been totally recovered.

During the early 1980s the author and his trusty band of 'Battlefield-Walkers' made their own pilgrimage to the immortal area, finding and photographing the John Chandos Monument at Lussac, erected in the fourteenth century by his friends and followers, near the bridge where he met his death. It bears the words, in French: 'This monument was erected by the English of the 14th century to the memory of Constable Jean Chandos, mortally wounded in combat on the bridge of Lussac, on 30th December 1369.'

There is another stone also, put in position in 1910. From Lussac we went to Morthemer, where Sir John's body was taken and where he is said to have been buried, but could find no trace of a grave nor mention in the chapel of the château. Disappointed, we walked from the imposing building, to be stopped in our tracks by a nameplate on the wall of a house on the corner of a nearby road. It said Rue John Chandos and, even more significant, it was fixed to the wall of Bar John Chandos! Over a beer, we talked to a pair of elderly Frenchmen sitting at the counter, who said: 'Oh, he's up there somewhere, but nobody knows where', and they added, somewhat darkly, 'We know ... we've seen him.' Nor does the fame of Sir John Chandos end at Morthemer, because streets bearing his name abound throughout England; in London there are five of them and, in Southampton there is one, which is not surprising as the fleets bearing the armies who triumphed at Crécy, Poitiers and Agincourt all sailed from that port. Before pub names became 'modernised' there were numerous hostelries called the Sir John Chandos, or The Chandos and, not so very long ago, there was such a pub in Colindale Lane in Hendon, London, called The New Chandos, with Sir John's coat-of-arms on its sign!

Baugé, 21 March 1421

In the years following the English victory at Agincourt in 1415, Henry V systematically conquered Normandy and consolidated northern France, but died suddenly in August 1422 as he was preparing to move into south-central France. John, Duke of Bedford, younger brother of Henry, continued the consolidation, encountering on numerous occasions the Scots army brought to France by the Earl of Buchan in 1420, auxiliaries who displayed signal gallantry on several occasions, particularly at the battle of Baugé in 1421.

A colourful account of this relatively small action is given by Victorian military historian and writer James Grant in his series British Battles on Land and Sea (1877):

From the chronicle of Monstrelet, we learn that the Duke of Clarence, who had been appointed Governor of Normandy, after being joined by Sir Thomas Beaufort and two Portuguese captains of Free Lances, marched on Easter-eve towards Anjou, to attack the Scots and Dauphinois, who were led by Lord Buchan, the Lord de la Fayette, who was Seneschal of the Bourbonnois, and the Vicomte de Narbonne, who so lately fought against the Duke of Bedford at Harfleur. Halting on his march to dine, he had barely sat down to table when he was informed by Andrea Fregosa, an Italian deserter, that the forces of the Earl of Buchan were encamped twenty-two miles eastward of Angers, at the small town of Baugé. On this the gallant Clarence sprang from table, and exclaimed, 'Let us attack them – they are ours! But let none follow me save the men-at-arms.'

He immediately set forth with all his knights and cavalry, 'beside his other gallant furniture and rich armour, wearing round his helmet a royal coronet set with many jewels. The Earl of Salisbury was to follow at all speed, with 4,000 infantry and archers. The Scots and the Dauphinois were, we have said, at Baugé, situated on the Couanon river, which was there crossed by an ancient bridge, and the battle which ensued there resembles in some of the features the greater one fought at Stirling by Wallace and the Earl of Surrey a hundred and twenty years before. The Couanon was both deep and rapid, and its narrow bridge was the only means by which these foes could approach each other. Under Sir John Stewart, of Darnley, and the Sieur de la Fontaine, Buchan had sent forward a reconnoitring party, who saw in time the glittering lances of Clarence advancing, and fell back duly to warn the camp, where the immediate cry was 'To arms!' and Buchan drew up his forces in order of battle in front of the town, on 22 March 1421. Clarence, we are told, was inspired by hot anger on finding the passage of the river disputed by the Scots; and he might have remembered at such a time the old English proverb, which Shakespeare afterwards introduced, in his *Henry V*:

> 'There's a saying very old and true –
> If that you will France win,
> Then with Scotland first begin.'

Salisbury had orders to cross the Couanon by a ford, and turn the flank of the Scots if he could; while Clarence came on direct for the bridge with a glittering array of men-at-arms, all clad in magnificent armour. To prevent its passage being forced, its defence was entrusted to Sir Robert Stewart, of Railston, with only thirty archers; and just as the skirmish began, Sir Hew Kennedy, son of the Knight of Dunure, who was quartered in a church close by, rushed forth at the head of 100 Scots, who, in their hurry, had their armour only half-buckled; but who, by a flanking shower of arrows, drove the English back for a space. The Earl of Buchan now dashed forward, at the head of 200 chosen knights, and in the high narrow passage of the ancient bridge there ensued a dreadful, and to Clarence most fatal, combat. Inspired by the mutual hate and rancour that more than a hundred years of war engendered between them, the English and Scots, now meeting on French soil, fought with the fury of madmen. The former, says Buchanan, 'took it in great disdain that they should be attacked by such an implacable enemy, not only at home, but beyond the seas; so they fought stoutly, but none more so than Clarence himself, who was well known by his armour.'

On the other hand, Buchan, a powerful man, in the forty-second year of his age, fought with all the courage and resolution of his race; but Clarence, being distinguished by his fatal coronet, was the mark of every weapon. In the close mêlée of mounted men upon the bridge, he was almost instantly assailed by Sir John Carmichael, ancestor of the future Earls of Hyndford, who, with helmet closed and lance in rest, spurred upon him with such fury that the tough ash shaft was broken to shivers upon the corselet of the prince, who at the same moment was wounded in the face by Sir John Swinton; then, just as he was falling from his high war-saddle, the Earl of Buchan dashed out his brains by one blow with an iron mace to which he had resorted after running him through the body with his lance. The fall of so gallant a prince filled the English knights and men-at-arms with greater fury, and they pressed in crowds upon the bridge to avenge him; in their haste and confusion, jostling and impeding each other in such a fashion that they were driven back, put to flight, and cut to pieces by the Scots, who continued the pursuit of the fugitive till night came on. Monstrelet has it that 3,000 English fell; Walter Bower says 1,700, while the French lost twelve, and the Scots only two, a disparity utterly incredible, as we find in the Chronicle of the former that the Dauphinois lost 1,100 men, among whom were Sir John Yvorin, Garin des Fontaines, and the good knight, Sir Charles le Bouteiller.

Among the English there fell Gilbert de Umphreville, titular Earl of Angus, in Scotland; the Lord de Roos, of Hamlake; the Lord of Tancarville; and Sir John Grey, of Heton. Two hundred, with their horses and armour, fell into the hands of the Scots; among them were John, Earl of Somerset, whose sister, Jane Beaufort, was afterwards Queen-Consort of Scotland, and Henry, Earl of Huntington, son of Richard II's half sister. Buchan bestowed the dead body of Clarence on the Earl of Salisbury, and John, the bastard of Clarence. They bore it unmolested to Rouen, and thence to England, where it was interred at the feet of his father, in Canterbury Cathedral, as the duke had directed by a will written before the battle, but his coronet was retained by the Scots. Sir John Stuart, of Darnley, purchased it from one of his soldiers for 1,000 angels, and Sir Robert Houston afterwards lent him five times that sum upon it. Buchanan, on the authority of the lost 'Book of Pluscardine', asserts that it was Sir Alexander Macauslan, a knight of the Lennox, who took the diadem from the helmet of Clarence. Sir John Carmichael, in memory of shivering his spear on the duke's breast, added to his arms a hand grasping a broken spear; though the honour of unhorsing him was claimed by Swinton and the Laird of Auchmar. To the shield of Sir Hew Kennedy the King of France added azure, three fleurs-de-lys or, in memory of his defence of the bridge, and these are still borne by all of the surname of Kennedy who are descended from him.

On the victor, Buchan, was now bestowed the sword and office of Constable of France, of which Charles of Lorraine had been the last holder. He was the first stranger to whom such an honour had been given, and it was followed by other gifts, such as castles and princely domains, stretching over all the territory between Chartres and Avranches.

The Earl of Buchan, after capturing the castle of the former place, laying siege to the old fortress of Alençon, and repulsing with the loss of 400 men Lord Salisbury, who attempted its relief, was compelled to return to Scotland, in consequence of the feuds which had broken out there. He left Stewart of Darnley commander, or, as he was named, 'Constable of the Scots in France'.

Henry V was now master of all northern France to the banks of the Loire. Save at Baugé no leaf had fallen from the laurels he had won at Agincourt; but just as he had almost won the summit of his ambition he died, and, surviving him by only two months, Charles VI of France also passed away on 21 October 1422. John of Bedford, the persecutor of Joan of Arc, immediately ordered his young nephew, Henry VI, to be proclaimed King of France; whilst the Dauphin, now Charles VII, to whom the Scots adhered, was called in mockery by the English and Burgundians, 'King of Bourges' as these two powers held all the provinces that lay between the Loire and the Scheldt.

Even though Henry V was dead, the struggle in France showed little sign of abating, despite a certain waning of Burgundian enthusiasm for English objectives. However, this countered within two years when a small English and Burgundian army exacted revenge for the débâcle at Baugé in 1421, as recounted by James Grant in his British Battles series:

Cravant, 21 July 1423

All the bravest captains in France and all the princes of the royal blood adhered to Charles; and we are told by Monstrelet that early in July, 1423, 'he ordered a large body of forces to cross the Loire, and besiege the town of Cravant. The chief of his expedition was', he adds, 'the Constable of Scotland' – a mistake of the chronicler, for Stewart of Darnley was simply Constable of the Scots, who had soon reason to regret the absence of their former leader, as Stewart, though brave, was destitute of military skill. Rapin states that the troops which crossed the Loire were commanded by the Maréchal de Severac; but he only led the French. Cravant, which they besieged, lies six miles south east of Auxerre, and the river Yonne was between them and the united English and Burgundians, at whose approach, 15,000 strong, Stewart drew up his forces in order of battle on the slope of a hill. The blockaded town was in his rear; before him rolled the river, which was crossed there by a stone bridge.

At Dijon the Duchess of Burgundy had urged that, at all hazards, Cravant should be saved from the Scots and French; whereupon the Lord de Toulongeon, Maréchal of Burgundy, united his forces to those of the Earls of Salisbury and Suffolk, with whom came Lord Willoughby, one of the heroes of Agincourt, and many other brave knights.

The troops of Lord Salisbury suffered much on their march, by the weight of their armour and the extreme heat of the sun, especially the gendarmerie, many of whom marched on foot, leading by the bridle their horses, that the latter might be more fresh for battle. As they drew near Cravant, 120 English and Burgundian horse, with the same number of archers, were sent forward as a reconnoitring party. Each archer had a pointed stake, to plant in the earth if necessary, to keep off cavalry. In Auxerre the English and Burgundians heard mass celebrated, 'drank a cup in much brother-like affection; and departed to fall upon the Scots and French, who had been under arms all night, and towards whom they advanced in handsome array, at ten o'clock on the morning of Saturday'.

Sir John Stewart had under his orders 3,000 Scots, with some French under Aumaury, the Maréchal de Severac, the Lord of Estissac, and the Comte de Ventadour. With their troops in solid array, and with all their armour shining in the morning sun, he and those leaders sat quietly in their saddles, while the adverse forces surveyed each other for three hours; after which 'they tamely permitted the English and their allies to defile across the bridge of the Yonne, and then to arrange their squares of foot and squadrons of men-at-arms, when they ought to have occupied the tête-du-point with cannon and crossbow-men, or have attacked them when half their strength was over. The most simple lessons of military art and tactics were forgotten by these leaders, and most disastrous was the result.'

Then, without striking a blow, nearly the whole of the French, the confidence of whose soldiery had been destroyed at Agincourt, fell back, under the Seigneur de Severac, and left the field to the Scots, who stood firm. A writer asserts that in most of the encounters at this time 'the French generally ran away, and left the Scots to fight for them'.

Overlapped and overwhelmed by the superior strength of the English and Burgundians, who assailed them in front and on both flanks, while a sortie from Cravant came upon their rear, the unlucky Scots fell into disorder. Stewart fought desperately to repair his first error, but lost an eye in the conflict, by a sword-thrust through the ventaille of his helmet; and becoming thereby blinded with blood, he surrendered himself to a Burgundian noble, Claude de Beauvoir, of Castellux.

Of the Scots, 1,200 were killed, and among them are enumerated by Monstrelet a nephew of the Earl of Buchan, Sir William Hamilton, and his son, Sir Thomas Swinton, and 'John Pillot, a Scots captain, and bastard to the king'; Sir William Crawford and 400 were taken prisoners. Among the English who fell were Sir Gilbert Halselle, Sir John Grey, Sir William Hall, and Richard Ap Murdoc. The English and Burgundians offered up solemn thanks in the churches of Cravant for this victory.

Sir John Stuart was exchanged for the Lord Pole; and after being made Lord of Aubigny, Concressault, and Evereux, with the right of quartering the arms of France with his own, he was slain in his old age at the siege of Orleans.

With some nostalgia, the author recalls sitting in the Relais de Deux Ponts, alongside the bridge at Cravant, some 561 years after the Scots were massacred there, during a 1984 'Battlefield-Walking Tour' of France. Around us were the walls and turrets of this timeless little town, with a backcloth of vineyard-cloaked hills above the area, as we satisfyingly discussed our noble and warlike ancestors who rarely lost a battle in France.

4. SEVENTEENTH AND EIGHTEENTH CENTURY EUROPE

The Lech, 15 April 1632

During the Thirty Years War (1618–48), the Swedish king Gustavus Adolphus sent his army across the River Lech over a bridge of boats, to attack General Graf von Tilly's imperial army in their entrenched camp. In the battle that followed, Tilly was mortally wounded and Maximilian of Bavaria led the army in retreat, abandoning most of the artillery and baggage.

Major H. G. Eady, in his book Historical Illustrations to Field Service Regulations 1929 tells the story of the river crossing on 15 April 1632:

In this remarkable example of a crossing of a river in face of an enemy, Gustavus Adolphus employed smoke on part of the front. The Imperialists, under Tilly and the Elector, had withdrawn before Gustavus and taken up a position behind the River Lech, with their right flank on the Danube and their left on the town of Rain. 'Redoubts had been built along the low-lying river-front and joined by entrenchments; and heavy guns in suitable batteries stood at intervals. The fords of the Lech, up to Augsburg, and this city also, were held by Tilly; the bridges had been destroyed and the towns occupied.' (Dodge.) Gustavus could turn Tilly's position by crossing the Lech above him, and might be able to coop him up in a corner and starve him out: but he wanted a decisive action. He decided to do the unexpected, and cross the river frontally in Tilly's teeth, before Wallenstein could reinforce him. Having made a close reconnaissance, he threw up a 72-gun battery on the left bank, where it could dominate part of the right bank; and under cover of a constant fire, directed by the King in person, a bridge was thrown in such a way that the artillery and musketeers on the banks could protect; and when it was nearly done, there was sent over a party of 300 Finns, who were concealed by burning damp straw to produce thick smoke. These, with this concealment, got across successfully, and formed a bridgehead of earth works, and eventually the whole force was passed across by means of this bridge.

Powick Bridge, 23 September 1642

Here occurred the very first fighting of the English Civil War (1642–51), predating the opening major battle of Edgehill by exactly a month. Royalist Sir John Byron, with his Regiment of Horse, were at Worcester escorting the plate of the University of Oxford, when it was reported that the Parliamentary leader, the Earl of Essex, was marching his force in that direction.

Charles sent Prince Rupert, with eight troops of Horse and ten companies of Dragoons, to reinforce Byron. Arriving at Worcester on 23 September, the prince realised that the derelict defences of the town made it untenable, and ordered a withdrawal, covering this manoeuvre by moving to Powick Bridge, a mile and a half south of Worcester. Dismounting his cavalry, he positioned them in a shallow depression just north of the River Teme, with the Dragoons lining hedges between them and the bridge, allowing them to relax and sleep.

However, Rupert was not to know that a Parliamentarian force was close at hand; leaving Essex at Allerton on the previous day, Colonel John Brown had marched his dragoon regiment, consisting of ten troops of horse and five companies of dragoons, via Upton-on-Severn, in an exhausting night march that brought them to Powick Ham, the meadow south of the bridge, before dawn on 23 September. He kept them mounted and watchful for the rest of the night, so that they were all tired out when, at daybreak, they were ordered to line the low ridge running from Ham Hill to Powick Church.

Brown neglected to put out patrols or investigate the bridge, so that no action occurred until about mid-afternoon, when a messenger from Essex told Brown that the main army were nearing Worcester. At once, Brown decided to march and, while the dragoons were brought in from their positions, he sent his second-in-command, Colonel Edwin Sandys, with a small party out on reconnaissance.

Arriving at the bridge, where only four men could move abreast, they crossed and rode up the lane, halting, almost within musket range of Rupert's dragoons, when Sandys ordered forward his advance-guard. The Royalist dragoons opened fire at point-blank range, but did not halt the daring Sandys, although it gave the Royalist cavalry time to mount. It was reported by the Royalist Earl of Clarendon (1600–74) contemporary historian of the Civil War, that Rupert's men were not wearing their armour at the moment of the attack, removing it to snatch some sleep; and such was the rapidity of the Parliamentarians' attack, they had no time to buckle on their back-and-breast armour. In fact, Sandys's speed of movement was such that his troops in the rear had to gallop in order to keep closed up. Emerging from the lane, he and his commanders hastened to deploy, but before the first five troops were through the field-gate and those already in the field had managed to form up, Rupert's men were on them.

The prince, with his younger brother Maurice and other officers, were resting under a tree when the enemy arrived on the scene, and he immediately decided to charge as soon as the enemy came in sight. So, Prince Maurice, Lord Digby, Wilmot and Byron, along with other officers, mounted and led their troops, in order, forward. Their charge was wholly successful, and Sandys was brought to the ground causing his troop to turn and flee; the Cavalier troop led by Sir Lewis Dyve fired pistols as they charged – in the continental manner – but were fired on by carbines and suffered in the subsequent mêlée.

Roundhead Fiennes's troop were badly cut up, and Fiennes, with his cornet and half-a-dozen of his men, were forced to make a dash for the bridge, which they managed to cross. The Parliamentarian leader Brown and his dragoons held the bridge and checked the pursuit of his broken men by the victorious Cavalier horse; the Parliamentary cavalry, having lost many of their officers, would not stand and dashed wildly for safety.

These fugitives from Powick Bridge galloped towards Pershore; crossing the Severn at Upton, they came up to Essex's advance troops whom they infected with their panic, so that the whole lot turned and dashed back to the earl's main body, believing the Cavaliers to be at their heels.

The forces at Powick were about equal – about 1,000 men each; Brown lost 100–150, including fifteen out of sixty officers; the Cavaliers lost far less, about twenty-five men, although many of their best-known officers were wounded. The first action of any campaign shows moral rather than physical results, and here the first blood was drawn by the king's army, setting the tone of much that was to follow, while enhancing greatly the name of Prince Rupert.

Cropredy Bridge, 29 June 1644

In early summer 1644 Charles I and his army, watched by Waller's Parliamentary army, was engaged in a series of marches and manoeuvres in Oxfordshire. On 29 June, after a small skirmish at Crouch near Banbury, the two armies were marching on parallel lines on either side of the River Cherwell, in sight of one another, although out of musket shot. The Royalist army was in three divisions: the van led by Lord Wilmot; the main body, with the King and the Prince of Wales; and the rearguard comprising Colonel Thelwell and 1,000 foot, and the lords Northampton and Cleveland, each with a brigade of horse. The Parliamentary army reached Cropredy Bridge, where the river bent sharply north-east and was crossed two miles farther on at Hays Bridge by the Banbury–Daventry road. The distance between the two armies led the Royalists to believe that they would not be attacked; nevertheless a party of Royalist dragoons are said to have been sent to hold Cropredy Bridge until the army had passed beyond it.

The vanguard had crossed Hays Bridge when they heard that some 300 enemy horsemen were less than two miles ahead. The Royal horse were sent after them, followed by the infantry of the vanguard, who proceeded without orders, and the main body crossed the bridge and joined the pursuit. But the rearguard maintained its original pace and a considerable gap developed between it and the main body; by the time the rearguard neared Cropredy Bridge the interval had lengthened to one and a half miles. Waller saw his chance of cutting off the Royalist rear and rushed Cropredy Bridge with two columns consisting of eight troops of Hazlerig's regiment of horse ('The Lobsters') and six troops of Vandruske's regiment, totalling some 1,500 troopers, supported by nine companies of infantry under Colonel Baines, four companies of Greencoats and five companies of Waller's own regiment. Eleven guns under James Wemyss, who had previously commanded Charles's guns but had defected to the Parliamentarians, were set up about 300 yards north of the bridge, just clear of the river bank. Lieutenant-General Middleton, with 1,000 horse, crossed the river about a mile below the bridge at Slat Ford. Once across the Cherwell, Hazlerig's horse galloped wildly in pursuit of the Royalist foot regiments of the rearguard, now approaching Hays Bridge, who saw them coming and drew up facing them, lining the bridge with musketeers and overthrowing a carriage as a barricade. Seeing this, and with no supporting infantry nearer than half a mile, the Parliamentary cavalry decided discretion to be the better part of valour and retired in the direction of Cropredy Bridge. Vandruske's regiment, although charged by Cleveland with some of the rearguard Royalist cavalry, was able to rally after being supported by infantry, but Cleveland's sweeping charge had cut off from Cropredy Bridge about 1,000 Parliamentary infantry, who were in disorderly retreat when overtaken and escorted by Hazlerig's retiring troopers. Farther south, Northampton and his horse boldly charged Middleton's cavalry and, although not inflicting heavy losses, forced them back to Slat Mill, where they remained for the rest of the engagement, evidently not fancying their chances of taking a second charge.

The van, now well beyond Hays Bridge, halted, and the King sent Lord Bernard Stuart with 100 Gentlemen of the King's Troop to aid the rearguard, now facing a second attack from the rallied Roundheads. Stuart came up to Cleveland and his cavalry, who were making a stand near a great ash tree (where the King had halted for refreshments some half an hour earlier), and the joint cavalry forces, in spite of considerable musketry and artillery fire, drove both Parliamentary foot and horse back over Cropredy Bridge in an untidy rabble. James Wemyss and his guns could not get away, and he was captured with five sakers, one 12 lb piece, one demi-culverin, two minions and two 3 lb pieces, besides other artillery equipment.

Waller retreated westward beyond the River Cherwell to take up a position on high ground near Bourton, leaving some foot and dragoons at Cropredy Bridge, as the Royalists did not pursue beyond that point, and at Slat Mill ford. But the King, apparently piqued by Waller's militancy, decided to capture Cropredy Bridge and Slat Mill, and a hot engagement took place on and around the bridge. Waller's men not only held off the Royalists but also recovered three pieces of their lost artillery, after managing to advance Birch, with the Kentish Regiment and Tower Hamlet regiments and two drakes, to the bridge. The Royalists had little trouble in crossing at the ford and taking Slat Mill.

Both armies faced each other from the opposite heights, the river and the water-meadows lying between them. As night approached, the Royalist foot and horse were drawn down to the river below the ford, and cannon were fired upon the enemy horse drawn up on Bourton Hill, causing them to retire in disorder. Then the two armies fell silent and the engagement was broken off. In this small but lively engagement the Roundheads appear to have misjudged their attack. Instead of cutting off the King's rearguard, they found themselves caught between two fires, and it seemed that the King, more by accident than design, had drawn the enemy over Cropredy Bridge and inflicted a sharp reverse upon them.

On today's A423 road from Oxford to Coventry, Cropredy lies five miles beyond Banbury; the bridge is on the road to Wardington, at the far end of the village. The surrounding fields remain much the same, but the river itself has been considerably narrowed through water being taken from it by the Oxford Canal.

Much repaired until restored in 1691, the bridge was completely rebuilt on its original site in 1937; a small plaque set in the parapet reveals that the first bridge was built in 1314 by the Bishop of Lincoln.

Preston, 17 August 1648

The second English Civil War lasted from 1648 until 1651, and during its first year – in July and August – James, Duke of Hamilton, led a Scottish invasion of 24,000 men into England, causing Cromwell to march, with 8,500 men, towards Preston. In the series of actions that followed, the ill-equipped and poorly led Scots took a general beating from the organised and well-led Parliamentary forces. On 17 August, the Duke of Hamilton's force on Preston Moor were advised by the Earl of Callander to fall back over Preston Bridge, so that the River Ribble would be between their reunited army and Cromwell's forces. General Baillie took the Scottish foot over the bridge, leaving two brigades to hold it against the Parliamentary forces, a necessary precaution because Cromwell's horse soon burst into Preston itself. Hamilton, Scots commander-in-chief, had remained on the moor with a small rearguard, who now found themselves cut off, with Hamilton himself separated from the bulk of his army. In the end, some of his men escaped from the moor, as Hamilton's small cavalry force fought bravely, until Hamilton was forced to swim the Ribble to make his escape.

Preston cleared of Scots, Cromwell was able to turn his attention to Preston Bridge, where the two Scots brigades were only able to hold out for two hours, allowing Baillie time to form his infantry just south of the Darwen, a tributary of the Ribble. Parliamentary infantry took the Darwen bridge soon after storming the Ribble bridge where both sides took heavy losses. The Parliamentarians pressed forward over the Darwen bridge, driving in

Baillie's outposts, to capture the Scots' supply wagons, abandoned by their civilian drivers on the slope leading up from the bridge.

By nightfall on 17 August, Cromwell had captured about 1,000 of Hamilton's men besides killing the same number, to give him a complete victory. Describing his defeat of Hamilton, in a letter to Parliament, written on 20 August, Cromwell says: 'The duke, with most of the Scots horse and foot, retreated over the bridge, where after a very hot dispute betwixt the Lancashire regiments ... they were beaten from the bridge and our horse and foot followed them, killed many and took divers prisoners.'

Within the space of one hundred years, the bridge over the Ribble played a prominent part in British military history. The first occasion has been described above. The second was during the siege of Preston in 1715, when 'General' Forster had omitted to guard the bridge and the narrow pass leading therefrom to the town, thus leaving the approach open to General Wills and the Royalist forces marching from Wigan.

The third historic occasion was when Prince Charles Edward's Scottish army passed over the bridge in safety on their retreat from Derby – threatened by Marshal Wade's northern army on their right flank, and the Duke of Cumberland's forces in the rear.

Bothwell Bridge, 22 June 1679

On June 1 1679 a Scottish rebel Covenanter force defeated and bloodily massacred a Royalist force under John Graham, Viscount Dundee, at Drumclog, in south-central Scotland. James Scott, Duke of Monmouth – illegitimate son of Charles II – was sent with a Royalist army to crush the rebels.

The detailed account that follows is taken from the well-known Victorian military history series British Battles on Land and Sea by James Grant:

As soon as Charles II heard of the affair at Drumclog and the spread of the insurrection, he ordered the celebrated and eventually unfortunate Duke of Monmouth to assume the command of the troops in Scotland. Forty copies of a speech made by Lord Shaftesbury in the English Parliament (to the effect 'that popery was intended to recede slavery in England, and that slavery had been the forerunner of popery in Scotland') were dispatched to Edinburgh for circulation, and it became, says Dalrymple, like the sound of a trumpet to the Scots.

On the proposal being made that some forces should accompany Monmouth, Shaftesbury started an objection 'that English troops could not be sent into Scotland without infringing the treaties between the two nations', and several of the Whig party refused to serve, among others Lord Grey, who was to have commanded the cavalry; and the city of London petitioned against any expedition into Scotland: so that ultimately only four troops of English cavalry, under Major Main, and 'clad in coats of a reddish hue', according to the old Cameronian ballad, accompanied the duke, who left London on 15 June, and on the 19th reached Edinburgh, a remarkable instance of speed when we consider what was then the state of the roads between these two cities. Prior to his arrival, on 6 June, the Earl of Linlithgow, on being appointed Major-General of the Scottish land forces in lieu of Sir George Munro, had ordered a rendezvous at Falkirk, where he was joined by Lord Ross and Claverhouse; and on marching to Larbert Muir he was joined by his own regiment, under his son, Lord Livingstone. The forces present were: Life Guards, one squadron; independent horse, three squadrons; the Foot Guards, two battalions; Lord Mar's Fusiliers, two battalions (21st Foot). In addition to these regulars were some militia from counties well affected to the Government, the most resolute of these being the Lennox Highlanders. The Haddingtonshire Regiment was led by George Seton, Earl of Winton. Those of Lothian were clad in blue uniforms; and about this time hats, in lieu of bonnets, were first worn by them. Save Main's dragoons, there were no English troops with the duke, though Scott, in his romance of *Old Mortality*, writes again and again of 'the English Foot Guards' at Bothwell Bridge; and the appearance of these dragoons did not add in Scotland to the popularity of the duke who, at the head of 10,000 men and a fine park of artillery, marched against the insurgents at midsummer.

The appearance of the royal army as it defiled over Bothwell Muir is said to have been so imposing – the regular aspect of the checkered squads of pikemen and musketeers, the guards, horse, dragoons and artillery, making up a glittering whole that it seemed as if nothing short of an actual miracle could prevent the total rout and destruction of the ill-equipped and ill-ordered forces of the insurgents, who had now taken possession of the bridge which led across the Clyde to the preaching camp which they had formed on the opposite side of the river. The famous General Dalzell was not present on this occasion with the army, though described as being so in Scott's romance. 'Upon the duke being made commander-in-chief, Dalzell refused to serve under him,' says Captain Crichton, 'and remained at his lodgings in Edinburgh till his Grace was superseded, which happened about a fortnight after.' According to the *London Gazette*, it was at seven in the morning when the Scottish regular troops began to approach the bridge of Bothwell; but prior to that the Covenanters had seen them advancing in the dark or before daybreak, by their lighted matches, which seemed like thousands of glow-worms in the moorland.

The Covenanters were now under 8,000 strong; but save those already named few gentlemen of note and not one of the nobility had joined them, the field-preachers being in fact their generals: though it is shrewdly suspected that they were secretly instigated to proceed to desperate measures by some influential men in Scotland, who acted in combination with Lord Shaftesbury and other popular leaders in England. Yet these poor people showed great judgment in their choice of a position, if they failed in skill or the means for defending it.

The ancient bridge, now so celebrated in history, was then very different from what it appears today. It was long and narrow, with four arches about 120 feet in length; but in breadth, exclusive of the parapets, it measured not more than 12 feet. It was paved with round unhewn stones, taken from the bed of the river which flows beneath it. In the centre was a fortified gateway, which was frequently the case on Scottish bridges in those days. This gateway rose from the pier nearest the southern bank, and the keeper's house occupied the other extremity. It also served as a kind of inn, or travellers' rest. Three-fourths of the bridge were left open and unprotected by the gateway upon that side from which annoyance might proceed.

On one side was a hollow, where the road is now filled up; and this gave the bridge a rise of twenty feet in its centre, and such was its aspect until 1826. The banks of the Clyde were fringed by thickets of hazel and alder trees. The ground occupied by the insurgents was a plain open field, interspersed by a few clumps of trees; consequently, as they were without efficient cavalry or artillery, on the defence of the bridge depended all their chances of success or of safety.

The appearance of the country around is different now from what it was then. The great muir or moor of Bothwell, over which the royal army advanced in such imposing order, is now a beautiful and fertile district; and a villa crowns the summit of the green knoll where the Duke of Monmouth, mounted on a superb white charger, and clad in all the Cavalier bravery of the day, with wig, and plume and breastplate, and with the Garter glistening on his breast, was seen, baton in hand, directing the motions of the troops and the fire of the artillery; and all the ground occupied by the insurgents is now turned into well-enclosed fields and thriving plantations.

Encouraged by the recent repulse of the Life Guards at Drumclog, the Covenanters prepared confidently to dispute the passage of the bridge. The central toll-house or gateway they had very strongly barricaded by stones, carts, wheels, and banks of earth; and to defend the hostelry of the warder was the special task of Hackston of Rathillet and Hall of Haughead, with 300 chosen marksmen. A cannon or two they had in position to sweep the approach to the bridge and gate; and along the bank of the river were all the horse they possessed, under Sergeant John Nisbet; and a body of matchlocks, under the grim and stern Balfour of Burleigh, occupied the thickets and bushes. The main body lay in dense masses within a quarter of a mile from the bridge. As the king's troops drew near, the insurgents could be seen in clamorous confusion. Instead of being in quiet order of battle, listening only to their officers or leaders, they were crowding around the preachers, while discord, timidity and irresolution began to prevail. Some proposed to lay their grievances before the Duke of Monmouth, a measure strongly opposed by Balfour and others, yet it took place.

Messengers with a flag of truce were sent to the duke, who received them on the green knoll with great courtesy; but he told them no negotiation would be entertained unless they surrendered as prisoners of war, unconditionally. They were further informed that if they would trust to the royal clemency they would be favourably received. 'Yes, and hung next!' was the scornful response of the messengers. They were allowed half an hour to consider the conditions, which eventually were fiercely and sorrowfully rejected by these desperate men, who were in no way suited to compete with the forces brought against them, and who were without order, and almost without ammunition; for one large barrel, which had come from a dealer in Hamilton, and was supposed to contain powder, on being opened was found to be filled with raisins!

While the royal troops formed in battalions and squadrons on one side of the Clyde, on the other could be seen the masses of the insurgents, with pikes glittering and banners displayed, but in no order. Thousands of tongues were vociferating, and no one was listening. To some parties the field-preachers were haranguing on their usual bitter topics, blending passages from the Old Testament with fierce denunciations of the king, of Claverhouse, of Erastians, Nullifidians, Prelatists and Anti-Covenanters. At length, when a few shots, at the expiry of the half hour, were exchanged between the advanced guard and the matchlock men at the bridge, they suffered themselves to be formed into ranks, and, after the manner of Drumclog, they struck up a psalm; but it was observed by the superstitious that it sounded more like 'a penitentiary stave than the bold strain which had resounded along the wild heath of Loudon Hill, in anticipation of that day's victory. The melancholy melody soon received a rough accompaniment, for the cannon began to fire on one side and the musketry on both, and the bridge of Bothwell, with the wooded banks adjacent, were involved in wreaths of smoke.'

Led by Lord Livingstone, the 1st and 2nd battalions of the Scots Foot Guards, and those of the Earl of Mar's Fusiliers, under cover of a fire from the artillery, formed in four contiguous close columns, rushed double quick, with colours flying, to the margin of the Clyde, and speedily deployed into line along its right bank, and then heavy file firing ensued from both ends of the bridge.

'I shall never forget the effect of our fire from our battery where my men stood,' says the Laird of Torfoot. 'We saw the line of the foe advance in all the military glory of brave and beautiful men; the horses pranced, the armour gleamed. In one moment nothing was seen but a shocking mass of mortality – human limbs, and the bodies and limbs of horses, mingled in one huge heap, or blown to a great distance. Another column attempted to cross above the bridge, and some threw themselves into the current; but one well directed fire from Burleigh's troops threw them into disorder, and drove them back.'

So resolute was the defence made on the long narrow bridge, swept as it was by the concentrated fire of 300 picked marksmen, that the Foot Guards gave way, on which the Duke of Monmouth leaped from his horse, and proceeded to rally and re-form them, sword in hand.

Then it was that the Macfarlane clan, with their badge, tufts of the cloud-berry bush in their bonnets, and led by their chief, raised their cathghairm, or shrill wild battle cry, of 'Lochsloy! Lochsloy!' taken from a lake at the head of Loch Lomond, the centre of their ancient possessions, and rushed on with sword and target to storm the gateway, at the very moment when the ammunition of its defenders began to fail. Over the killed and wounded of the Foot Guards they sprang lightly, and with axes and hammers beat the portal to pieces; the trees, carts, wheels and other obstructions which formed the barricade were cast into the river. Then the roll of the musketry had ceased, for the ammunition was done on one hand, and on the other the infantry battalions had plugged their bayonets, as was still the fashion, in the muzzles of their matchlocks. The Lennox Highlanders now led the way, opposing their targets, claymores and poleaxes to the halberts, pikes and partisans of those who came on, under Burleigh and others, to succour the men who fought under Rathillet and Haughead.

A brief but bloody conflict ensued; the Covenanters were driven back in front, and many of those in the rear began to fly, while the troops with all speed continued to defile across the bridge, and form by regiments on the opposite bank, unscrewing their wooden-hafted bayonets, and opening fire as they came up upon the recoiling masses.

The moment the last man of the infantry was over, the fiery Claverhouse, 'who, like a hawk perched on a rock, and eyeing the time to pounce upon its prey, had watched the event of the action from the opposite bank', now, with reins loose and brandished sword, led over all the cavalry, forming them in squadrons almost at a gallop, and then wheeling them at full speed in the open ground round the flanks of the Foot Guards and Line, fell upon the Covenanters, whose loose and dis-

71

heartened masses were in no condition to encounter a charge of horse, with all its terrible accompaniments of speed, sight and sound.

Burning to avenge their recent defeat at Drumclog, the terrible Life Guards, cuirassed and plumed, and armed with swords of enormous length, were first among them, cutting down the unfortunates on all hands. The latter gave one disorderly or scattered volley, made one attempt to form a stand of pikes, and then all was over, and the Guards, the mounted Militia, and Main's English dragoons, called by some Oglethorpe's Horse, were riding through the living masses as through a field of ripened corn. The slaughter was terrible; the screams and cries of the wounded and dying were heard at a vast distance, and the Duke of Monmouth, on his white charger, was seen to ride in every direction to arrest the pursuit of the fugitives, and save their lives if possible.

A column of 1,200 men, on finding themselves surrounded and cut off, surrendered at discretion, though in most instances they had better have died on the field, as the axe and the gibbet, torture by steel boots and thumbscrews, captivity, slavery and shipwreck were before them. In this battle, as in many others, the numbers present, killed or taken vary in every account.

In Blackadder's *Memoirs*, we are told that the Life Guards in the pursuit could not resist cutting down some of Main's dragoons and certain of the mounted militia, 'being grieved to see the English men delighting so much to shed their countrymen's blood'. The pursuit continued long after the trumpets had sounded a retreat, and in their despair the fugitives made a last attempt to rally and defend the streets of Hamilton, under the command of John Balfour of Burleigh and Captain Paton, when the former received a bullet which broke his right arm.

'May the hand that fired the shot be withered!' he exclaimed, fiercely, as the sword fell from his grasp. 'I can fight no longer now.'

Turning his horse's head, he galloped away, and made his escape to Holland. According to the *London Gazette*, about 800 were killed on the field. Many of the fugitives found a refuge in the leafy recesses of Cadzow Forest and the wooded domain of Hamilton Palace, where they were defiantly protected by the Duchess Anne, the eldest surviving daughter of James, Duke of Hamilton and Chatelherault, who had been beheaded for his loyalty to Charles, in March 1649. Her Grace sent a message to the Duke of Monmouth desiring him ' to prevent his soldiers from trespassing upon her grounds'.

Robert Hamilton, of Preston, the commander, reached Ayrshire in safety, and died a baronet in 1701; but Hackston of Rathillet, and Sergeant Nisbet, taken at different times, with two of the field-preachers, were executed at Edinburgh, and their heads were fixed on the Tolbooth wall.

On the field of Bothwell, the pursuit was scarcely over and the troops had just returned to their colours, when old General Dalzell arrived on horseback from Edinburgh, in hot haste, lest he should be too late for the fighting. He brought with him a new commission, appointing him commander-in chief, but not entirely superseding the Duke of Monmouth, whom he is said to have upbraided for his clemency to the prisoners, and especially for the orders he had issued that morning. These were 'to yield quarter to all who asked it; to take as many prisoners as possible, and to spare life'. 'Had my commission come before the battle,' said Sir Thomas, grimly, 'these rogues should never more have troubled king or country.'

He then marched the troops to Glasgow, all save Main's dragoons. These returned to England with Monmouth, who en route received, says Lord Kingston, a splendid banquet, on 6 July, from the Earl of Winton, at his house of Seton. The *London Gazette* announces that the news of the victory at Bothwell Bridge was received in the capital with intense satisfaction. Bonfires were set ablaze, bells pealed and cannon boomed, with other signs of rejoicing over the defeat of those unfortunates whose wrongs the citizens cared not to comprehend, and who had come forth to do battle 'for an oppressed Kirk and broken Covenant'; and it must be acknowledged that for the sake of their religious opinions the Scots have made bloody sacrifices, to which there is no parallel in the records of England; and well did their Church assume the motto, 'Behold the bush burned with fire, and the bush was not consumed.'

Crossing of the River Duna, 6 October 1700

During the Great Northern War (1700–21), Russia, Poland and Denmark entered into a secret alliance to end Sweden's domination of the Baltic. Charles XII, the sixteen-year-old King of Sweden, displaying military talents far beyond his years, was consistently successful throughout the war, beginning in 1700 when he invaded Livonia. The subsequent events arising from his crossing of the River Duna on 6 October 1700 are related by Major H. G. Eady in his Historical Illustrations to Field Service Regulations:

Poland and Russia, under Peter the Great, had just formed an alliance against Charles XII, who, after having passed the winter at Narva, appeared in Livonia, in the neighbourhood of Riga.

Voltaire, in his History of Charles XII, writes:

'The Saxon troops, hired by the King of Poland, were posted along the River Duna, which is very broad at that place. Charles, who was on the other side of the river, was obliged to dispute the passage. The King of

Sweden had caused some large boats to be built on a new plan, the sides of which were much higher than ordinary, and could be raised or let down like a drawbridge. When raised, they covered the troops on board; and when let down, they served as bridges to land them.' (Compare these with Admiral Bacon's pontoons for the protected landing on the Belgian coast in the Great War.) 'He made use also of another artifice. Having remarked that the wind blew from the north, where he lay, to the south, where the enemy's camps were, he ordered that they should set fire to a quantity of wet straw. From this a thick smoke arose, and so spread itself over the river, that the Saxons were prevented from seeing his troops, and observing what he was about. Under the cover of this cloud, he ordered several boats to put off full of the like wet fuel; so that the cloud always increased, and was driven by the wind into the eyes of the enemy, making it impossible for them to know whether the King was passing the river or not. Meanwhile he conducted the execution of his stratagem alone. In a quarter of an hour, he had effected the crossing.' He immediately landed his cannon, and formed a line of battle, while the enemy, blinded with smoke, could not oppose him, except by a few random shot. The wind having dispersed the smoke, the Saxons saw the King of Sweden already advancing towards them.'

Oudenarde, 11 July 1708

During the War of the Spanish Succession (1701–14), the Duke of Marlborough won fame with his quartet of victories at Blenheim (1704), Ramillies (1706), Oudenarde (1708) and Malplaquet (1709). At Oudenarde, Marlborough's plans of action entailed the provision and crossing of a bridge over the River Scheldt. Brief mentions of this river crossing are contained in two well-known series of books on British military history.

From British Battles on Land and Sea, edited by Field Marshal Sir Evelyn Wood, comes the following:

The town of Oudenarde lies on low ground in the valley of the Scheldt, which flows there from south-west to north-east. The Norken river, which rises near Oycke, runs nearly parallel to the Scheldt, which it joins below Gavre. From Oycke, which stands on the highest ground of the battlefield and about three miles to the west of Oudenarde, two small streams rising near the Norken run nearly at right angles away from it, and through Eyne into the Scheldt.

There is a succession of hamlets facing the Scheldt and parallel to it, Mooreghem, Bevere, Groenewald and Heurne, the former being a mile upstream of Oudenarde, and the latter three miles down the Scheldt, all about a mile from the water-line.

When Marshal Vendôme learnt that the Allies' cavalry were across the Scheldt, he rode towards the river, and from the high ground above Eyne saw that the enemy's infantry were still far back and he directed that all the hamlets facing the Scheldt should be occupied, sending seven battalions to hold Heurne.

And from James Grant's British Battles on Land and Sea:

Oudenarde was invested by the French on 9 July, and the Duke of Burgundy and Marshal Vendôme intended to occupy the strong camp at Lessines, on the Dender, to cover the siege; but they were opposed by a commander whose promptitude and decision were only equalled by those of the 'Great Duke' of the succeeding century, and whose resources were called forth by the magnitude of the stake for which he was contending. By gaining Lessines before them, and passing the Scheldt, as stated, he compelled them to march in the direction of Gavre; and in order to force on a general engagement, Major-General Cadogan, with sixteen battalions and some cavalry, was detached to throw bridges over the Scheldt near Oudenarde, for the passage of the army.

The Allies marched with such expedition that about two o'clock in the afternoon of 11 July the advanced guard reached the bridges over which the battalions of Cadogan were passing. The French had thrown seven battalions into the village of Heynom, or Eynem, through which the long level highway runs along the margin of the Scheldt, and about three o'clock this battle, in which scarcely any artillery was used, and which was almost decided by musketry alone, was commenced by General Cadogan driving in some of the French foragers with his cavalry.

He was in turn charged by a corps of French dragoons, under the Count de Chimarault, upon which he retired to a position where he became an object of doubt and suspicion to Burgundy and Vendôme, who believed that the whole allied army, and not a solitary advanced column, was before them.

They accordingly halted, and observing a heavy column of horse crossing the river, drew in their pickets, in order to avoid exposing them to the attack of a superior force.

It was fortunate for Cadogan and his corps that a difference of opinion among the French leaders, already confounded by finding themselves out-generalled, kept them from either falling on more boldly towards their front, or hazarding an attack on the bridge. Had either step been taken, this column, with the advanced guard, must have been cut off; for the main body of the army was yet in the rear, and not all the exertions of Marlborough and Eugene could get it into the line of battle for the space of two hours.

At the head of his cavalry, as soon as Cadogan's peril became known, Marlborough came pressing on; but the infantry, worn with past toil, encumbered with knapsacks, greatcoats, blankets and the heavy musket of those days (weighing fourteen pounds) proceeded more slowly, and at this time the officers of the Scotch and Welsh Fusiliers were armed with very ponderous partisans. Hence the leading companies did not reach the bridge until past three in the afternoon. The uniform of those days, with its heavy square skirt and huge-cuffed coat, coarse braided hat and feather, long gaiters, and thick crossbelts, was cumbersome to the soldier; but each corps as it arrived, whether horse or foot, moved promptly into position, and six guns being planted in battery on an eminence, the whole assumed by degrees an imposing attitude.

Fortunately for Marlborough the Duke of Burgundy, heir to Louis XIV, and Commander-in-Chief of all his armies, was present, and, exercising his right, he determined to form a line of battle on the left bank of the Norken, two and a half miles from the Scheldt. The seven battalions ordered by Marshal Vendôme to hold Heurne marched in error to Eyne, three-quarters of a mile farther south.

The advanced guard of the Allied infantry reached the Scheldt at 2 p.m., crossing by the Oudenarde bridge and pontoons, which had been thrown over the river by Lord Cadogan. A brigade, under General Sabine, consisting of the Liverpool Regiment, Royal Welsh and Iniskilling Fusiliers, attacked Eyne vigorously in front, and the cavalry which had passed through Oudenarde, forming up in the rear, so demoralised the seven battalions that three surrendered, four broke up, and were pursued and slaughtered by the cavalry under Prince George of Hanover (later George II). He, having broken some French squadrons, drove them across the Norken.

At 4 p.m., when the Allied infantry were still crossing the Scheldt and Cadogan had only two battalions in Groenewald, one mile in advance of Eyne, the Duke of Burgundy advanced his right wing, and Marshal Vendôme, conforming, brought forward his left, but the Duke sent him orders to entrench.

Marlborough sent up twelve battalions to Groenewald, and the Prussian cavalry formed up to the north of Heurne, the British infantry occupying Bevere, on the left flank, at the same time.

The two battalions of Prussians, although attacked by thirty of the French, held on with grand courage in Groenewald until supports came up, which prolonged the line to Schaerken, on the left or south flank, where much hand to hand fighting took place, in which the Royal Scots (Lothian Regiment) and the Buffs (East Kent Regiment) were hotly engaged.

76

5. THE NAPOLEONIC WARS

The battles of the Napoleonic Era produced generals endowed with great qualities of leadership, in command of soldiers who displayed outstanding courage and endurance. The period of the French Revolutionary Wars (1792–1800) witnessed numerous military engagements which entailed a wide range of tactical skills, including the passage and capture of bridges. The two that follow are taken from Lieutenant-Colonel Clery's book Minor Tactics.

River Po, 6 May 1796

At the outset of the campaign of 1796 in Italy, a French force under Bonaparte, of about 35,000 men, was opposed to an Austro-Sardinian force, under Beaulieu, of about 60,000. The theatre of war was the country south of the Po, between Genoa and the Alps. The Sardinians occupied a line from the Stura river to Mellesimo, with headquarters at Ceva. The Austrians prolonged this line to the left as far as Voltaggio. Bonaparte concentrated against this extended line at Savona.

In the first important engagement of the campaign (Montenotte), the French, victorious, penetrated between the Austrians and Sardinians; following up this success the next day, they completely separated them.

Bonaparte left one division to observe the Austrians driven back on Mondovi, where they were again defeated. This led to an armistice with the Sardinians, in which they separated themselves from the Austrians, and ceded to the French the fortresses of Alessandria, Tortoni, Coni and Ceva. Bonaparte now turned against the Austrians.

Beaulieu had withdrawn across the Po at Valenza, destroying the bridge, and had taken up a position to defend Lombardy and cover Milan. The Po, increasing considerably in width from Casale downwards, is a formidable barrier in this direction.

Bonaparte aimed at driving the Austrians out of Lombardy, but to do this he must throw his army across the Po. In the armistice with the Sardinians, he stipulated for the right of passing the river at Valenza. This led Beaulieu to infer that the French would attempt the passage at that point. He accordingly took up a position with his main body on the Ogogna at Vallegro; an advanced guard on the Sesia; a division (General Liptay) on the left bank of the Ticino near its confluence with the Po; a division at Buffalova, a brigade at Somma. He also threw up some fortifications along the line of the Ogogva.

To attempt the passage at Valenza would be to do so in face of an army in position on the other bank. This would entail great loss, and be of doubtful success. Further, even were the passage effected, the subsequent advance on Milan would lead the French directly against a number of smaller rivers, affording good defensive positions to the enemy.

Clearly, therefore, if the Austrian position could be turned, what was aimed at would be best effected. Could that turning movement be carried out on the enemy's left, then not only would the passage be gained, but his line of retreat to the Mincio seriously endangered.

But below Pavia the Po increased in size and difficulty. Moreover, Bonaparte had no pontooning equipage. Still he determined to attempt a passage at Piacenza. For this it was essential to deceive the Austrians to the last.

The position of the French on 5 May was: one division threatening Valenza, half a division at Sale Cambio, and the remainder echeloned towards Voghera.

Bonaparte collected 3,000 infantry and 1,500 cavalry at Casteggio, and on 6 May led them in a forced march by S. Giovanni on Piacenza. At the same time a hundred cavalry moved along the river bank to seize any boats that could be found, of which they secured several and brought them to Piacenza. This advanced party reached Piacenza the following morning, the 7th, and the infantry at once commenced crossing. There were only two squadrons of Austrian cavalry to oppose them, and these they quickly obliged to retire.

As soon as this movement on Piacenza had been sufficiently pronounced, three divisions of the French followed in forced marches. The division before Valenza was still retained there to mask the movement. By the evening two divisions had effected a crossing, and during the night the third.

When Beaulieu detected this movement of the French, he ordered Liptay to move with eight battalions and eight squadrons towards Pizzighetone to oppose it. He followed himself in the same direction with ten battalions and twenty-two squadrons.

On the 8th, the French attacked Liptay at Fombio before Beaulieu came up, and drove him back on Pizzighetone.

Beaulieu, coming up, divided his force, seeking to establish communication with Liptay. After a night affair with the French outposts, in which he was repulsed, he fell back on Lodi.

The French were now securely established on the left bank.

The bridge of Lodi, 10 May 1796

In the campaign of 1796, in Italy, the Austrians under Beaulieu, after a succession of defeats by the French, were first forced across the Po, and finally driven back on the Mincio. In retiring over the Adda, Beaulieu left about 10,000 men under Sebottendorf to defend the bridge over that river at Lodi.

Lodi was a small town surrounded by a high wall, distant from the bridge about 200 yards. Sebottendorf placed one battalion and two squadrons in Lodi, and, with the remainder withdrew to the other side of the river.

Bonaparte, having crossed the Po at Piacenza, pushed on in pursuit of Beaulieu with the Augereau and Masséna divisions. His leading troops drove the small Austrian force out of Lodi and across the river, but their further advance was checked by Sebottendorf's attitude at the other side.

On finding Lodi occupied, Bonaparte at once argued that the bridge had not been destroyed. So, pushing rapidly on, he himself, under a heavy fire, placed two light guns in position, to enfilade the bridge and prevent the enemy from blowing it up.

As more guns came up a heavy cannonade commenced on both sides. Bonaparte determined, after his troops had a couple of hours' rest, to storm the bridge. To defend it Sebottendorf had placed three battalions and fourteen guns in first line, holding five battalions and six squadrons in reserve.

To storm the bridge Bonaparte formed the grenadiers, about 4,000 strong, into a close column. They were drawn up behind the wall of the town running along the river, until the moment arrived for them to move against the bridge. This column was to be supported by Masséna's division. The mass of the cavalry was sent up the river about a mile and a half, to cross by a ford and fall on the flank of the Austrians. The fire of the whole of the disposable artillery was concentrated on the Austrian guns enfilading the bridge. The islands in the river were occupied with French skirmishers.

The bridge was about 200 yards long and very narrow. It rested, about a third of the way from the French side, on a sand-bank.

At a given signal the column of grenadiers moved from behind their cover and pushed rapidly on to the bridge. The whole of the Austrian guns at once opened on them with grape, and under this crushing fire the column staggered and showed signs of falling back. Alive to the danger of a moment's hesitation, Berthier, Masséna, Dallemagne and Ceroni rushed to the front to lead their men on.

Some soldiers, perceiving that the water shallowed towards the other side, slid down to the sand-bank in the river, and, followed by others, waded across, and advanced in skirmishing order against the enemy. The column on the bridge again pushed forward at the double, overthrew Sebottendorf's first line and captured the guns.

79

At the same time a body of 300 cavalry swam the river, charged the enemy, and took two guns. The Austrians now fell back, leaving the French in possession of the bridge. The French lost over 200 men on the bridge alone.

The next account of a river crossing by French forces comes from General Sir Edward Hamley'sThe Operations of Wars:

Moreau's passages of the Rhine, 24–26 June 1796

In 1796 it was arranged that the passage of the Rhine should take place a little above Kehl – the fortifications of that place forbidding a direct passage.

The river Ill runs nearly parallel to the Rhine past Strasbourg. A canal unites it to the small branch of the Rhine called the Bras Mabile.

The materials for the passage were to be collected in Strasbourg, and to be taken by canal to the Bras Mabile, where the attacking force was to embark. On the opposite bank the river was watched by the Swabian troops in the camp of Wilstett, the works of Kehl, and along the course of the Rhine for several miles on each side, 7,500 men in all, of which about half were near enough to oppose the passage. The Austrians had about 9,000 men between the Rench and Murg, and about 4,000 extending from above Kehl to Brisach.

All being ready, a false attack was made on 20 June on the Austrian camp at Mannheim. On the same day the troops for the first embarkation quitted the neighbourhood of Mannheim for Strasbourg. The French right wing from the Upper Rhine also closed on Strasbourg. All the troops were to arrive near there on 23 June.

Some 16,000 French, for the main attack, were assembled in Strasbourg, while 12,000 were to make a secondary passage at Gambsheim. Between these places, three false attacks were to be made to confuse and distract the Austrians.

The width of the main branch of the Rhine is from 200 to 300 yards near Kehl. The numerous islands diminishing the total breadth of the stream, the woody banks, and the dikes along the shores, forming at once lines of defence for the first troops that might cross, were all circumstances in favour of the passage.

About 2,500 embarked at half-past one. The guns at the points of false attacks then opened. The flotilla ascended the Bras Mabile, and got into the main stream; the main body landed on the wooded islands nearest Kehl – a detachment of 1,500 men seized the bridge connecting the Erlen-Rhin with the Kehl shore; another attacked and carried the batteries on the Erlen-Rhin, and a fourth attacked the two small islands on the stream. The boats, having landed all these, returned for fresh troops.

The Austrians, from their camp at Wilstett, marched to this point in time to oppose the troops first landed, who maintained themselves behind the dikes.

A flying bridge from the French shore to the Erlen-Rhin was established by six in the morning. Infantry passed incessantly there, and by boats. Sufficient troops having passed, they moved on to Kehl. A detachment attacked the Austrian works, aided by heavy artillery from the Strasbourg bank. The enemy were driven out, on the Buhl road, and had no time to destroy the bridges of the Kinzig.

The bridge of boats opposite Kehl was commenced at six in the evening and finished next morning. The communications were thereby assured, and cavalry and artillery passed.

25 June: Moreau reconnoitred the enemy.

26 June: The French pushed out on Goldschir, Korck, and Wilstett.

The Austrians, who had been driven back on Wilstett on the 24th, retired on Buhl.

Had Moreau brought Laborde's division from the Upper Rhine, where it was now useless, he might have assembled at Wilstett, on the 26th, 45,000 men – enough to guard the passages, and to crush all the troops between him and the Murg.

The Austrians after the passage were scattered thus: 4,000 on the Rench, 8,000 at Buhl and 2,000 on the Murg.

About 4,000, separated from the rest, moved up the river towards Friburg.

Arcola, 15 November 1796

Situated some 40 kilometres south-east of Verona, amid marshes at the confluence of the rivers Adige and Alpone, the town of Arcola was the scene of one of the most colourful battles fought and won by Napoleon during the Italian campaign of 1796. On the night of 14 November, leaving a mere 3,000 troops to hold Verona, Napoleon led his 18,000 men along the south bank of the River Adige, to force a surprise crossing at Ronco, about seven kilometres south-west of Arcola. By dawn on the following day, General Andreossy, commanding the bridging-train of the Army of Italy, had managed to place a pontoon bridge across the river. This allowed French troops to pour across into the marshes beyond as though to threaten the Austrian commander Alvinczy's lines of communication running east from Verona.

Masséna sent a force to cover the French left at Porcile, as Bonaparte led forward 6,000 men of Augereau's division towards the Alpone bridge at Arcola, to begin a battle for the crossing that lasted all day against the reinforced Austrian defenders, who succeeded in holding the bridge. Exposing himself recklessly throughout the fight, at one point Napoleon, colour in hand, was almost drowned as he was pushed into the water by one of his over-excited commanders.

Next morning the struggle was resumed and although they secured Por-cile, the French were still not successful at the bridge. On the third day, Napoleon continued the attack, as Masséna was sent to occupy the Aus-trians on the north bank of the Adige, while Augereau attempted to cross the river at Alberedo and take Arcola from the rear.

Masséna sent half his force over the Adige, using a shaky pontoon bridge, a hazardous business because it collapsed and was repaired to tie down the Austrian defenders in the Porcile area: the remainder of his force were concealed amid dikes and marshes, with but a single unit purposefully left in view. As anticipated, the Austrians attacked them, falling straight into the ambush, and were sent fleeing in disorder, chased across the Arcola bridge by French troops who took possession of part of the town. Mean-while the Alboredo crossing was proving very difficult for Augereau's men, so that part of the force were sent south to find another crossing near Leg-nano. To aid the crossing attempt at Alberedo, Napoleon quickly despatched a small force of mounted guides across a ford over the Alpone, the four trumpeters with the party making a distracting din to unsettle the Austrians holding the positions at Alberedo and Arcola. Seizing the oppor-tunity, Augereau launched a full-scale attack and captured Alberedo, caus-ing Alvinczy to order a general retreat northwards in the direction of Vicenza. By next morning all the Austrian forces had left the area of Arcola.

The lead-up to the battle and a concise version of subsequent events is described by Major Eady:

During the fighting for Mantua, the Austrian leader, the Archduke Charles, by October 1796, had completely defeated Jourdan at Wurzburg, and thrown back both his army and that of Moreau on the Rhine. The Imperialists then decided to make another attempt to retake Lombardy. The French had only 40,000, of whom 8,000 were contained opposite Mantua, while Alvinczy disposed of 60,000. Alvinczy with 35,000 was to advance due west towards the Brenta, and Davidovich through Tyrol by the valley of the Adige to meet him at Verona. On 12 November, Masséna was severely handled by Alvinczy at Caldiero, and forced into Verona with considerable loss.

Napoleon was now in a difficult position. It was necessary at all costs to drive Alvinczy from the heights of Caldiero before the Tyrolese columns should overpower Vaubois's detachment at Rivoli and debouch in the plains west of Verona. But, as Caldiero could not be taken by a front attack, it must be turned by a flanking movement. To any other general than Bonaparte, this would have appeared hopeless; but where others saw nothing but difficulties, his eye discerned a means of safety.

South and south-east of those hills lies a large depression swamped by the flood waters of the Alpone and the Adige. Morasses stretch for some miles west of the village of Arcola, through which runs a road up the eastern bank of the Alpone, crossing that stream at the afore-named village and leading to the banks of the Adige opposite the village of Ronco; another causeway, diverging from the former a little to the north of Ronco, leads in a north-westerly direction towards Porcile. By advancing from Ronco along these causeways, and by seizing Arcola, Bonaparte designed to outflank the Austrians and tempt them into an arena where the personal prowess of the French veterans would have ample scope, and where numbers would be of secondary importance. Only heads of columns could come into direct contact; and the formidable Austrian cavalry could not display its usual prowess. On these facts Bonaparte counted as a set-off to his slight inferiority in numbers.

In the dead of night the divisions of Augereau and Masséna retired through Verona. Officers and soldiers were alike deeply discouraged by this movement, which seemed to presage a retreat towards the Mincio and the abandonment of Lombardy. To their surprise, when outside the gate, they received the order to turn to the left down the western bank of the Adige. At Ronco the mystery was solved. A bridge of boats had there been thrown across the Adige; and crossing this without opposition, Augereau's troops rapidly advanced along the causeway leading to Arcola and menaced the Austrian rear, while Masséna's column defiled north-west so as directly to threaten his flank at Caldiero.

Actually, the surprise was not complete, and the ensuing fight was of a desperate nature...

Victory again declared for the troops who could dare the longest, and whose general was never at a loss in face of any definite danger. Both armies suffered severely in these desperate conflicts; but, while the Austrians felt that the cup of victory had been snatched from their very lips, the French soldiery were dazzled by this transcendent exploit of their chief.

Despite Napoleon's personal efforts to lead the attack across the bridge over the Alpone at Arcola – flag in hand – it was to no avail and continuous French attacks were repulsed. On the third day of the battle, Augereau's men crossed over a trestle-bridge below the village, while Masséna made yet another assault on the main bridge. Coinciding with this, a detachment of French cavalry rode round to the Austrian rear, giving the impression of being a much larger force by blowing bugles and creating a din, causing the Austrians to fear they were encircled, so that they broke and retreated.

In 1796 Carnot planned a pincer-operation against Austria, waging war in the two major theatres of Germany and Italy, the character changing from defence to conquest. The armies of the Sambre-and-Meuse and of the Rhine-and-Moselle were to drive through Germany and unite with the Army of Italy, now commanded by General Napoleon Bonaparte, aged twenty-seven. The sullen and semi-mutinous troops of the army in Italy were ragged and half-starved and their revolutionary fervour had long since vanished. Within a month of taking command, Bonaparte had won them over and led his 40,000 men (including 3,000 cavalry) with 60 guns against Colli's Piedmontese force of 25,000 and Beaulieu's 30,000 Austrians, with 150 guns, who were covering the cities of Turin and Milan.

On 12 April 1796 Bonaparte struck north between his opponents to drive in Beaulieu's right flank at Montenotte; two days later, he again defeated the Austrians at Dego so that they retreated and widened the gap between the Allied armies. Bonaparte turned west on Colli's army and at Mondoviso defeated the Piedmontese that they asked for an armistice and went out of the war.

A French force marched 44 miles in thirty-six hours to cross the River Po and turn Beaulieu's left so that he retreated, leaving a rearguard to hold the bridge at Lodi, where Bonaparte personally led the charge which took the bridge. After defeating two armies in detail in seventeen days, Bonaparte entered Milan on 15 May. After again defeating Beaulieu at Borghetto, the whole of Northern Italy was now in Bonaparte's hands with the exception of the great fortress of Mantua and its garrison of 11,000 Austrians with 316 guns.

General Wurmser with 24,000 men marched down the Adige Valley east of Lake Garde to relieve Mantua while Quasdanovich led 18,000 west of the lake. Abandoning the siege, Bonaparte concentrated 47,000 men against Quasdanovich and left Augereau's division to check Wurmser and, for forty-eight hours, the French battled in front and rear. Bonaparte defeated Quasdanovich at Lunate on 3 August and then turned on Wurmser at Castiglione on 5 August where, in an old-fashioned style pitched battle, Bonaparte engaged the whole Austrian front; while the French reserves marched all night to strike the enemy rear as their left-centre was decisively attacked and defeated. In five confused days Bonaparte had thrown himself between two enemy forces, concentrated in turn on each and defeated them in detail, to capture 70 guns and inflict 20,000 casualties.

Wurmser and General Davidovich regrouped the Austrian army, leaving Davidovich with 20,000 to defend the Tyrol while Wurmser attempted to relieve Mantua with 26,000. Leaving 8,000 men without siege artillery to blockade Mantua (the French spiked their 140 guns when raising the siege), Bonaparte marched northward to defeat Davidovich at Colin on 5

September, and then turned southward in pursuit of Wurmser – in six days Masséna marched 100 miles and Augereau marched 114 miles, and both fought three actions. On 8 September, Wurmser was heavily defeated at Bison when each of the French generals attacked an Austrian flank; the 12,000 Austrian survivors fought their way into Mantua, swelling the garrison to between 26,000 and 28,000 troops.

Early in November the Austrians made a third attempt to relieve Mantua, when, intending to unite at Verona, Davidovich with 16,000 men marched down the Adige while Baron Alvinczy moved on Venousness with 27,000 men. Leaving 9,000 men to contain Wurmser's 28,000 in Mantua, Bonaparte sent General Dobbs with 8,000 to delay Davidovich and hurried east with 18,000 to meet Alvinczy at Caldiero. Here he lost the first battle of his career when, clashing at dusk in a sleet storm, the French were checked by a rapid Austrian build-up and withdrew unpriced to Verona. Undeterred, Bonaparte tried to swing south and fall on Alvinczy's rear, but the French advance through swampy country was held up for three days at Arcola where a force of Croats held the bridge and the causeway over the Alpone. Finally Augereau crossed by a trestle bridge below the village as Masséna made an assault on the main bridge; French cavalry buglers from Augereau's force sounded the 'charge!' in the rear of the Austrian position and panicked the defenders into retreating. Davidovich was driving Dobbs back towards Verona but was chased off by Bonaparte on 19 November. Alvinczy retired eastward across the Brenta and Wurmser withdrew into Mantua after several abortive sorties so that the Arcola campaign ended inconclusively with both sides fought out.

In November of 1796 Napoleon planned to attack the Austrian army of General Alvinczy, a force outnumbering the French, being 24,000 strong, lying east of the French base at Verona. At nightfall on 14 November, Napoleon's army of 19,000 men moved wide to the south, crossed the Adige to threaten the Austrian rear. But on the following day the French were brought to a halt by a strongly held bridge over the Alpone at Arcola; the bridge had to be forced as surrounding swampy terrain made manoeuvre impossible. Every attack made by the French on 15 November was repulsed, but on the following day, although no breakthrough was achieved, French pressure caused Alvinczy to move back from Verona to defend his left-rear. On the third day of the French attack, the Alpone was crossed below Arcola by Augereau's division, causing a widened front that finally squeezed the Austrians out of Arcola and to fall back to the east.

The 'tactical techniques' for an action such as that of Arcola are discussed by Clery:

A position on the causeway itself has the usual disadvantage of a restricted front without power to manoeuvre. It is also liable to a flank and cross fire; if the force be large its strength cannot be utilised in such a position, and a defeat may be made destructive. This was proved on the third day at Arcola by an Austrian column advancing along the causeway against the bridge at Ronco. Headed in front, and attacked with fire on both flanks, its rout was complete, with a loss of from two to three thousand prisoners. But if the force be small, and be secured from flank fire, it may act in such a position very effectively against a superior one. On the second day at Arcola an Austrian column, moving by a causeway from San Bonifacio against Augereau's flank and rear, was completely arrested by a company of infantry and four guns sent along the causeway to oppose it.

But as with a bridge, a position in rear is here the strongest for defence; it has the additional advantage of having the enemy under fire for a proportionately longer time in his advance, and of being itself further removed from the action of his artillery preparatory to attack. How difficult it is to force a position of this kind was proved by Bonaparte's unsuccessful efforts during two days to force the defence at Arcola.

Taufers, 25 March 1799
An action during the War of the Second Coalition (1798–1800), between two relatively small forces of Austrians and French, is also discussed by Clery in his book:

In March 1799, an Austrian force of 6,300 men under General Loudon was encamped about Taufers in the Munster valley, defending the approaches to Glurns and the Upper Adige.

A French force under Dessolles, of about 4,500 strong, had fought its way to Ste Maria in the same valley, and was preparing to follow up its success. Dessolles' orders were to attack Taufers and reach Glurns.

The road from Ste Maria to Glurns passes through the villages of Munster and Taufers, and thence along a narrow valley by the Rambach stream, which flows through a steep and deep ravine. On the right bank the mountains run down to the river, and their sides are so rugged that it is only possible to advance there by a difficult footpath. On the left the country is more open, particularly between Munster and the stream of Vallarola. At the village of Rawail the valley again closes, and becomes so narrow farther back that the road is forced across the stream at a point where the other bank widens. After continuing along the right bank the road branches in two directions, one leading to Glurns, the other to Laatsch. The mountains overlooking Taufers send spurs towards the Rambach, and their slopes get less rugged between

Rawail and Munster. A footpath leads upwards from Taufers along the stream of Vallarola.

The Vallarola and Rambach were at this time almost dry. The bed of the former was deep and rocky, and it was difficult of passage except by the existing bridge. The bed of the Rambach was deep, and so wide that a column of troops could advance along it and be still hidden from an enemy occupying the left bank. To defend the defile leading to Glurns the Austrians took up a position between Taufers and the stream of Vallarola.

A line of entrenchment was constructed about 150 yards behind the stream, running across the high road and resting its left on the Rambach. This line was flanked by two redoubts. A second line of entrenchment ran parallel to the first about 300 yards in rear, and formed an echelon to protect the right flank. It bordered the crest of a ravine, having its right on a rocky slope, and was connected on both flanks with a redoubt.

But the bed of the Rambach had been altogether neglected: it was neither occupied, swept by fire, nor overlooked from any point. Filled by a mountain torrent it was a strong point to rest a flank on; dried up as it now was, it offered an open road to turn the whole line of defence.

The defensive force comprised eight battalions and sixteen guns. Four of these, with the guns, occupied the entrenchments, furnishing the outposts and a detachment of 500 men for the heights. The four other battalions were encamped in rear of the second line to the right of Taufers. The heights on each side of the valley were occupied chiefly by organised mountaineers, there being in all about four companies on the right, three on the left, and four more detached into a neighbouring valley. The outposts were about 1,500 yards beyond the Vallarola, watching the road from Munster. There was but one bridge over this stream, and it was covered by a small field-work.

On the night of 24 March Dessolles moved with 4,500 men and two guns from Sta Maria through Munster, pushing forward his right along the Rambach, while he held back his left near the village.

At daybreak the following morning he drove in the enemy's outposts and engaged him along his whole line with skirmishers. At the same time three battalions on the right entered the bed of the Rambach near Bundweil and advanced to turn the enemy's left; three more followed in echelon to cover their inner flank.

As soon as this turning movement was sufficiently pronounced, Dessolles moved rapidly against the front of the position and attacked the Vallarola bridge, while the turning party issuing from the bed of the Rambach took the enemy in rear, causing universal alarm and disorder. Part of this column carried Taufers, and part moved rapidly on Rawail to intercept Loudon's retreat, sending a strong detachment through the defile on Glurns.

The Austrians were driven from one work after another, and when Taufers was taken the French broke through at all points and dispersed them completely. Loudon, with about 400 men, escaped over the mountains, as did also the light troops posted on the heights. About a thousand were killed or wounded, and the remainder, with the whole of the guns, were taken prisoners.

The dispositions of the Austrians were here so faulty that to this, as much as to the position they selected to fight in, their disaster must be attributed. Their left was made to rest on the bed of the Rambach, which was no obstacle, and yet was neither defended nor observed. It was in fact a defile, and one gun, of which they had sixteen, would have barred its passage. The direct road to Rawail led in rear of the left, yet the reserve was posted behind the right, already protected by the heights it rested on and the fire of the troops occupying them. The mouth of the defile was therefore left completely unguarded, so the front line once turned, there was nothing to prevent the enemy from seizing it. The outposts were so close that they were useless against surprise, for when they were attacked the main body found itself attacked also. The low ground was the weak part of the position, for though the heights overhung, they did not command it. This was proved by the troops holding them taking little or no part in the action. The usual rule for attacking mountain defiles was here disregarded, for if the defence of the valley, the easiest to attack, were forced, that of the heights, being turned, would fall in at the same time.

The Austrians took up this position for a contemplated movement against the French, and wished on that account to hold the outlet of the defile. But such a position is at all times one of danger, and their measures for protection were insufficient and ill-judged. For simple defence a position between Glurns and Laatsch, with outposts along the roads leading from these points to Taufers, and the defile itself blocked, would have best effected the purpose of barring the enemy's advance.

The War of the Second Coalition was fought in various parts of Central Europe – in Italy, in Germany and the Netherlands, and in Switzerland and the Alps. Clery now tells of the passage of a river during the third battle of Zurich:

Crossing of the Limat, 25 September 1799

In September 1799, the centre and left of Massena's army was cantoned along the left bank of the Linth and Limat. These rivers were in effect one, that part above Lake Zurich being called the Linth, that below the Limat.

Opposed to Masséna was an Austrian force under Hotze on the Linth, and a Russian force under Korsakov on the Limat. Masséna selected the point of Dietikon for forcing the passage of the latter.

The line of the Limat was short and very strong, and the points suitable for a passage few. The right bank commanded the left throughout, so that all movements on the latter were entirely exposed to view. The width of the river was from 90 to 100 yards.

The point of Dietikon was chosen for the following reasons. Here the river bent on both sides so decidedly towards the enemy that an effective cross fire was obtained to sweep the opposite bank, while the positions for the artillery were excellent. The peninsula formed by this winding of the river narrowed the front on which a force landing could be opposed, and containing a wood that ran down to the river, formed a strong position for an advanced party to cover the passage of the remainder. Moreover this wood effectively screened the point selected for the bridge. The anchorage appeared good, and the course of the river, at other points excessively rapid, was here considerably lessened by the winding of its bed. In rear the peninsula was closed by a high ridge covered with pine trees, but between this ridge and the small wood in front, the ground was so open as to be everywhere swept by artillery from the left bank.

But this point had also its disadvantages. There was no protecting island, nor was there any auxiliary stream in which to collect the boats and cover the embarkation of the advanced party. This latter might have been obtained higher up or lower down, but then all the advantages of the positions for artillery should be abandoned, as also the important one of having the point for the bridge hidden from the enemy. It therefore became necessary that the boats should be brought by land, on carriages, to the river-side; that they should be unloaded, launched, and the troops embarked within view and under fire of the enemy. For his posts were thick on the other bank, and supported from a large camp close in rear of the pine wood.

The obstacles to be contended with were:

1. The difficulty of moving by land all the appliances for crossing when no adequate pontoon train existed.

2. The unloading of boats on the river-side in the presence, and possibly under fire of the enemy, when the horses and men employed were those requisitioned in the country.

3. The small number of boats it was possible to unload together at the required point for the transport of the advanced troops, and the advantage this delay would give the enemy in assembling to resist the passage.

4. The confusion and impediment to embarkation unavoidable with an unorganised body of drivers, horses, and carriages, crowded on the

river-side. The means available for effecting the passage consisted of sixteen large boats, at the moment forming a bridge at Rothensweil on the Reuss. This river ran nearly parallel to the Limat, and was separated from it by a range of mountains joining on to the Albis. These boats were to form the bridge.

For the passage of the first troops, to cover its construction, there were no boats available except what could be procured in the country. Of these, such only were useful as could be conveyed on carriages. With great difficulty thirty-seven in all were procured, the largest carrying forty-five men, the smallest about twenty. They were collected at the small town of Bremgarten on the Reuss, whither it was intended to float down the boats forming the bridge at Rothensweil, and thence the whole were to be conveyed over the mountain to Dietikon. But this journey over the mountain was one of great difficulty. For the road was very narrow, always bad, and now almost destroyed from the incessant rain of a wet summer. The bridge and streets of Bremgarten were narrow, with sharp turns and steep slopes, and almost impracticable for the long and awkward carriage loads. Yet this was the only road available, where a single breakdown would have completely blocked the passage of the remainder.

The transport available amounted in all to only twenty-four carriages. It became therefore impossible to transport the whole of the boats in one journey. It was accordingly arranged that those for conveying the covering party should be first brought over the mountain in two detachments, and that to avoid arousing the enemy's suspicions, those for the bridge should continue in their present position at Rothensweil until the day for the passage of the Limat was definitely fixed on.

The work of transport was performed with the artillery horses of the division charged with effecting the crossing. The convoy arrived at Dietikon without being observed by the enemy. It was halted behind a wood until nightfall, and then moved up near the village, unloaded, and the boats placed in concealment under cover of a small camp already existing about a thousand yards from the point of crossing.

Lorge's division, supported by one of Mesnard's brigades, in all about 15,000 men, were appointed for forcing the passage. This division had its right at Altstetten, its left near Baden. On the right of Lorge was Mortier's division, about 6,000 men from Altstetten to Aldesweil on the Sihl. On his left was Mesnard's division, along the Limat, from Baden to the Aar.

Opposed to the French was Korsakov's corps – the main body encamped between the town of Zurich and the Silh, with outposts pushed forward to Altstetten, where a small stream separated the sentries of both armies.

On the right bank of the Limat the enemy had a camp of 2,000 strong in rear of the pine-wood before mentioned, and close to the point selected for crossing. Nearer to the bank in the same neighbourhood was an additional body of 400 Cossacks, posted in the small wood.

To the right, at Wurenlos, was another camp of about 6,000 men, closing the defile leading to that village. Further to the right was a third camp of about 2,000 men near Wettingen.

In addition to these, parties were distributed in the different villages on the Zurich–Baden road, while along the river the posts were so numerous that the sentries were nowhere more than a hundred yards apart.

Korsakov's force, actually on the Limat, was about 25,000 men. Thus to oppose the French there were close to the point of crossing 2,400 men. Within four miles, at Wurenlos on the left, 6,000 men. Within six miles, at Zurich on the right, the main body of the army.

It became a matter of great moment therefore for the French general to conceal the point of crossing to the last.

Masséna fixed the morning of 26 September for the passage, but on the 23rd circumstances made him suddenly alter it to twenty-four hours earlier. This was an important change, as the boats for the bridge were still at their old place at Rothensweil, for every precaution was deemed necessary to avoid arousing the suspicions of the enemy. So it was not intended to move them till the last moment, and nothing was as yet done.

Yet now such activity was displayed that the bridge was dismounted and the boats floated down to Bremgarten, where they were drawn on shore, loaded on carriages and thence transported to Dietikon, so as to arrive there the following evening by nightfall.

The convoy consisted of one small boat and sixteen large ones (bateaux d'arsenal), loaded on their carriages and drawn by the artillery horses of Lorge's division. About sixty country carts, chiefly drawn by oxen, were requisitioned to carry the tackle and equipment, and formed part of the convoy. It marched in sections of two boats, each section followed immediately by its equipment complete. Some cavalry were distributed amongst the requisitioned carts, to ensure that none lagged behind.

At nightfall on the 24th the immediate preliminary work of crossing began. The boats for conveying the first troops were, as we have seen, already on the spot. When darkness set in they were moved on the shoulders of infantry told off for the purpose, to the bank. Here they were arranged in three divisions not far apart. The men to work them, also in three divisions, lay down by them, where they awaited in perfect silence the signal to attack. The lightest boats, as most quickly launched, were placed on the right, to enable the first troops to surprise the Cossack post in the wood, and so secure the passage of the others. The medium-sized boats were on the left, to quickly overpower the enemy's post on the island whence the point of passage was taken in reverse. The heaviest boats were in the centre.

Some sappers were posted at the points of embarkation to make ramps for launching the boats, as the bank was steep and some seven feet above the water. This work was completed by midnight, and apparently without being observed by the enemy. The boats for the bridge were kept for the present behind the village of Dietikon.

To cover the passage, artillery was placed on the plateau in front of Nieder Urdoff, which would take the enemy in flank and rear and sweep the ground between the two woods. This fire would powerfully aid in preventing an offensive return when the enemy was once driven from the small wood.

Below Dietikon guns were also placed along the bend of the river to take the enemy in flank and rear on that side, throw shells into his camp, and cross their fire with those on the right. In the centre some guns were distributed in the neighbourhood of the crossing, while some more were held in reserve for possible use in the plain towards Schlieren.

On the high ground over the river opposite Odweil, a battery of heavy guns was established to command the defile leading from Wuren- los, and thus close the road against reinforcements attempting to advance on that side.

The infantry forming the advanced guard were drawn up by the time appointed about fifty yards from the bank. The arrangements were made with a view to throwing 600 men across in the first passage. All these dispositions were effected in such perfect order and silence that the enemy did not take the least alarm.

So far, all preliminaries for the passage were complete. But we have seen that the enemy's main body at Zurich had its outposts at Altstet- ten, less than four miles distant from the point of passage. Thus had he the power of taking the attacking force in rear, and so placing it between two fires. To provide against this a strong body of infantry and cavalry of Klein's division was moved up towards Schlieren.

As a diversion, Mortier, on the right, was to attack the Russian camp at Wollichsofen, and on the left, Mesnard was to keep the enemy occu- pied as far as the Aar, and attempt a false passage at Bruck.

At daybreak the signal was given for the small boats on the right, destined to carry the head of the advanced guard, to launch and push across against the small wood. This party consisted of about 180 men. The remainder were in the meantime held back. But the water on the right was not deep enough near the shore, and the boats, when weighted with the troops, stuck fast. But the delay occasioned only lasted a few minutes.

In the meantime the enemy was alarmed, and a musketry fire was opened along the whole line. Instantly the remainder of the advanced guard, seizing the other boats, launched them so rapidly that no time was allowed the sappers to attempt cutting ramps.

Within three minutes of the first shot, not a single boat remained on the left bank, and six hundred men were on their way across the river. The enemy kept up a sharp musketry and artillery fire on the boats, yet not one was sunk nor was there a man drowned.

The French artillery, aided by infantry interspersed between the batteries, quickly cleared the opposite bank of the enemy. But this fire had soon to cease, from the progress made by the attacking force in the wood. All efforts were now directed to accelerating the passage of more infantry.

When the work had so far advanced that the infantry thrown across seemed certain to hold their ground, the bridge equipage, hitherto held back, was rapidly brought forward and the bridge commenced notwithstanding that the enemy's artillery still commanded this ground.

While this was proceeding, the boats had so quickly increased the numbers on the right bank that the French advanced to attack the enemy, now strongly posted in the pine-wood and on the ridge in rear. After some very obstinate fighting this position was carried and seven guns captured.

Within an hour from the commencement of the operation the pine-wood ridge and the enemy's camp, still standing, was in the hands of the French.

Some sappers were now employed to make a road practicable for cavalry and artillery through the small wood of the peninsula. The bridge, commenced about five o'clock, was finished by half-past seven, and this without impeding the passage of the infantry in the boats, as by that time 8,000 men had crossed over. The whole force destined to cross (about 15,000 men) was on the other bank by nine o'clock – within four hours of the commencement of the passage.

Crossing of the Beresina River, 26–28 November 1812

Beginning on 19 October 1812, the French army's retreat from Moscow rapidly took on the aspects of a nightmare, as the Grande Armée, harassed on both flanks and in the rear, relentlessly fell apart under the cruel conditions. Towards the end of November, they reached the Beresina River area, which had to be crossed in the face of vastly superior numbers of Russians.

How it was done is told graphically by Clery:

In the retreat from Moscow in 1812, Napoleon learned on arriving at Toloczin, about 40 miles from the Beresina, that the only bridge by which he could pass that river was in the hands of the enemy.

This point, Borisov, was held by a Russian force of about 30,000 men under Chichagov, while pressing on the French right was another force of about equal numbers under Wittgenstein, and on their left rear followed closely the advanced guard of the main Russian army of Kutuzov.

What was left of the French army did not exceed 35,000 men, and it was attended by an immense horde of unarmed stragglers and camp followers.

The Beresina was in this neighbourhood unfordable. Its banks throughout its course were marshy and wooded.

The French had no longer a bridge equipage left, as the last had been burned some days previously at Orcha, the horses being required for the guns. High up the river towards its source, fordable points could have been obtained, but this would entail a march open to a flank attack from Wittgenstein, while Chichagov and Kutuzov closed in on the rear. Below Borisov the country was still more wooded and marshy than above; the bridges leading to the river across these marshes had been destroyed.

The situation of the French seemed desperate. An army worn down by famine and disorganised by retreat, with an unfordable river in front and no appliances for throwing a bridge; an enemy of equal force defending the opposite bank; a superior enemy pressing on its rear.

The Emperor determined to move straight on Borisov, recapture that passage if possible, and if he failed, search for one in the neighbourhood.

The corps of Victor and Oudinot had been hitherto opposed to Wittgenstein and were now about Czereja. These corps, though greatly reduced in numbers, had as yet escaped the disorganisation of the rest.

Oudinot was now ordered to retake Borisov. Victor, with a much inferior force, was to continue holding Wittgenstein in check. Napoleon, with the remainder, followed Oudinot. On the 23rd, Oudinot surprised the Russians at Borisov, drove them from the town, but in retreating they burnt the bridge. Chichagov took up a position on the opposite bank.

On this day an accident revealed the existence of a ford by which cavalry with much difficulty could pass, about eight miles above Borisov. Napoleon determined to construct a trestle bridge at this point.

Everything now depended on concealing the true point of crossing long enough from Chichagov to prevent his interfering with the work, and on completing it before the pressure on their flanks and rear would drive the French into the river.

Directions were at once sent to Oudinot at Borisov to prepare secretly for a passage at the true point, and at the same time make demonstrations along the river below Borisov to attract Chichagov's attention to that side. He was also to allow the rumour to spread in his own force that the passage would take place below Borisov, so as to draw in that direction the crowd of camp followers that encumbered the army. To further fix the enemy's attention on the lower part of the river, the Emperor moved forward the guard to Borisov.

On the 24th, General Eblé, with about 400 men that remained of the pontoon train, started from Lochnitza for Studianka, the point of crossing, where they arrived about midday on the 25th. Six carriages containing tools, nails, etc, had been fortunately preserved on the destruction of the pontoon equipage, and there were besides, two forges and two wagons of charcoal.

As time did not admit of cutting down trees and then preparing the wood, the village of Studianka was pulled down for the purpose, and the timber of the houses used for making trestles. The iron necessary for binding them was forged on the spot. By daybreak on the 26th, a considerable number of trestles were completed.

The enemy's posts were now visible on the other bank, and it became important, before commencing the bridge, to know in what force he was present. An aide-de-camp of Marshal Oudinot (Jaqueminot), accompanied by a few troopers, each having a light infantry soldier behind, half swam, half forded the river, gaining with great difficulty the opposite bank. He only found a Cossack post, which he dispersed, and recrossed the river to report to the Emperor.

But information that the enemy was not in force on the other bank was not enough for Napoleon; he wished to know where he was in force, and for this required a prisoner. The same officer again crossed the river with a few more troopers, and pushing forward, surprised an enemy's post, capturing an under officer. Forcing the latter to mount behind him, he recrossed the river and took his prisoner to the Emperor. It was learnt from his answers that Chichagov with his main force was still watching the river below Borisov, and that there were only outposts opposite Studianka.

Corbineau's cavalry brigade was now sent across to occupy a small wood on the further bank and cover the construction of the bridge. Forty guns were established on the left bank in support.

Two bridges were now commenced, one for infantry and cavalry, one for guns and carriages. As it was desirable to get infantry over quickly, the smaller bridge was first gone on with. But to fix the trestles the men

95

had to enter the river, and the water freezing round their legs and arms added greatly to their labour and sufferings. They were without food or drink of any kind; except some thin soup.

The river was here about a hundred yards wide, and required twenty three trestles to span it. The first bridge was finished about one o'clock on the afternoon of the 26th.

In the meantime Oudinot's corps had been moved up from Borisov and replaced by other troops from the rear. His cavalry and infantry were now sent across the river, and two light guns were also moved with great care over the small bridge. Oudinot attacked and defeated a detachment from Chichagov's force, and took up a position to cover the crossing.

About four o'clock the same day, the larger bridge was completed and artillery commenced to cross. In constructing this bridge, time did not admit of squaring the round beams so as to make a smooth roadway. But as the concussion in moving carriages over the unequal surface was likely to create a strain dangerous to the bridge, it was sought to supply a remedy by filling up the intervals with moss, etc. The horses, however, carried this away in their feet, and the strain from the sustained concussions increasing, the trestles, where the bottom was softest, began to yield, and at about eight o'clock they entirely gave way, precipitating their burden into the river. But General Eblé, as soon as the bridge had been finished, made his men take rest, while of the remainder some guarded the bridges and some set to work to make reserve trestles.

It was now necessary for these men to again enter the river and replace the broken trestles with fresh ones. But it was freezing so hard that the ice had to be broken with axes, and even when broken it quickly refroze. Yet the damage was repaired and the bridge again in working order by eleven o'clock p.m. About two o'clock in the night, three more trestles gave way about the centre of the bridge, where the water was from seven to eight feet deep. The same work of repair had again to be gone through, which taxed to the utmost the energies of the half-frozen and more than half-famished workmen. By great efforts the bridge was once more made practicable by six o'clock a.m. (27th). About two o'clock in the afternoon this bridge gave way for the third time, but was, as before, very quickly restored again.

The day of the 27th was spent in passing over the remnant of the different corps as they arrived, while Victor still held Wittgenstein in check. But there remained an immense crowd of stragglers, camp followers, and carriages on the left bank who had yet to cross.

Chichagov had hitherto been completely deceived as to the true point of passage, and was still with his main body about Borisov, watching the lower river. Wittgenstein was closely following Victor, who was slowly falling back on Studianka.

Kutuzov's advanced guard under Miloradovitch had reached Lochnitza, and was moving to join Wittgenstein.

To continue deceiving Chichagov, Victor was ordered to leave one of his divisions (Partonneaux's) at Borisov. With the remainder he took up a position between the latter place and Studianka, covering the bridges.

But Chichagov at length became alive to the true movements of the French, yet he hesitated to attack without the co-operation of the other corps. A combined attack on both banks was arranged for the following day.

To meet this attack, Oudinot's corps, with the remnants of Ney's and Poniatowsky's, in all about 13,000 men, was to oppose Chichagov, who had over 30,000. Victor's corps, amounting (including Partonneaux's Division) to about 13,000, was to hold in check the combined forces of Wittgenstein, Strenghel and Miloradovitch, about 40,000. The Old and Young Guard, about 6,000, the Emperor held in reserve at his own disposal.

The remnants of the other corps were sent forward on the Zembin road to secure those important defiles on the future line of retreat. But Wittgenstein's and Miloradovitch's movements in pursuit of Victor seriously endangered Partonneaux's division at Borisov and on the night of the 27th the latter tried to rejoin Victor through the woods and marshes separating Borisov from Studianka. Taking the wrong road, he fell on Wittgenstein's corps, and the whole of his division, except about one battalion, was killed or captured. This disaster reduced Victor's force to 9,000 men, to cover the bridges.

On the morning of the 28th the Russians attacked on both banks. On the right bank Oudinot and Ney held their ground against Chichagov with varying success, and finally repulsed him. On the left bank Victor, in a desperate struggle, defeated all Wittgenstein's efforts to drive him into the river or separate him from the bridges. Darkness terminated the battle, and during the night Victor withdrew his whole force, unmolested, to the other bank. Here he took up a position with his guns to continue the defence of the bridges.

About nine o'clock the following morning the bridges were destroyed, and the French continued their retreat to Wilna.

Wavre, 18 June 1815

After being defeated by Napoleon's French army at Ligny on 16 June, in the first battle of the Waterloo Campaign, Blücher's Prussians fell back northward to Wavre. Napoleon considered this to be sufficiently distant from the Allied army at Waterloo for him to be able to concentrate offensive action against Wellington. To guard against any possible attack on his right flank by the Prussians, Napoleon sent Marshal Grouchy with 33,000 men to pursue Blücher, who left Thielmann with about 15,000 men as a rearguard to preoccupy Grouchy. Uncertain of the Prussians' whereabouts, Grouchy moved slowly before beginning an all-out attack on Wavre.

Clery comments as follows upon the action at Wavre:

The bridge over the Dyle near the village of Bierges was defended by two companies lining the banks and occupying a mill on the defenders' side, supported by a battalion, with a battery in action on the slope in rear. This combined fire swept the approaches with such effect that repeated attempts of the French, led by Gérard and Grouchy in person, failed to force the passage.

Major A. F. Becke, a retired officer of the Royal Field Artillery, was a great admirer of Napoleon, and in 1915 wrote what he called a 'detailed and very fully documented work' on the Waterloo Campaign. From his revised single-volume edition of Napoleon and Waterloo, published in 1936, comes this account of the battle of Wavre:

The Dyle from Limal to Basse Wavre was unfordable below Limelette. The river was about 30 feet wide and its low parallel banks made it look like a 'muddy canal'. The low-lying ground intersected by deep ditches, full to the brim with storm-water, had become a serious obstacle to the free movement of assaulting troops, and the whole valley bottom was soft and treacherous. Consequently the wooden bridges at Limal, Bierges and Basse Wavre, and the two stone bridges at Wavre, and the approaches to these bridges, were of paramount value to an assailant.

Thielemann, with 16,000 men and 36 guns, held the river-line from Limal to Basse Wavre. The general had disposed his troops as follows: one brigade (Stülpnagel's) and one battery of horse artillery were on the high ground behind Bierges, with one company placed to cover the bridge. Another brigade (Kemphen's) was on the heights behind Wavre, to the left of Stülpnagel's. In rear of Wavre, a third brigade (Luck's) was halted astride the Brussels road. The cavalry (Hobe) were in reserve, formed in column on the southern side of the Brussels road, and the guns were on the heights above Wavre. Leaving a detachment to hold Basse Wavre, Borcke dropped three battalions and two squadrons in Wavre, and with the rest of his brigade he followed the II Corps to Waterloo. Similarly Ziethen left three battalions and three squadrons (under Stengel) to cover Limal bridge. In addition, from Bierges to Basse Wavre, the river bank was lined with Prussian skirmishers. Thielemann's whole front covered about three miles and he could only deploy about 5,000 to the mile to oppose Grouchy's very superior force. The general, perforce, had to rely on rearguard tactics in order to neutralise Grouchy all day and gain the time for Blücher to intervene at Waterloo.

At first Thielemann mistook Exelmans' dragoons for a mere screen. Impressed by the heavy cannonade, the general had decided to follow Ziethen westward, leaving a rearguard of two battalions to hold Wavre to cover this movement. Just as he reached this decision, Vandamme launched his attack. Thielemann promptly counter-marched the troops who had started and they took up their recently vacated positions, except the officer in command in Wavre (Zeppelin) who had not time to complete his arrangements before the French attacked.

Vandamme was as impetuous as ever. He disregarded the orders which he had received from Grouchy, undertook no preliminary reconnaissance, and dispensed with even a semblance of any preparatory bombardment. Only at 4 p.m., when Habert's infantry attacked Wavre, did three French batteries open fire on the town from the high ground some 600 yards from the river. The attack was delivered with great dash. The French at once drove the Prussians out of the suburb on the right bank but then came to a standstill in front of the Dyle. The barricaded bridges were swept with grape from guns placed in the steep streets overlooking them, and the houses on the left bank were crammed with Prussian sharpshooters. The affair was short and deadly. In a few minutes Habert's division lost 600 men, including the general. Retirement was impracticable. The streets behind the French were swept by fire from end to end, and Grouchy arrived to find Habert's luckless division 'wedged in a real cul-de-sac'. Luckily Hulot's division (Gérard) was near at hand.

Grouchy surveyed the scene. After some deliberation he decided to assist Vandamme's effort by two other attacks, one above and one below Wavre. Habert's division was reinforced, and Lefol (Vandamme) was ordered to take one of his battalions and storm the bridge at Bierges while Exelmans' dragoons threatened Basse Wavre. Hardly had Grouchy made these arrangements when he received Soult's despatch timed 1.30 p.m. This informed him that battle had been joined with Wellington at Waterloo. In the postscript of this letter Grouchy was told the alarming news that Bülow's corps was in sight near Chapelle St Lambert; and the Marshal was ordered to march westward at once and crush Bülow before the Prussian corps effected its concentration with Wellington.

This 1.30 p.m. despatch was imperative and precise enough. At last, when it was too late, Grouchy realised the situation. Just as Ney at Quatre Bras was powerless to comply with the emperor's demands on the 16th, after he appreciated the full significance of Major Baudus's message, so, on the 18th, Grouchy was impotent when at last he perceived his duty. It was 5 p.m. already. The marshal had no troops on the Dyle's left bank. Not a single river-passage was in his hands, and to force the river at once a heavy blow was requisite. Even so, Grouchy's efforts at this moment were not very brilliant.

The Prussians in Wavre and at Bierges might have been neutralised by Habert and the three batteries, supported by Lefol's division. Basse Wavre could have been neglected; and Berthezène and Exelmans should have been ordered to storm the bridge at Limal. The Limal bridge was the all-important one to gain, so as to allow the right wing to march to Waterloo without delay or counter-marching. Directly it was captured Grouchy could threaten the flank of the Prussian columns as they marched to the Lasne. Habert and Lefol could have covered the rest of the right wing as it passed across the Dyle at Limal. It was, however, not on the 18th that the marshal was to retrieve his reputation as, unfortunately, he only adopted half measures. Grouchy was still determined to carry Wavre and he decided to allow half his force to continue the attack, whilst the other half was to move on St Lambert after crossing the Dyle at Limal. To effect this, Grouchy left Exelmans and Vandamme to attack Basse Wavre and Wavre and he despatched an order to Pajol to hasten his advance on Limal. The marshal then rode over to La Baraque to order Gérard to take the IV Corps and storm the Limal bridge. Possibly the head of Gérard's column had gone astray and made for Wavre so as to avoid undue loss of time, since Gérard brought Vichery's and Pecheux's divisions to Wavre instead of to Limal. As matters were, this mistake was of no importance. Previously Gérard's other division (Hulot) had reached the heights above Wavre about 5 p.m.

Meanwhile the fight raged along the Dyle. Lefol failed to carry Bierges bridge, but this failure only stimulated Grouchy to fresh exertions. Determined to master this bridge, which was only suitable for infantry, the marshal ordered Gérard to renew the attack with one of Hulot's battalions. Gérard pointed out that it would be a better arrangement to support Lefol with troops drawn from the same corps (the III) as the assailants. Grouchy rejected this advice, and Gérard then ordered Hulot to co-operate with Lefol. Hulot led the attack in person. The assailants had to cross broad, deep ditches (over 4 feet deep) running perpendicular to the line of advance, and the attack was so delayed and broken up that the battalion fell back. Grouchy, and Gérard who was leading up a supporting battalion, appeared at this juncture. Gérard himself led the next attack, in which he was severely wounded by a musket ball which struck him in the chest. Grouchy then ordered General Baron Baltus (commanding the artillery of the IV Corps) to take Gérard's place and lead the assault. Baltus declined. Marshal Grouchy never lacked personal courage. Without a moment's hesitation, he sprang from his charger and headed the assault himself. Nevertheless this attack failed. Grouchy then left Hulot's division at Bierges and rode off to lead Gérard's two other divisions towards Limal. Although one may admire the courage of Marshal Grouchy, who in his long and honourable career was wounded twenty-three times, yet the same admiration can hardly be accorded to the marshal's handling of the action of Wavre. In this fight Grouchy degenerated into a mere troop leader. He was everywhere at once and ready to head any attack. For too long he had been a subordinate. When he was perplexed and anxious he did what was second nature to him, and his efforts at Wavre were the mechanical and methodical ones of a subordinate.

Whilst skirmishing continued at Basse Wavre a desperate fight was being waged for the possession of Wavre. Vandamme's thirty-one battalions delivered thirteen assaults on the town, yet they failed to wrest the place from its defenders who fought fiercely and stubbornly to hold the French at bay. More than once Vandamme's men stormed the bridges and entered the nearby houses. But, even when they were driven from the bottom floors, the Prussians retreated to the upper storeys and fought on with great determination. The French could neither penetrate into the town nor make good their foothold on the left bank. Each time this obstinate defence allowed the Prussian reserves to arrive and drive back the assailants over the bridges. Actually not more than four Prussian battalions were engaged in holding up Vandamme's corps for seven hours, so the fight raged on for the remainder of the day and at 11 p.m. was still raging.

But the Dyle was forced elsewhere. When the marshal reached Limal with Gérard's two divisions he found the bridge had been captured by Pajol's horsemen. Pajol decided to attempt at Limal the daring expedient which had been employed at Montereau in 1814, showing once again that in war the happiest inspiration is often only a recollection. Pajol charged the bridge with Vallin's hussars (Gérard's corps cavalry), although it was only wide enough to allow four horses abreast and was defended by a Prussian battalion. The audacious adventure succeeded. The Prussians were ridden into, broken through, and dispersed. Teste's division then crossed to the left bank in the wake of the hussars and made permanent the temporary success achieved by Vallin's gallant horsemen.

Had the Limal bridge been barricaded this bold manoeuvre would never have been attempted. This oversight lost the river crossing to the Prussians, and probably the failing light may also help to explain the success which was gained. The rest of Pajol's cavalry corps followed Teste to the left bank; but Stengel, realising the importance of time, fought truculently to retain the village of Limal and stem a French advance. At last, under the pressure of superior numbers, Stengel relinquished Limal, but, rallying his men, he took up another position on the high ground to the north of the village. Despite the poor light Teste attacked at once; and Grouchy came up with Gérard's two divisions in the nick of time, just as Thielemann moved Stülpnagel's brigade and Hohe's cavalry to support Stengel. In the growing darkness the Prussian reinforcements encountered a ravine, their advance was stopped by the fire of infantry, and French cavalry threatening to outflank their right, the Prussians drew back into the large woods.

The fight went on until 11 p.m. when the French succeeded in obtaining possession of the plateau. At last the road to Mt St Jean lay open and Grouchy could move to his master's assistance when he pleased. But the cannonade had died away and a death-like silence reigned to the westward. No one could tell what this silence presaged.

The critical hours of Waterloo had passed before Grouchy succeeded in wresting one of the Dyle passages from its defenders. This reflects the greatest credit on Thielemann's excellent dispositions and the desperate fight which his troops made to hold back Grouchy's very superior forces at this vital time.

When the French debouched on the left bank of the Dyle it was too late to affect the main issue, because at 8 p.m. the great struggle was over and the fate of the day had been decided. Even if Grouchy had been able to march westward at 5 p.m., when he received Soult's 1.30 p.m. despatch, yet he could have effected nothing of importance. Bülow was already attacking Plancenoit and it was too late to detain Pirch I or Ziethen. Grouchy would have reached the fatal field only to find his master defeated and the Armée du Nord spread-eagled over southern Brabant. Grouchy must then have shared in their disaster, and by no means could he have altered the fortunes of the day. But the precise order given in the postscript of Soult's despatch made clear to the marshal that a crisis had been reached. This did galvanise Grouchy into action and awoke his cavalry spirit. Immediately he was up and doing. He struck hard at last, albeit he struck unskilfully. It is fair to ask what might have happened, had as definite orders been issued at daybreak on the 18th, and received by Marshal Grouchy before he left Gembloux?

As darkness had fallen, Thielemann's and Grouchy's troops bivouacked in front of one another. The French left rested in squares on the plateau which they had won, whilst the Prussians occupied the woods to the north of them. The opposing outposts bickered all night and the repose of the troops was constantly disturbed by outbursts of musketry. About 11.30 p.m. Grouchy sent orders to Vandamme to bring the III Corps to Limal. The marshal's idea was to finish off the action by rolling up the river line from the south. Then he would move on Brussels so as to join the Armée du Nord, as a rumour spread that Napoleon had beaten Wellington.

Marshal Grouchy must have forgotten Blücher, or where did he expect the Prussian field-marshal was? Thielemann, however, knew the true state of affairs. He had received the reassuring news that the Allies had gained a crushing victory and the French army was in full retreat. Thielemann could take a justifiable pride in his share of the great day's work. With only 16,000 Prussians he had kept at bay the French right wing of 33,000 men commanded by a marshal of France.

THE PENINSULAR WAR, 1807–14

The Peninsular War – eight years of incessant campaigning in Portugal, Spain, the Pyrenees and southern France involving the armies of Britain, Spain, France and Portugal – became known as the 'Spanish Ulcer' and played a major part in Napoleon's eventual downfall. Led throughout by Sir Arthur Wellesley (later Duke of Wellington), the British armies embodied Portuguese regiments as integral parts of their formations. After Sir John Moore's retreat to Corunna in January 1809, they enjoyed an almost unbroken series of victories, beginning with Rolica in August 1808 and ending with Toulouse in April 1814.

Moore's retreat to Corunna, December 1808

Since Moore had changed his base to Corunna, he could not be caught between Valladolid and Salamanca, as he would have been if retreating on Portugal; but he might be intercepted between Valladolid and Astorga by following the direct road from Medina del Campo to Benavente, and by seizing the bridge of Castro-Gonzalo over the Esla, before the British could occupy it. If the British were still at Valladolid when the French were at Tordesillas and Colbert's cavalry was already close to Tordesillas, then the French were nearer to the bridge of the Esla than were their adversaries, and the British were trapped.

On 24 December Moore began his retreat in two columns, Baird's division moving by Valencia de Don Juan and crossing the Esla there by ferry and ford; while the divisions of Hope and Fraser, with most of the artillery, took the road by Mayorga and Valderas to cross the Esla by the bridge of Castro Gonzalo on the way to Benavente.

Realising now, however, that the British were retreating, Napoleon resolved to fall upon their flank before they could reach Benavente, or at any rate to keep them engaged until the rest of his army could come up and crush them.

He therefore ordered that Marshal Bessières should march at six o'clock on the following morning for Aguilar de Campos on the road to Mayorga, with all the cavalry that he could collect – some four thousand sabres – and that at the same time General Lefebvre Desnoëttes should push on with two regiments straight upon Benavente. This would give the emperor no more than fifteen thousand or sixteen thousand men for immediate action; but these, he hoped, would suffice at any rate to arrest Moore's further retreat until the Infantry of the Guard, with the divisions of Lapisse and Dessolles, should struggle forward and drive the British into the Esla. The weather on the 28th was almost the worst that the French had encountered. Rain fell unceasingly, and the soil was already so much soaked since the thaw of the 24th that the roads were knee-deep, and even waist-deep, in mud. Nevertheless the troops, guessing from the presence of the Emperor in their midst that a battle was at hand, marched on with indomitable spirit. It was all to no purpose. Not a redcoat was found about Mayorga or Valderas; and the Emperor realised that the British had crossed the Esla and were gone.

Moore, as we have seen, had arranged to pass the Eslain with two columns at Valencia de Don Juan and Castro Gonzalo. On the 26th Baird's division reached the river at the former point, and with some danger, for the water was rising rapidly, succeeded in taking their vehicles and some of the infantry over by the ford. On the same day the divisions of Hope and Fraser crossed by the bridge of Castro-Gonzalo and reached Benavente. All day the rain poured down, and the roads were knee-deep in clay. Panic had spread among the people owing to rumours of the French advance. The peasants deserted the villages, and the drivers of the hired wagons absconded with their teams. Many of the oxen that remained were broken down by fatigue, and many of their wagons were in the worst repair.

At nightfall Paget's regiments halted at Valderas and Villalon, but continued their retreat upon Benavente before dawn of the next day. Soult's cavalry clung to their heels but was driven back from time to time in a succession of brilliant little attacks; and by the evening four out of the five regiments had passed over the bridge of Castro-Gonzalo. Craufurd's brigade, which had meanwhile guarded the bridge, now began the destruction of it, labouring in torrents of rain and under the very eyes of the French cavalry. The masonry was so good that the work took much time; but the rearguard was never seriously molested. In the course of the following afternoon the whole of the huge force of cavalry under Bessières came up before the bridge; but beyond a trifling skirmish with the hussars of the King's German Legion, who remained on the east bank of the river, there was no engagement. Colbert wandered up and down beside the water, seeking for a ford, but could find none in the swollen state of the stream. In the evening Lefebvre-Desnoëttes attempted to force the bridge with some dismounted men, but was easily repulsed. The German hussars then passed over the river; a little after midnight the bridge was successfully blown up; and the French were left fuming with impatience on the wrong side of the flood.

Though disappointed of his great enveloping movement, Napoleon still hoped to overtake the British and perhaps to force them into action; and he therefore gave orders to his cavalry and one division of infantry to pass the river as soon as possible, so as to ascertain whether Moore had retired on Zamora or on Astorga. The water, however, was still high, and it was found impracticable to execute his commands.

Balagny, a contemporary French military historian, author of Campaigne de l'empereur Napoleon en Espagne, criticises Moore's action in taking the bulk of his army on the road by Benevente, on the ground that this was the route that lay nearest the enemy. The way by the bridge of Mansilla was, he maintains, nearer; the presence of the Spaniards there was no sufficient reason for avoiding it; and the excuse – that Moore needed the bulk of his army to cover the evacuation of his magazines, will not stand examination.

By 28 December, except for Paget's 2,000 strong cavalry force, all of Moore's army were west of the River Esla; to facilitate their crossing by the bridge at Castro Gonzalo, Crauford's light brigade had to hold the bridge and, after the cavalry had crossed, blow the bridge. With the rain still falling heavily in the rapidly failing light of the late afternoon of the 28th, Crauford's riflemen were ranked on the eastern side of the bridge, watching the cavalry clatter past to safety. In their turn, they were under surveillance by strong forces of French cavalry hovering in the vicinity and occasionally making sporadic attacks on light brigade piquets lying in the hills to their front. The main British force lay behind barricades of tree-trunks, carts and other available material, while others placed explosives on and around the bridge. Moving among his men, Craufurd warned them to be ready to dash across the bridge when the orders were given.

It was midnight before the time came for this, the darkness and rain aiding the riflemen as they came tumbling down from their positions above the bridge. First, the connecting buttresses were blown, masonry dropping into the foaming waters of the swollen river amid a cloud of dust; men making a perilous passage, in single file, over planks placed across the shattered arches, with the river roaring beneath them. As soon as the last man had passed over, the engineers blew up the central arch, with every man safely across and ready to resume the march to Benavente.

The engineers blew the bridge with such good effect that it took the French more than a day to make it reasonably serviceable, a delay which, coupled with the flooding of the fords by the rain, gave Moore's exhausted troops the opportunity to have a much-needed rest at Benavente.

As Moore anxiously awaited the ships that were to carry them to safety, their engineers did everything possible to hinder the French, delaying them so that the British could load salvageable material onto the boats that had arrived. Among these activities was the blowing of the bridge at El Burgos, carried out with such enthusiasm that far more gunpowder was used than was necessary, so that the structure disappeared in a huge cloud of smoke and dust, with massive masonry slabs hurling through the air, killing and wounding men of the nearby 28th Regiment.

Soult's close pursuit had left his men as exhausted as their enemies, and the blowing of the bridge prevented the French from crossing the flooded river, leaving them with the solitary solace of being able hurl verbal abuse across the obstacle.

The bridge at Cacabelos, 3 January 1809

During Sir John Moore's retreat to Corunna in late 1808 and early 1809, his rearguard fought frequent actions against the French pressing upon them. One such skirmish occurred during the crossing of the small but flooded stream of the Cua near Cacabelos, where the French cavalry, charging down the slope to the fringe of the village, drove back the handful of 15th Hussars opposing them, but were eventually driven back by the British infantry in the village. While the French General Colbert reinforced his mounted force, a general withdrawal began over the small stone bridge crossing the Cua, covered by two small field-pieces brought up by the Horse Artillery, which opened fire upon the advancing French cavalry supported by the riflemen of the 52nd and 95th Regiments from behind low stone walls. Shaken by the fire brought upon them, causing several casualties, the cavalry began to waver but were repeatedly rallied by their General Colbert, conspicuous on a white horse as he fearlessly moved about on the river bank.

It was a challenge impossible to withstand by the riflemen, both regiments' marksmen employing their skills as they tried to bring down the French commander, but without success until a notable sharpshooter of the 95th – Rifleman Thomas Plunket – ran forward and flung himself down on the ground, to take careful aim at the colourfully uniformed cavalryman.

Above the noise of battle there came a sharp detonation and a small cloud of smoke, immediately followed by the suddenly inert figure of General Colbert tumbling from the saddle into the river's muddy water. Seeing the French trumpet-major riding to the aid of his commander, Plunket waited until he came within range and dropped him with a ball in his head, then rose and ran desperately for the protection of a nearby stone wall, pursued by a large group of French cavalrymen whose charge carried them over the bridge and into the waiting 95th riflemen. A fierce mêlée ensued with sword-bayonets clashing against slashing sabres, while on the fringes from behind stone walls the riflemen kept up a deadly fire that forced the horsemen to withdraw, leaving the road and bridge strewn with their casu-

106

alties. Almost at once they attacked again, and again were beaten back, not to return as the fighting died away with the failing light, allowing the gallant rearguard to resume their withdrawal.

The Douro, 12 May 1809

In May 1809, Sir Arthur Wellesley advanced from the Mondego against Marshal Soult at Oporto, holding the line of the Douro. The French advance parties fell back fighting, and on the night of the 11th retired over the Douro, destroying the bridge of boats at Oporto. Soult intended to defend the passage, and had about 10,000 men on the opposite bank. He had collected all the boats on the river and secured them on his own side, thinking thus his safety was provided for. He judged that any attempt by the English to cross would be made with their own ships at the mouth of the river.

It was of extreme importance to Wellesley, from the plan of his campaign, to effect a crossing without delay. Still the Douro was unfordable, more than 300 yards wide, and the other bank occupied by a veteran army. On the morning of the 12th the English army was secretly collected behind the Serra height.

In reconnoitring from this rock, the English commander remarked the excessive paucity of the French outposts, and the general want of vigilance apparent on the other bank. Opposite him stood a large isolated building called the Seminary, surrounded by a high wall, which on the river side ran down to the bank. This building commanded all the neighbouring ground and was unoccupied. Moreover, the winding of the river round the Serra rock would conceal a passage at this point from the city. Sir Arthur determined, if he could get any boats, to attempt a passage here, seizing that building as a first point of defence.

A staff officer sent up the left bank to look for boats found a small one about two miles off, lying on the mud. In this he crossed over to the other bank, and succeeded with difficulty in inducing some peasants to accompany him. In a short time he returned with three large boats. In the meantime a brigade of infantry, a regiment of cavalry, and two guns, under General Murray, were sent about three miles up the river, to effect a crossing, if they could, at Barca de Avintas.

When the first boat arrived at the point of crossing, an officer and twenty-five men embarked, and in a quarter of an hour were on the other bank and in possession of the isolated building. The two other boats closely followed, taking in all three companies. Eighteen guns were now in battery on the British side, on the Serra height. These guns swept the ground to the left of the Seminary, and so would confine an attack to the single entrance in front of the building.

By this time the British movement had been detected. One French battalion and then another moved down rapidly against the Seminary, and notwithstanding the fire of the English guns from the other bank, the struggle became desperate and the moment critical. The French succeeded in getting one gun up to batter down the building, but the English charged and captured it. At last Murray's force appeared moving down the right bank from Barca de Avintas, and Sherbrooke's division had begun to cross at Villa Nova in boats brought over by the citizens. Three battalions of the other divisions, too, had now gained the Seminary.

Their efforts to drive the English from the Seminary being unavailing, taken in rear through the town by Sherbrooke's division, and their line of retreat to Amarante threatened by Murray's force, the French now drew off, and the passage of the river was secured.

The following passage from Clery's Minor Tactics is entitled 'Example of forcing the passage of river in immediate vicinity of the enemy's main body':

The Coa, 23 July 1810

In late July 1810 General Craufurd's Light Division was engaged in an action usually referred to as the 'Combat on the Coa'. The British force, numbering less than 5,000 horse, foot and guns, held off French troops six times their number. Suffering some 3,000 casualties, they inflicted twice that number on the enemy. It was a most gallant and successful action, and when in 1848 a medal was granted to survivors of the Peninsular War, Lieutenant Frederick, who lost a leg in the affair, put in a claim to it. However, he was refused the medal on the grounds that he had not been present in a 'general action'.

Wellington's army wintered in northern Portugal, save for Robert Craufurd's Light Division (their new title from 1 March 1810) pushed forward to lie amid the villages around Almeida on the Spanish frontier. Here he was in contact with Ney's corps along the line of the River Agueda, a dangerous and solitary position forty miles in advance of the main army; his orders were to retain communications with the fortress town of Ciudad Rodrigo (Spanish garrisoned) until it fell, to cover the smaller walled town of Almeida as long as was prudent, and to keep Wellington informed of every enemy move. Here, from March to July 1810, Craufurd, in charge of the army's whole outpost system, guarded a front of forty miles in the face of a force six times stronger than his own, without once having his line pierced or allowing Ney any indications of events to his rear.

Masséna now wished to besiege Almeida, twenty-one miles from Ciudad Rodrigo and ordered Ney to drive Craufurd back onto that area. In the face of overwhelming numbers, Craufurd reluctantly blew up Fort Concepcion, the isolated Spanish fortress on the frontier facing Almeida, where he had been established, and withdrew to a position on the River Coa, with his left flank on Almeida. On 22 July Wellington sent Craufurd a 'strong suggestion' (not an order) that he bring his force back behind the Coa.

'I am not desirous of engaging an affair beyond the Coa. Under these circumstances, if you are not covered from the sun where you are, would it not be better that you should come to this side of it, with your infantry at least?' (Wellington to Craufurd, from Alverca, 16 July 1810.)

But Craufurd, confident of his own judgment and ability, aware that the French had never attacked him with more than a division, and never at a very brisk rate, believed it would be possible, under stress, to make an orderly retreat properly covered by a moderate rearguard. So, he hung on two days longer by the glacis of Almeida, with what could have been disastrous results.

Sir John Fortescue describes the situation in his History of the British Army:

The ridge upon which Almeida stands forms the western boundary of the great upraised plain of León, the altitude of the town above the sea exceeding two thousand feet. The summit is broad, flat and sound, an ideal country for cavalry, and to eastward the upland rolls away in broad billows which are furrowed by little rapid streams. But on the westward side of the fortress the ground plunges down rapidly to the gorge of the Coa, the distance from the walls to the river in a direct line being almost three thousand yards, and the difference in height over three hundred feet. The whole of its hillside is seamed by hollows, about three in every mile of ground, each carrying its trickle of water to the sea. From the southern face of the fortification there descends to the Coa a road, narrow and fairly steep indeed, but by no means bad, being for the most part paved and enclosed between fairly high stone walls. It would, however, be too slippery for horses to descend it safely at high speed, particularly after rain. This road follows a leading spur very nearly to its foot and the final descent to the bridge, upon which Craufurd's salvation depended, is a comparatively easy slope. The ridges immediately to right and left of the leading spur both tend to converge upon the bridge. The ground along the upper part of the declivity is broken by countless vineyards, high walls, and little enclosures, but the soil steadily becomes poorer as the water is approached. The rock crops up more and more thickly through the heather and broom, the enclosures become less frequent, and for the last few hundred yards the ground is open and the rock is everywhere. At a short distance from the water the road for wheeled traffic is forced aside by many obstacles, and after turning for a little way upstream doubles back to its final access to the bridge. But for men and pack-animals the track leads perfectly straight down, and upon each flank of this final descent to the bridge rise two rocky knolls, covered with heather and broom. The Coa itself is a boiling torrent which, at the point where the road touches it, has cleft its way through the rock and turned the valley into a chasm.

The bridge consists of two lofty arches, and the roadway runs nearly forty feet above the highest flood mark. The left or western bank offers above the bridge a fairly easy slope, which becomes far steeper below; immediately opposite to the ridge itself it presents a sheer cliff over one hundred feet high.

Around Almeida the vast Plains of León lie in a low and rolling, treeless expanse, strangely contrasting with the wild, rocky and picturesque ground where it falls away to the gorge of the River Coa, only a mile or so away, where rushing water swirls under the old curved bridge set amid rocks and fir trees. This was the stage nature set for Craufurd's combat on the Coa, claimed by no less an authority than Fortescue to be as sharp a fight, on its own scale, as was seen in the entire course of the war.

With his left based on one of the many windmills in the area, Craufurd had his line formed across the slope of the hill, facing roughly east, his left 500–700 yards south of the town of Almeida, where half a company of the 52nd with two of Ross's guns held the windmill, then came the 43rd, followed in succession by the 95th; 1st Caçadores; 3rd Caçadores, and the remainder of the 52nd nearest to the river – the whole line in convex formation covering a front of about a mile and a half, with cavalry piquets dispersed out in front. Ney believed Craufurd's position, with the defile to its rear and only a single narrow bridge for retreat, to be faulty. Before dawn on 24 July 1810, he arranged his whole corps of 24,000 men in a broad and deep column fronted by the two cavalry brigades of Lamotte (3rd Hussars and 15th Chasseurs) and Gardanne (15th and 25th Dragoons). Then came the thirteen battalions of Loison's division in line of columns, behind them Mermet with eleven battalions while three regiments of Marchand's division formed the reserve. After taking over an hour deploying for action, the French infantry then came forward rapidly as the French cavalry in line of fifteen squadrons bore down on the much smaller British mounted force to send them and Ross's advanced guns flying back over the plain. Then came the overwhelming infantry assault with Craufurd's line of three British and two Portuguese battalions being suddenly hit by Loison's thirteen battalions, coming on at the pas-de-charge, their loud cries and shouts rising above the monotonous beating of numerous drums. Their first rush was momentarily halted by rolling volleys, then the French 3rd Hussars, in bearskin caps and light-coloured pelisses, braved the gunfire from the ramparts of Almeida to sweep across the interval between Craufurd's left and the fortress walls down onto the flank of the Light Division. Flurried by this sudden charge, gunners in Almeida fired so wildly as to cause few casualties so that the cavalry were able to fall upon a company of the 95th and then sweep along the rear of Craufurd's line, rolling it up until checked by volleys from the 43rd and from riflemen behind stone walls.

Seeing he was turned on what he thought to be his safest flank, Craufurd realised he must retreat at once, so ordered cavalry and guns to gallop to the bridge, followed by the Caçadores. The rest of the British infantry were to fall back in echelon from the left, defending each enclosure and hillock, with the 52nd holding fast on the right flank. Marching westward straight upon the British line, the French, due to the smoke and the nature of the ground, were unable to see Craufurd's enforced change of front more or less to the south. Preserving their direction, they struck the British line in an oblique grazing blow. This was fortunate for Craufurd, because had the French fully hit his right at the same time as they closed with his left, they would have overwhelmed the 52nd and reached the bridge before the main body of the retreating force. Coming successively into action, Loison's battalions struck first and hardest against the British left, nearest the top of the hill; a wing of the 43rd, hotly pressed, found themselves trapped within the ten-feet-high stone walls of an enclosure and were only able to escape by throwing down the wall by the sheer strength of many desperate hands. It is hard to make a fighting retreat when pressed by an overwhelming foe. The British companies dared not stand too long in a position for fear of turned flanks cutting off retreat to the bridge, besides having to watch for French cavalry who were cantering down the paved road, sabreing everyone encountered. Delayed by the sharp turn in the road near the bridge, the guns and cavalry were further impeded when an artillery caisson overturned at the bend and had to be righted by hand. At the same time they were harried by French artillery unlimbering in the rest of the ridge to pour shot down on them. They were still choking the passage of the bridge when Craufurd's left was gradually forced down upon them and the Caçadores. The situation was eased when Major McLeod of the 43rd rallied four companies on one of the pine-covered knolls which lay above the bridge, while two companies of the 95th positioned themselves on a corresponding hillock on the other side of the track. Holding firm, they allowed Craufurd to range the guns and Caçadores on the slopes on the far side of the bridge, in order to command the passage when all had crossed. Then it was seen that the five companies of the 52nd holding the right wing were still making their way along the river bank. Hoping to cut them off, the French made a supreme effort and dislodged McLeod from his knoll, but he rallied and, aided by everyone within reach, threw the French from the hillock which was held until the

111

52nd had reached safety. Then the rearguard dropped down from the knolls, ran swiftly across the bridge and allowed the French infantry to reoccupy the wooden eminences.

On the far bank the British infantry strung themselves out behind rocks and walls on the lower slopes commanding the bridge, with Ross's guns unlimbered on upper slopes to sweep the passage. The cavalry were sent off to watch the fords six miles south in case of an attempted enemy crossing that would cut them off. Just as a wargamer might, in the full flush of triumph, Ney decided to force the bridge, but the wargamer only loses metal figures whereas the impetuous French general was playing with flesh and blood, and first sacrificed a mounted officer in a vain attempt to find a shallow crossing of the river. French skirmishers came down to the water's edge and took cover behind rocks, engaging in a lively musketry duel with riflemen across the river, while guns thundered at each other across the valley. Next, Ney ordered the 66th, a leading regiment of Loison's division, to carry the bridge. Quickly they formed and, led by grenadiers, the column rushed gallantly forward, to be mown down until bodies rose almost as high as the top of the bridge's parapets, before they fell back. But the blood of the fiery red-headed Ney was up and he ordered an élite battalion of picked marksmen to take the bridge; however, they only added to the heaps of dead until the bridge was quite blocked. Out of 300 men, 90 were killed and 147 wounded in less than ten minutes, and a third attack by the 66th, delivered with little dash or enthusiasm, was easily beaten back.

The duel of artillery and musketry across the valley was resumed, until at four o'clock a rainstorm of tropical intensity caused it to cease. Craufurd remained in position until midnight before retiring on Pinhel, having lost 36 killed, 206 wounded, and 75 missing in an action he had handled very badly. Ney, had he been wise and contented himself with driving in the Light Division for small loss, would not have lost 527 men, mostly in mad attempts to rush the bridge.

George Simmons was twenty-five years of age and a lieutenant in the 1st Battalion 95th Regiment (Rifle Corps), part of Craufurd's Light Division on the Coa in July 1810. During his entire service, Simmons kept a journal, described by Lieutenant Colonel Willoughy Verner in his book A British Rifleman, published in 1899, and containing Simmons's journals and letters to his parents. Simmons wrote graphically of the combat on the Coa on 24 July 1810, both in his journal and in a letter to his parents:

A little after daybreak the enemy advanced against our piquets and drove them in. The division was put into position, the left upon Almeida and the right in rugged ground upon the Coa, which river was running furiously in its course; several companies of riflemen and the 43rd Light Infantry were placed behind stone walls. The enemy now advanced in vast bodies. The whole plain in our front was covered with horse and foot advancing towards us. The enemy's infantry formed line and, with an innumerable multitude of skirmishers, attacked us fiercely; we repulsed them; they came on again, yelling, with drums beating, frequently the drummers leading, often in front of the line, French officers like mountebanks running forward and placing their hats upon their swords, and capering about like madmen, saying, as they turned to their men, 'Come on, children of our country. The first that advances, Napoleon will recompense him.' Numbers returned to the attack. We kept up a very brisk fire. Several guns began to play upon us, and as the force kept increasing every moment in our front, and columns of infantry were also moving upon our right flank, we were ordered to retire half the company. Captain O'Hare's retired, and the remainder, under Lieutenant Johnston, still remained fighting for a few moments longer. I was with this party. We moved from the field into the road, our men falling all round us, when the body of hussars in bearskin caps and light-coloured pelisses got amongst the few remaining riflemen and began to sabre them. Several attempted to cut me down, but I avoided their kind intentions by stepping on one side. I had a large cloak rolled up and strapped across my body; my haversack was filled with little necessary articles for immediate use; thus I got clear off. A volley was now fired by a party of the 43rd under Captain Wells, which brought several of the hussars to the ground. In the scuffle I took to my heels and ran to the 43rd, Wells calling out, 'Mind the rifleman! Do not hit him, for heaven's sake.' As I was compelled to run into their fire to escape, he seized me by the hand and was delighted beyond measure at my escape. The road to a small bridge across the Coa, which the division would have to retire over, was very bad and rocky. Our gallant fellows disputed manfully every inch of ground and retired towards the river. Every place we left was covered with the enemy's light infantry in ten times our number. As we got near the river the enemy made several attempts to cut us off. General Craufurd ordered a number of riflemen who had occupied a place that prevented the French from stopping our retreat over the bridge to evacuate it before half the 52nd, who were on the right, had filed over. The enemy directly brought up their infantry to this hill, which commanded the bridge, and kept up a terrible fire. Colonel Beckwith, a most gallant and clever soldier, saw this frightful mistake and ordered us to retake the wall and hill instantly, which we did in good style, but suffered severely in men and offices. Lieutenant Harry Smith, Lieutenant Thomas Smith and

Lieutenant Pratt were wounded, and I was shot through the thigh close to the wall, which caused me to fall with great force. Being wounded in this way was quite a new thing to me. For a few moments I could not collect my ideas, and was feeling about my arms and body for a wound, until my eye caught the stream of blood rushing through the hole in my trousers, and my leg and thigh appeared so heavy that I could not move it. Captain Napier took off his neckerchief and gave it to a sergeant, who put it round my thigh and twisted it tight with a ramrod, to stop the bleeding. The firing was so severe that the sergeant, on finishing the job for me, fell with a shot through the head. Captain Napier [William Napier, 43rd Light Infantry, author of *History of the War in the Peninsula*] was also about the same time wounded in the side. The division had now nearly got over the bridge; some men put me into a blanket and carried me off. Our general had placed himself some distance from the fight to observe the enemy's movements. I passed him in the blanket. The general had still in his remembrance the loss of his light cart. He told the men this was no time to be taking away wounded officers, and ordered them back. They observed, 'This is an officer of ours, and we must see him in safety before we leave him.' The last party of our men retired over the bridge and occupied it. The ground was very rugged, so that riflemen were placed behind every stone, and two companies of the 43rd hid themselves and were ready to support our men. Several Frenchmen held up calabashes as much as to say, 'Let us get some water to drink.' Our men allowed some of the enemy to get water, and did not fire upon them, but the cunning rogues made lodgements between the stones, and when their party was ready to storm the bridge, they commenced firing upon our men.

A number of French officers and other drummers headed the storming party. Our fellows allowed them to come close to the bridge. Some officers got over before they fell, but few went back to tell the tale, either men or officers. They attempted to force the bridge several times before the evening, and finding it impossible to effect their purpose, they made a signal to cease firing. An officer came forward waving a white handkerchief and requested to be allowed to remove their wounded, as the bridge and its vicinity were covered with their killed and wounded. This request was granted. The officer said he had heard of the English fighting well, but he could not have supposed men would have fought against such fearful odds. He complimented our men much upon their gallantry, and observed what a pity it was we were enemies. During this day it rained occasionally, and towards evening more so, which made the arms frequently miss fire. After dark the Light Division marched to Carvalha.

Fortescue provides the epilogue to Craufurd's combat on the Coa:

Wellington was extremely and rightly annoyed at his subordinate's escapade, but he accepted his report of it and transmitted it to England without comment. Only to his brother, Wellesley Pole, did he reveal the full measure of his vexation not only over the combat of the Coa but over the other 'foolish affairs in which Craufurd had involved his outposts'. Yet he added, 'If I am to be hanged for it, I cannot accuse a man who, I believe, has meant well, and whose error is one of judgment and not of intention; and indeed I must add that, although my errors and those of others also are visited heavily upon me, that is not the way in which any, much less a British, army can be commanded.' There spoke a true ruler of men, who knows what representative assemblies can rarely grasp – that a chief must not be extreme to mark what is done amiss by an honest and zealous subordinate. With all his faults Craufurd was a really good soldier; and it behoved a wise commander to make the best of him.

Sir William Napier, at that time serving in the 43rd Regiment, describes the aftermath of the engagement on the Coa in English Battles and Sieges in the Peninsula:

Craufurd's enforced retirement left the fortress of Almeida completely isolated and, on 15 August 1810 Ney's corps began the investment, setting up his siege-train and beginning the digging of parallels, made very difficult by thin soil and rocky ground. Almeida was a neat little fortress of six bastions, a covered way, a dry ditch cut out of solid rock, and six lunettes; nearly circular, it had a diameter of 700 yards. Its weak points were a glacis that was too low and an inadequately protected magazine situated in a dilapidated medieval castle set in the middle of the little town. The commandant was British Brigadier Cox, in Portuguese service, who had a garrison of 5,000, half of whom were regular troops; its fortifications mounted more than 100 guns, and it was abundantly supplied. In better material condition than Ciudad Rodrigo, there seemed to be every chance of Almeida holding out for at least two months; circumstances and the nature of the ground for an approach made it almost certain that Wellington would not make any attempt to relieve the besieged town. After ten days the first parallel had been completed and eleven batteries mounted, which opened fire on 26 August and seemingly did little damage in twelve hours of firing. However, on the following morning a falling shell kindled a train of powder leaked from a barrel in its passage from the magazine to the ramparts, practically destroying the town, killing 500 men, including more than half the gunners, and leaving little if any powder for the remaining guns.

Brigadier Cox had little alternative but to surrender which, after attempting to brazen things out, he did on 28 August.

When the last of the retreating troops had passed over the bridge (of the Coa), an Irishman of the 43rd named Pigot – a bold turbulent fellow – leaned on his firelock, regarded the advancing enemy for some time, and then in the author's hearing [at that time serving in the 43rd Regiment] thus delivered his opinion of the action: 'General Craufurd wanted glory, so he stopped on the wrong side of the river, and now he is knocked over to the right side. The French general won't be content until his men try to get on the wrong side also, and then they will be knocked back. Well! Both will claim a victory, which is neither here nor there, but just in the middle of the river!'

Then, firing his musket he fell into the ranks. Even to the letter was his prediction verified, for General Craufurd published a contradiction of General Masséna's despatch.

Clery saw the action at the Coa as a classic example of the defence of a bridge from a position to its rear:

When driven over the river, Craufurd's infantry ranged themselves in loose order along the side of the mountain looking down on the bridge. The artillery took up a position on the summit. The cavalry was moved to watch some fords and a bridge further up the river to the right. For General Craufurd had good reason to apprehend that he might be turned in that direction.

The French skirmishers quickly gathered along the right bank in swarms, and opened a sharp fire, while the artillery on both sides again came into action.The river, which had been rising, was now unfordable. Soon a dense column of French infantry advanced to the bridge, which they tried to clear at a run.

The steepness of the ravine seems to have at first affected the fire of the British, for it did not begin to tell until the French had passed two-thirds of the bridge. But then 'the whole leading French section fell as one man'. ('The column still pressed forward, yet could not pass that terrible line – the killed and wounded rolled together until the heap rose nearly even with the parapet – the living mass behind melted rather than give back.' Napier.) In half an hour after this repulse another still stronger column repeated the attempt, but this time it only succeeded in getting half-way across. A third attempt met with similar unsuccess. A desultory fire was kept up for some time longer, when all further attempt to force the passage was abandoned by the French.

Major Eady, in his Historical Illustrations, describes the dangerous situation of Craufurd's Light Division on the Coa in 1810.

In June 1810, the French were obviously about to invade Portugal, and Wellington had distributed his force with the bulk under his own command about Viseu, Celorico, Guarda and Pinhel, while Craufurd with 2,000 of the Light Division watched Ciudad Rodrigo, between the Rivers Coa and Agueda. Craufurd was instructed to retire behind the Coa and not to risk a serious action on the right bank, if the French advanced in any strength.

Early in June, Ney crossed the Agueda to invest Ciudad Rodrigo, and Craufurd fell back fighting rearguard actions with great skill. Ney took Ciudad, and advanced, threatening Almeida. Craufurd, anxious to delay its fall, remained in position on the right bank of the Coa. He was then in the position of a small force 'accepting battle in a position which is liable to envelopment' as Ney's corps was six times his strength. The result was that he was nearly surrounded, and was obliged to draw off his force hastily over the Coa on 24 July by one narrow bridge, suffering very heavy casualties for very little object.

The Redinha, 11 March 1811
Napier offers the following account of the battle at the bridge of Redinha:

Soon after the Barosa fight, Wellington and Masséna were again pitted in attack and defence. Masséna had kept Santarem until 6 March expecting Soult's co-operation, and retreated when that marshal, after defeating twenty thousand Spaniards on the Gebora, and taking Olivenza, Badajos, Albuquerque and Campo Mayor, was coming to his aid; of this, however, he was ignorant, because Wellington's forces on the south bank of the Tagus had intercepted all communication. Hence when Soult was invading Portugal on one side of that river, Masséna abandoned the other side and was pursued by the Allied army.

Strong positions crossed Masséna's line of retreat, which was confined by mountains, every village being a defile: and Ney governing the rearguard, lost no advantage. He was driven by the Light Division with a sharp skirmish from Pombal on the 10th, but on the 11th he offered battle at Redinha with five thousand infantry, some cavalry and guns; his wings were covered by pine-woods which, hanging on the brow of the table-land he occupied, were filled with light troops; the deep bed of the Soure protected his right, his left rested on the village of Redinha, lying in a hollow, masking a narrow bridge, and on a rugged height beyond a reserve was so posted as to seem a great force.

The Light Division under Sir William Erskine soon won the wooded slopes covering Ney's right, and the skirmishers pushed into the open plain, but were there checked by a heavy rolling file, and a squadron of hussars, charging, took fourteen prisoners. Erskine then formed his line, which, outflanking the French right, was reinforced with two regiments of dragoons. Picton had also seized the wood covering the French left, and Ney's position was laid bare; but he observed that Wellington, deceived by the reserve beyond the bridge, was bringing all the Allied troops into line, and would not retire; he even charged Picton's skirmishers and held his ground, though the third division was nearer to the bridge on the right, and there were troops and guns enough on the plain to overwhelm him. In this posture both sides remained for an hour, but then three cannon shots, fired from the British centre, gave the signal for a splendid spectacle of war. The woods seemed alive with troops, and suddenly thirty thousand men, presenting three gorgeous lines of battle, were stretched across the plain, bending on a gentle curve and moving majestically onwards, while horsemen and guns, springing simultaneously from the centre and left, charged under a general volley from the French battalions, who were thus covered with smoke, and when that cleared away none were to be seen!

Ney, keenly watching the progress of this grand formation, had opposed Picton's skirmishers with his left, while he withdrew the rest of his people so rapidly as to gain the village before even the cavalry could touch him, the utmost efforts of the light troops and horse artillery only enabling them to gall the hindmost with fire.

One howitzer was dismounted, but the village of Redinha was in flames between it and the pursuers, and Ney in person carried off the injured piece; yet with a loss of fifteen of twenty men and great danger to himself; for the British guns were thundering on his rear, and the light troops, chasing like heated bloodhounds, almost passed the river with his men; his reserve beyond the bridge then opened a cannonade, but fresh dispositions soon made it fall back ten miles. Twelve officers and two hundred men were killed and wounded in this combat. Ney lost as many, but he might have been destroyed, Wellington paid him too much respect.

The stone bridge over the Dos Casas stream at Fuentes de Oñoro, 5 May 1811

On 11 April 1811, Wellington drove the French General Masséna and his army from Portugal, only the fortified town of Almeida remaining in French hands, blockaded by the Allies. Masséna intended re-victualling Almeida and, in early May, crossed the River Aguedo at Ciudad Rodrigo. Anticipating the move, Wellington had discovered an excellent position east of Almeida and the Coa to give battle. He placed his army on high ground between the Torones and the Dos Casas streams, two miles apart, the main road from Ciudad Rodrigo crossing the Dos Casas at the village of

Fuentes de Oñoro. This was a narrow village straggling between the Dos Casas and a hill to the west; there were a few buildings on the right bank of the stream and some enclosed gardens; inside the village was a maze of stone wall restricted narrow crooked streets.

Today, the village of Fuentes de Oñoro remains almost exactly as it was in 1811 at the time of the fierce battle which raged through its narrow streets and over the stone-slab bridge, still in position over the semi dried-up stream.

Considering the sprawling village to be the key to his position, Wellington had garrisoned it with 28 light and rifle companies and a weak line battalion – 2,260 men, many of them picked marksmen with accurate rifles. They were deployed in a thick line on the western bank of the stream, under cover of garden walls and buildings. At 2 p.m. on 5 May 1811, Masséna sent forward a ten-battalion division, more than 4,000 men in a deep line, over the bridge and fording the knee-deep stream and, despite heavy losses, initially gained a foothold on the left bank but was thrown back. Further attacks followed and eventually the Allies were driven out of the village on to the ridge behind.

Close at hand, Wellington sent in two battalions supported by a third who retook the village, crossed the stream and then repulsed a cavalry attack. But Masséna was not done and sent in fresh infantry units who could only take and occupy a few walled gardens and a small chapel on the eastern bank. Darkness fell with the Allies in possession of the whole village west of the Dos Casas stream.

Reconstruction of the Alcantara bridge, April 1812

After the fall of Badajoz on 16 April 1812, the French held central Spain, with much of the rest of that country in Allied hands. This allowed Wellington to consolidate and to improve his communication, one such effort being to make the Roman bridge at Alcantara serviceable. The bridge had been damaged to the extent of losing 39 yards of its central arch, 140 feet above the river, which had to be replaced; this was done in brilliant fashion by Colonel Sturgeon of the Royal Service Corps, using a form of suspension well known to Wellington in India. Sturgeon was required to transport some seventeen cartloads of bridging material from Elvas to Alcantara (60–70 miles) and used it to such good effect that, within a few days, the bridge was capable of carrying heavy artillery. The cables used in the suspension could be removed or replaced within a few hours when necessary, and hand-operated capstans could adjust the cables for changes in length due to dampness.

The bridge of Almaraz, 18 May 1812

At this time the main French crossing-place over the Tagus west of Toledo was at Almaraz, where the original bridge was broken and unserviceable, causing the French to use a temporary pontoon structure. It was an important crossing because alternative crossing-places such as that at Talavera and Arzobispo were served by almost impassable roads south of the Tagus. If the French could be thrown from Almaraz, then direct communications between Soult and Marmont would be severed, so on 12 May Wellington sent General Hill to capture the fortified positions on both banks of the Tagus at Almaraz. Hill's force was made up of three brigades of British and Portuguese infantry, a cavalry regiment, and a battery of heavy artillery.

Sir William Napier relates the stirring story of Hill's foray:

So many obstacles, military and political, were to be overcome before Andalusia could be invaded, 1812, that Lord Wellington finally resigned that project and meditated instead operations against Marmont's army. To obtain success it was essential to isolate him as much as possible, and in that view various combinations were matured; but the most important stroke was to destroy the bridge and forts at Almaraz on the Tagus. Strong in works, that place was also a great depot for stores and boats, and not only facilitated the passage of the Tagus for reinforcements coming from Soult, but was sufficient to serve as a base and place of arms for an army to operate on the rear and flank of the British, if they engaged with Marmont in Castile. General Hill, who remained with a force in the Alemtejo, was charged with this great and dangerous enterprise, for a clear understanding of which the nature of the country must be described.

The left bank of the Tagus, from Toledo to Almaraz, is lined with rugged mountains, difficult for small bodies, impracticable for an army. From Almaraz to the frontier of Portugal the banks are more open, yet still difficult, and the Tagus was only to be crossed at certain points, to which bad roads led. From Almaraz to Alcantara the bridges, both those included, were ruined, and those of Arzobispo and Talavera above Almaraz were of little value because of the rugged mountains. Soult's pontoon equipage had been captured in Badajoz, and the French could only cross the Tagus between Toledo and the frontier of Portugal by Marmont's boat bridge at Almaraz, to secure which he had constructed three strong forts and a bridgehead.

The first, called Ragusa, contained stores and provisions, and was, though not finished, exceedingly strong; it had a loopholed stone tower twenty-five feet high within, and was flanked without by a field-work near the bridge. This was on the north bank. On the south bank the bridge had a fortified head of masonry, which was again flanked by a redoubt called Fort Napoleon, placed on a height a little in advance; imperfectly constructed, however, inasmuch as a wide berm in the middle of the scalp furnished a landing-place for troops escalading. It was yet strong, because it contained a second interior defence or retrenchment, with a loopholed stone tower, a ditch, drawbridge, and palisades.

These forts and the bridgehead were armed with eighteen guns and garrisoned with eleven hundred men, which ensured command of the river; but the mountains on the left bank precluded the passage of an army towards Lower Estremadura, save by the royal road to Truxillo, which, five miles from the Tagus, went over the lofty rugged Mirabete ridge: to secure the summit of this, the French had drawn a line of works across the throat of the pass; that is to say, a large fortified house was connected by smaller posts with the ancient watch-tower of Mirabete, which contained eight guns and was surrounded by a rampart twelve feet high.

If all these works, and a road, which Marmont, following the traces of an ancient Roman way, was now opening across the Gredos mountains had been finished, the communication of the French, though circuitous, would have been very good and secure. Wellington feared that accomplishment and designed to surprise Almaraz previous to the siege of Badajoz, when the redoubts were far from complete; but the Portuguese government then baffled him by neglecting to furnish the means of transporting the artillery from Lisbon. Hill now marched to attempt it with a force of six thousand men, including four hundred cavalry, two field brigades of artillery, a pontoon equipage, and a battering train of six iron twenty-four-pound howitzers. The enterprise was become more difficult. For when the army was round Badajoz, only the resistance of the forts was to be looked to; now Foy's division of Marmont's army was in the valley of the Tagus, and troops from the king's army occupied Talavera. Drouet was also with eight or nine thousand men near Medellin, and closer to Merida than Hill was to Almaraz; he might therefore intercept the latter's retreat, and the king's orders were imperative that he should hang on the English force in Estremadura. Hill had therefore to steer, going and coming, through all these forces with an unwieldy convoy, and as it were, blot out the strong place without a battle, but Wellington took many precautions to divert the French attention to other points, and to furnish support without indicating the true object. Hill, though dangerously delayed by the difficulty of restoring the bridge of Merida, which he had himself destroyed during the siege of Badajoz, crossed the Guadiana with six thousand men, twelve field-pieces, pontoons, battering-train and fifty country carts, conveying material and ammunition. On the 15th he reached Truxillo, and during his march the guerrillas of the Guadalupe mountains made demonstrations at different points, between Almaraz and Arzobispo, as if seeking a place to cast a bridge that he might join Wellington. Foy was deceived by these feints, for his spies at Truxillo, while reporting the passage of the Guadiana, said Hill had fifteen thousand men, and that two brigades of cavalry were following: one report even stated that thirty thousand men had entered Truxillo, whereas there were less than six thousand of all arms.

Early on the 16th the armament reached Jaraicejo, formed three columns, and made a night march, intending to surprise at the same moment, the tower of Mirabete, the fortified house in the pass, and the forts at the bridge of Almarez. The left column, directed against the tower, was commanded by General Chowne. The centre, with the dragoons and artillery, moved by the royal road under General Long. The light, composed of the 50th, 71st and 92nd regiments, under Hill in person, was to penetrate by the narrow and difficult way of Roman Gordo against the forts of the bridge; but day broke before any column reached its destination, and all hopes of a surprise were extinguished. This was an untoward beginning, unavoidable with the light and centre column because of the bad roads, but Chowne was negligent, for the Milabete tower might have been assaulted before daylight.

Hill now saw that to reduce the Mirabete works in the pass he must incur more loss than was justifiable, and be in such plight that he could not finally carry the forts below; yet it was only through the pass the artillery could move against the bridge. In this dilemma, after losing the 17th and part of the 18th, in fruitless attempts to discover some opening through which to reach Almaraz with his guns, he resolved to leave them on the Sierra with the centre column, make a false attack on the tower with Chowne's troops, and in person, with the right column, secretly penetrate by the scarcely practicable line of Roman Gordo to the bridge, intent, with infantry alone, to storm works which were defended by eighteen pieces of artillery and powerful garrisons!

This resolution was even more hardy than it appears, without a reference to the general state of affairs. His march had been one of secrecy, amidst various divisions of the enemy; he was four days' journey from Merida, his first point of retreat; he expected Drouet to be reinforced and advance, and hence, whether defeated or victorious at Almaraz, his retreat would be very dangerous; exceedingly so if defeated, because his fine British troops could not be repulsed with a small loss, and he would have to fall back through a difficult country, with his best soldiers dispirited by failure and burdened by numbers of wounded men. Then, harassed on one side by Drouet, pursued by Foy and D'Armagnac on the other, he would have been exposed to the greatest misfortunes, every slanderous tongue would have been let loose on the rashness of attacking impregnable forts, and a military career, hitherto so glorious, might have terminated in shame. Devoid of interested ambition, he was unshaken by such fears, and remained concealed until the evening of the 18th, when he commenced the descent, with design to escalade the Fort Napoleon before daylight. The march was less than six miles, but the head of the troops only reached the fort a little before daylight, the rear was distant, and it was doubtful if the scaling ladders, cut in halves to thread the short narrow turns in the precipitous descent, would serve for an assault. Some small hills concealed the head of the column, and at that moment Chowne commenced his false attack at Mirabete. Pillars of white smoke rose on the lofty brow of the Sierra, the heavy sound of artillery came rolling over the valley, and the garrison of Fort Napoleon, crowding on the ramparts, were gazing at those portentous signs of war, when, quick and loud, a British shout broke on their ears, and the 50th Regiment, with a wing of the 71st, came bounding over the low hills. Surprised the French were to see an enemy so close while the Mirabete was still defended, yet they were not unprepared; a patrol of English cavalry had been seen from the fort on the 17th, and in the evening of the 18th a woman had given exact information of Hill's numbers and designs. This intelligence had caused the commandant, Aubort, to march in the night with reinforcements to Fort Napoleon, which was therefore defended by six companies ready to fight, and when the first shot was heard they smote with musketry and artillery on the British front, while the guns of Fort Ragusa took them in flank. A rise of ground, twenty yards from the ramparts, soon covered the assailants from the front fire, and General Howard, leading the foremost into the ditch, commenced the escalade. The breadth of the berm kept off the ends of the shortened ladders from the parapet, but the first men jumped on to the berm itself and drawing up the ladders planted them there; then with a second escalade they won the rampart and, closely fighting, all went together into the retrenchment round the stone tower. Aubert was wounded and taken, and the garrison fled towards the bridgehead, but the victorious troops would not be shaken off, they entered that work also in one confused mass with the fugitives, who continued their flight over the bridge itself. Still the British soldiers pushed their headlong charge, slaying the hindmost, and would have passed the river if some of the boats had not been destroyed by stray shots from the forts, which were now sharply cannonading each other, for the artillery-men had turned the guns of Napoleon on Fort Ragusa.

Many French, leaping into the water, were drowned, but the greatest part were made prisoners, and to the amazement of the conquerors the panic pervaded the other side of the river, where the garrison of Ragusa, though perfectly safe, fled with the others! Some grenadiers of the 92nd, then swimming over, brought back boats, with which the bridge was restored and the towers and works of Ragusa were destroyed, and the stores, ammunition, provisions and boats, burned. In the night the troops returned to the Mirabete ridge with the colours of the foreign regiment, and two hundred and fifty prisoners, including a commandant and sixteen other officers, their own loss being a hundred and eighty.

The bridges at Vitoria, 21 June 1813

Forced by events elsewhere in Europe, not the least being Russia, Napoleon withdrew troops from the Peninsula to reinforce his armies fighting on other fronts. Taking advantage of this reduction in the forces opposing him, Wellington marched his army from the Portuguese frontier into the north of Spain, with 79,000 British, Portuguese and Spanish troops crossing the upper Ebro to outflank the French positions. At Vitoria, 175 miles north-east of Madrid, on 21 June 1813 Wellington attacked Jourdan's army in a three-pronged assault, disconcerting Jourdan, who expected an Allied attack from the west after crossing the Zadorra River which encompasses the area of most fighting in a series of loops. In June this river can be forded in numerous places and was crossed by at least a dozen small bridges within the valley, none of which had been destroyed.

But Wellington had no intention of attacking head-on and divided his army into four columns, personally accompanying the right-centre column formed of Lowry Cole's 4th Division, which entered the valley by crossing the bridge over the Zadorra at Nanclares. Once across, he halted the column under cover while he surveyed the field from the top of a hill west of the Zadorra. As he waited for the 3rd and 7th Divisions, which had not yet reached the point for a combined attack, a Spanish peasant came in haste to Wellington, telling him that the bridge of Tres Puntes had been left unguarded, and offered to guide troops across it.

Immediately, Kempt's brigade of the Light Division were ordered to that area and, concealed by rocks, crossed the narrow bridge at double-quick pace, muskets at the trail, to mount a ridge where they lay close to the line of battle. Two cannon shots were fired at them, one of which cut in two the Spanish peasant who had guided them.

Meanwhile in the centre, where Wellington himself controlled the fight, General Picton, who commanded the impatient 'Fighting Third' Division, was fretting under his enforced inaction. He had advanced from Anda, on the Bayas River, and was to work in connection with the Light and 4th Divisions, then on his right. His soldiers were eager, and their equally fiery leader had some difficulty in restraining them. As the day wore on, and the fight waxed ever warmer on his right, Picton became furious and observed to an officer, 'Damn it! Lord Wellington must have forgotten us.' When an officer galloped up from Lord Wellington Picton's face began to glow with animation at the prospect of being ordered into action; but it suddenly grew black again on the officer simply asking whether he had seen Lord Dalhousie. 'No, sir,' answered Picton sharply, 'but have you any orders for me?' 'None,' replied the aide-de-camp. 'Then pray, sir,' continued the irate general, 'what are the orders you do bring?' 'That as soon as Lord Dalhousie, with the 7th Division, commences an attack on the bridge,' (pointing to one on the left) 'the 4th and 6th are to support him.'

Picton could not understand the idea of any other division fighting in his front, so, drawing himself up to his full height, he said to the astonished aide-de-camp, with some heat: 'You may tell Lord Wellington for me, sir, that the 3rd Division under my command shall, in less than ten minutes, attack the bridge and carry it, and the 4th and 6th Divisions may support me if they choose.' Saying which, he turned from the aide-de-camp and put himself at the head of his eager men, with a wave of his hand towards the bridge and the cry of 'Come on, ye rascals! Come on, ye fighting villains!'

He well fulfilled his promise. Under a heavy fire of artillery his 'fighting' division moved steadily on, his leading companies rushing over the bridge, where they formed up in open columns. Then they moved to their left, so as to attack the enemy's centre. Still advancing in the same order, they pressed up the heights, where they quickly deployed into line. The foe hardly awaited the attack, for so rapidly were these manoeuvres carried out that the French for the moment were as if paralysed. Picton had gained the heights in front of him, but the division on his right had not yet made sufficient progress to come into line with and support him. Halting his impatient 'rascals', he waited for the advance of the 7th Division (Lord Dalhousie's) and part of the 'Lights', while the 4th (under General Cole) passed the Zadorra a little farther to the right by the Nanclares bridge.

The bridge at Sorauren, 28 July 1813

After the battles of Maya and Roncesvalles, lacking Wellington's resolution, Cole and Picton became alarmed at these French incursions with superior numbers, and so they pulled back helter-skelter towards Pamplona. Here Picton actually intended taking position on ridges within artillery range of French guns on the walls of the blockaded town. Luckily Cole noticed the Sorauren-Zabaldica Ridge about 5 km from Pamplona and persuaded Picton to stand there where Wellington found them at about midday on 27 July.

The duke, accompanied by his military secretary Fitzroy Somerset and Murray, his quartermaster-general, travelled on the Pamplona road which they had been traversing since dawn looking for the army; at Velate they came up with the 6th Division moving south, and ordered them to hasten to join Cole and Picton – wherever they were. The QMG was left at the small village of Olague to hasten reinforcements – although at that moment the duke knew the fastest reinforcements he could send Cole and Picton was himself! With only Fitzroy Somerset riding by his side, the duke carried on until reaching the little village of Sorauren and saw his army massed on a ridge to the south-east; he also noted Reille's columns pouring onto a ridge in front of them, directly in the path of his reinforcements. Despite French light troops coming through the village towards them, he halted on the stone bridge over the narrow River Ulzama and scribbled a message to QMG Murray telling him to détour southwards, marching 6th Division on a minor road through Lizaso.

Bearing the despatch, Fitzroy Somerset turned his horse and galloped back on the road to Olague. He was the same soldier who had his arm amputated at Waterloo and then sent for the limb to recover a ring he had left on a finger; forty years later he reappears in history as the kindly but bumbling Lord Raglan in command of the British army in the Crimea, where he died.

It would be difficult for any playwright or producer to stage-manage the dramatic entrance of the Duke of Wellington as, with the nearest enemy only about a hundred yards away, he turned his horse's head toward the steep slope of Cole's Ridge and galloped ostentatiously upwards – a solitary horseman unmistakable in a low hat, plain blue jacket and short white cape. The first to see him were men of Campbell's Portuguese brigade who set up the cry 'Douro! Douro!' – the name they knew him by since his feat across that river four years earlier; then British infantry joined in the cheering until every man knew Old Nosey had arrived – everything would be all right now! Putting his horse to the steep slope, the duke knew he had done what had to be done – he had made his presence vividly felt by his army – and by the French!

This small and relatively unimportant event was made notable not by the thirteen lines that were hastily scrawled, but by the character and stature of the man who scrawled them, and is well documented. An officer recalled that Wellington was 'wearing his grey frock coat buttoned close-up to the chin, with his little cocked hat, covered with oilskin, without a feather. I cannot adequately express the sense of confidence and assurance that was revived by his presence in the midst of a single division of his army; cheers were vehemently raised along the whole line.'

The ever-present William Napier described it thus:

When the solitary horseman, Wellington, reached the summit of the ridge above the village of Sorauren, he was greeted by 'that stern and appalling shout which the British soldier is wont to give upon the edge of battle, and which no enemy has ever heard unmoved. In a conspicuous place he stopped, desirous that both armies should know he was there. A spy who was present pointed out Soult, then so near that his features could be plainly distinguished. Finding his eyes attentively upon that formidable man, Wellington thus spoke: 'Yonder is a great commander, but he is a cautious one and will delay his attack to ascertain the cause of these shouts; that will give time for the 6th Division to arrive and I shall beat him!'

A week later, Wellington (using rather terse language) described his ride to Larpent, his judge-advocate-general: 'At one time it was rather alarming certainly, and a close run thing. When I came to the bridge of Sorauren I saw French on the hills on one side, and it was clear that we could make a stand on the other hill, in our position of the 28th, but I found that we could not keep Sorauren, as it was exposed to their fire and not to ours. I was obliged to write my orders accordingly at Sorauren, to be sent back instantly. For if they had not been despatched back directly, by the way I had come, l must have sent them four leagues round, a quarter of an hour later. I stopped therefore to write accordingly, people saying to me all the time, "The French are coming! The French are coming!" I looked pretty sharp after them every now and then, till I had completed my orders, and then set off. I saw them just near the one end of the village as I went out of it at the other end. And then we took up our ground.'

The bridge at Vera, 7 October 1813

If the bridge at Arnhem, defended by Johnny Frost and his paratroopers in September 1944, was considered 'A Bridge Too Far', then the bridge at Vera 131 years earlier, held by Captain Dan Cadoux and a detachment of the 95th Rifles, may be said to have been 'A Bridge Too Near'. Vera took place on 7 October, but it had an overture on 1 September, after Soult had sent a strong force across the Bidasoa on 31 August which failed to achieve much and was forced to withdraw. During that day Soult ordered Clausel to retire under cover of darkness and a fierce rainstorm, which caused the river to rise until there was six feet of water over the fords used by the French invaders earlier in the day. Trapped on the south bank was General Vandermaesen with his division and a brigade each from those of Taupin and Darmagnac – more than 10,000 men who would be overwhelmed if they did not re-cross before daybreak. Vandermaesen led them upstream to force a crossing of the bridge at Vera, and marched into one of those imperishable incidents that colour British military history.

An anonymous chronicler records the scene:

Toward night it began to thunder and lighten (sic) horribly and poured with torrents of rain. I was on piquet and observed Johnny (the French) by the lightning's glare retracing his steps back on this horrid night. At 2 a.m. Johnny attacked a bridge where we had a piquet of riflemen – two companies – who fought so handsomely that, with this small number, they checked them for an hour. A captain of ours, Dan Cadoux, who stood upon the bridge rallying his men around him received several musket balls in his breast and fell like a soldier. Five officers of ours were wounded and Lieutenant Llewellyn had his jaw shattered – all fought most heroically.

Harry Smith, a Light Division officer who had a colourful military career and played a notable part as a general in the Sikh War of 1845–6, tells what subsequently occurred:

The evening came on very wet. We knew that the enemy had crossed the Bidasoa [31 August], and that his retreat would be impossible from the swollen state of the river. We knew pretty well the Duke would shove him into the river if he could; this very bridge, therefore, was of the utmost importance, and no exertion should have been spared on our part so to occupy it after dark as to prevent the passage being seized. The rain was falling in torrents. I proposed that the whole of the 2nd Battalion Rifle Brigade should be posted in the houses, the bridge should be barricaded, and the 52nd Regiment should be close at hand in support. Skerrett positively laughed outright, ordered the whole battalion into our position, but said, 'You may leave a piquet of one officer and thirty men at the bridge.' He was in the house on the heights he previously occupied. I had a little memorandum-book in my pocket; I took it out for the first time in my life to note my general's orders. I read what he said, asking if that was his order. He said, 'Yes, I have already told you so.' I said most wickedly, 'We shall repent this before daylight.' He was callous to anything. I galloped down to the houses, ordered the battalion to retire, told my brother Tom, the adjutant, to call to me a piquet of an officer and thirty men for the bridge. Every officer and soldier thought I was mad. Tom said, 'Cadoux's company is for piquet.' Up rode poor Cadoux, a noble soldier, who could scarcely believe what I said, began to abuse me for not supporting them in the morning. I said, 'Scold away, all true; but no fault of mine. But come, no time for jaw, the piquet!' Cadoux, noble fellow, says, 'My company is so reduced this morning, I will stay with it if I may. There are about fifty men.' I gladly consented, for I had great faith in Cadoux's ability and watchfulness, and I told him he might rest assured he would be attacked an hour or two before daylight. He said, 'Most certainly I shall and I will now strengthen myself, and block up the bridge as well as I can, and I will, if possible, hold the bridge until supported; so, when the attack commences, instantly send the whole battalion to me, and, please God, I will keep the bridge.' It was then dark, and I rode as fast as I could to tell Colborne, in whom we had all

128

Above: The Battle of Stirling Bridge, 1297.

Right: Preston Bridge during the English Civil War, 1648.

Above: The bridge at Lodi, 1796 (Lejeune). (P. J. Haythornthwaite)

Left: Napoleon at Arcola, 1796 (Vernet). (P. J. Haythornthwaite)

Right: The bridge over the Coa, taken from the far side and showing the two knolls and the track running between them, up to the field of action in 1810.

Below: The bridge over the Beresina, 1812. (de Myrbach)

Above: The Roman bridge at Alcantara. (Porter) (P. J. Haythornthwaite)

Left: The bridge at Vitoria.

Top right: The bridge at Sorauren.

Right: The bridge at Vera.

Left: Orthez.

Below: The Battle of Antietam, 1862.

Top right: French troops crossing the Canal du Marne during the Sedan Campaign in the Franco-Prussian War.

Centre right: The Norvals Pont railway bridge on the Orange River in South Africa.

Bottom right: The battle of Colenso. The broken bridge and the trestle bridge over the Tugela.

Above: The Pontoon bridge over the Tugela.

Below: Pegasus Bridge at Benouville, Calvados. Taken by troops of the British 5th Airborne Division on the night of 5/6 June 1944 – the first bridge in France to be captured.

complete faith and confidence. He was astonished and read my memo-
randum. We agreed that, so soon as the attack commenced, his battalion should move down the heights on the flank of the 2nd Battalion
Rifle Brigade, which would rush to support Cadoux, and thus we
parted. I was as sulky as my hot nature would admit, knowing some
disaster would befall my dear old brigade heretofore so judiciously
handled. In the course of the night, as we were lying before the fire, I
far from asleep, General Skerrett received a communication from General Aken to the purport 'that the enemy were retiring over the swollen
river; it was, therefore, to be apprehended he would before daylight
endeavour to possess himself of the bridge; that every precaution must
be taken to prevent him.' I, now being reinforced in opinion, said, 'Now,
General, let me do so.' As he was still as obstinate as ever, we were dis-
cussing the matter (I fear as far as I am concerned, very hotly) when the
'En avant, en avant! L'Empereur recompensera le premier qu'avancera,'
was screeched into our very ears and Cadoux's fire was as hot as ever
fifty men's was on earth. 'Now,' says I, 'General, who is right?' I knew
what the troops would do. My only hope was that Cadoux could keep
the bridge as he anticipated. The fire of the enemy was very severe, and
the rushes of his columns most determined; still Cadoux's fire was
from his post. Three successive times, with half his gallant band, did
he charge and drive back the enemy over the bridge, the other half
remaining in houses as support. His hope and confidence in support
and the importance of his position sustained him until a melancholy
shot pierced his head and he fell lifeless from his horse. A more gallant soul never left its mortal abode. His company at this critical
moment were driven back, the French column and rearguard crossed,
and, by keeping near the bed of the river, succeeded in escaping,
although the riflemen were in support of poor Cadoux with as much
rapidity a distance allowed, and daylight saw Colborne where he said
he would be. I was soon at the bridge. Such a scene of mortal strife
from the fire of fifty men was never witnessed. The bridge was almost
choked with the dead; the enemy's loss was enormous, and many of his
men were drowned, and all his guns were left in the river a mile or two
below the bridge. The number of dead was so great, the bodies were
thrown into the rapid stream in hope that the current would carry
them, but many rocks impeded them, and when the river subsided, we
had great cause to lament our precipitancy in hurling the bodies, for
the stench soon after was awful. The Duke was awfully annoyed, as
well he might be, but, as was his rule, never said anything when disaster could not be amended. I have never told my tale till now. Skerrett
was a bilious fellow (a gallant grenadier, I must readily avow), and I
hope his annoyance so affected his liver it precipitated a step he had

desired – as his father was just dead, and he was heir to an immense property – to retire home on sick leave. You may rely on it, I threw no impediment in his way, for when he was gone, Colonel Colborne was my brigadier, whom we all regarded inferior to no one but the Duke. Many is the conversation he and I have had over the lamentable affair which killed poor Cadoux. I really believe, had he survived, he would have held the bridge, although the enemy attacked it in desperation, and although each time the column was driven back, a few men in the dark succeeded in crossing, and these fellows all practised soldiers, posted themselves under cover on the banks of the river below the bridge, and caused the loss our people sustained, that of noble Cadoux among the rest, with impunity. Cadoux's manner was effeminate, and, as a boy, I used to quiz him. He and I were, therefore, although not enemies, not friends, until the battle of Vitoria, when I saw him most conspicuous. He was ahead of me on his gallant war horse, which he took at Barosa with the holsters full of doubloons, as the story went. I was badly mounted that day, and my horse would not cross a brook which his was scrambling over. I leaped from my saddle over my horse's head (I was very active in those days), seized his horse by the tail, and I believe few, if any, were as soon in the middle of the Frenchmen's twelve guns as we were in support of the 7th Division. From that day we were comrades in every sense of the term, and I wept over his gallant remains with a bursting heart, as, with his company who adored him, I consigned to the grave the last external appearance of Daniel Cadoux. His fame can never die.

An account derived from a Colonel Thomas Smith, of whom no details are known, tells a rather different story:

Skerrett sent to desire Cadoux to evacuate his post. Cadoux refused, saying that he could hold it. At 2 a.m. the French made a rush, but Cadoux, by his fire from the bridge house, kept the head of the advancing column in check. Skerrett now peremptorily ordered Cadoux to leave the bridge-house. Cadoux could only comply, but remarked that 'but few of his party would reach the camp'. And as a matter of fact every officer present was either killed or wounded (Cadoux being killed), besides 11 sergeants and 48 rank and file out of a total strength of 100 men. Until the party left the bridge-house, Cadoux had not lost a man except the double sentries on the bridge, who were killed in the rush made by the French.

Accordingly, while Harry Smith in the text blames Skerrett for leaving Cadoux in an almost impossible position without support, Thomas Smith's charge against Skerrett is that he recalled Cadoux when he was well able to hold his own.

The bridge of boats across the River Adour, December 1813 to February 1814

The Allies crossed the River Nive on 9 December 1813. The battle is described by the Victorian military historian James Grant:

A double bridge at Ustaritz, on the Nive, had been broken down, but an island which connected them was possessed by a detachment of our troops. Marshal Beresford had quietly laid his pontoons on the hither side in the night; and on the morning of the 9th a beacon suddenly flaring up on a height above Cambo gave the signal of action, and Colonel John Cameron threw himself into the river at the head of the 92nd Highlanders, which belonged to Hill's division. The latter forced the passage in three columns, above and below the river, but not without resistance, and the winter fords were so deep that some of the cavalry were drowned; and the French were strongly posted, especially at Halzou, where a deep and strong mill-race had to be crossed as well as the river, along the banks of which the red fire of the musketry sparkled out upon the gloom of the wintry dawn.

Bayonne was now closely invested south of the River Adour, whose width allowed the French to continue to use river-boats from inland and coasting vessels from the sea, by night. Wellington was considering bridging the river west of Bayonne with a bridge of boats made from vessels larger and stronger than pontoons, protected by booms and land batteries against French waterborne attacks. That same Colonel Sturgeon who had repaired the Alcantara bridge twenty months before had designed a structure using larger-than-normal pontoons, ships' cables and special securing devices, to cope with the heavy tides and strong currents in the lower Adour. Coasting vessels, secured by anchors at each end, had five large cables held rigidly in place on each vessel, running across them to capstans on the shore; across these vessels a gangway was to be constructed by lashing three-inch oak planks to the outer cables. Thus the Adour, inland from Bayonne, would be impractical for river-boats if Allied artillery was positioned on the south bank.

The weather, however, was not suitable for such operations and did not clear until early in February, but Soult's army had to be manoeuvred further east from its concentration in Bayonne, before bridge-building operations could begin. An Allied offensive began on 14 February, and within a few days Hill had forced Soult to withdraw two of his three field divisions from Bayonne, with which he had given up direct contact. On the

19th Wellington visited the Bayonne area, intending to supervise the construction of the bridge, but bad weather made it impossible. The weather moderated on the 23rd when Hope advanced into the area with enough equipment to ferry a force across the Adour and hold its bridgehead. On the following day, the navy got sufficient vessels across the bar into the Adour to allow bridge construction to be started and, despite losses of men and material, it was completed and guns were moving across the bridge on the afternoon of the 26th.

There were other bridges involved in these operations, as the area involved in the operations was divided by four rivers all flowing parallel to the Nive, and to the east was the Gave de Pau. Hill crossed the Joyeuse river easily but encountered resistance in front of the next one, the Bidouse, but repaired the bridge over it at St Palais and so continued his advance. Then came the Saison, which Hill crossed, while the French were concentrating behind the last river, the Gave de Pau near the town of Orthez. Beresford crossed the Gave de Pau with 4th and 7th Divisions in the vicinity of Peyrehorade, while Picton managed to cross only four miles below Orthez and seized a permanent bridge, which was repaired quickly. Early on the 27th Wellington had five divisions and cavalry north of the river, some 31,000 men, an exceptional feat considering that he had reconnoitred the French positions from the southern bank only the previous day!

Orthez: the crossing of the Gave de Pau, 27 February 1814
The following account is from Hamley's The Operations of War:

In 1814, Soult held the Gave de Pau against Wellington. Above Orthez the river spread wide with flat banks. The bridge of Orthez was difficult to force, having a tower in the centre, the gateway of which was built up. The houses on both sides were occupied by the French, and the river there was deep and full of pointed rocks.

Five miles below Orthez was the broken bridge of Berenx, from whence a narrow defile led up to the main road on the right bank. Soult designed to fall in force on the head of the first column that should cross. His line extended from near Baigts on the right, to above Orthez on the left, where, as the river was less defensible, he had placed strong bodies of troops.

Soult had 40,000 troops, of which 3,000 were cavalry, and 40 guns. Wellington had 37,000, of which 4,000 were cavalry, and 48 guns. Of the seven English infantry divisions, four were massed opposite Orthez, with five regiments of cavalry and eighteen guns; an infantry division, with a brigade of cavalry in front of the broken bridge of Berenx; and two divisions of infantry and a division of cavalry under Beresford in front of Peyrehorade.

Beresford crossed the Gave by a pontoon bridge and fords, and advanced with the main part of his force on the Pau road, throwing a detachment to his left to threaten Soult's communications with Dax, where he had a magazine. Simultaneously a pontoon bridge was commenced at Berenx. Beresford, halting for the night near Baigts, covered the construction of the bridge. Communications were thus established between the centre and left.

Soult did not receive intelligence of Beresford's movements till he was near Baigts. By that time two divisions drawn from the right were approaching the bridge of Berenx, and that which had before been despatched there was about to cross. Thus five of the seven English divisions were massed opposite Soult's right, astride the river.

Soult now hesitated whether to fall upon Beresford, and the column crossing at Berenx, or to take a defensive position in rear. He finally decided on the latter course. Doubtless he was swayed partly by the strength of that position, but powerfully also by the circumstance that he could not know for certain the proportion of troops at each point. If he withdrew too many troops from left to right, the English right passing above Orthez might strike at his rear; if he attacked the English left with insufficient numbers, he might suffer losses to no purpose, and lose the Dax road. The screen of the river, veiling in some degree the assailant's movements, told against the defender.

In taking his new position he pivoted on Orthez with his left, and swung his centre and right backward from the river in front of the Dax road. Wellington's divisions, when all had passed to the right bank, attacked the front of the position, dislodging the enemy by main force; and towards the close of the action, the English right, passing above Orthez, turned the French left, and accelerated the retreat.

The attack on Toulouse, 4–7 April 1814

To get within striking distance of the actual fortifications of Toulouse it was necessary for the Allied army to cross the River Garonne. On 27 March, the army marched to where, five miles south of the city, pontoons were being formed into a bridge by the engineers, who then discovered that with the materials at their disposal the finished bridge would be about 80 feet too short to cross the Garonne at that point. Three nights later the bridge was successfully laid over the river a considerable distance further south, and Hill, with 13,000 men and three batteries, pushed across, only to discover that he was west of the Ariège, a branch of the Garonne in an area lacking suitable roads for his artillery. Wellington visited the area and ordered Hill back across the river, and the pontoon bridge was taken up and transported north again.

A spot was found 15 miles north of Toulouse where the Garonne could be crossed with the available equipment, although it meant stretching it beyond the limit of safety, with the pontoons spaced further apart than usual. The bridge was laid on the evening of 4 April and Beresford, with 19,000 men, including cavalry and artillery, crossed at dawn. Then the weather broke and a flood sweeping down the Garonne broke the bridge, marooning Beresford. However, the French did not venture out to attack him and, by the afternoon of 7 April, the river had fallen and the pontoon bridge was repaired and back in service.

6. AMERICAN WARS

THE WAR OF AMERICAN INDEPENDENCE

Lexington and Concord, 1775

It was on 19 April 1775 that the smouldering discontent in the British-ruled American colonies flared into open hostilities when, on a stretch of country road outside Boston, a dragging skirmish took place between American militiamen and British redcoats that was to start the American War of Independence. It was triggered off when General Thomas Gage, commanding a British army in Boston, sent a force under Lieutenant-Colonel Francis Smith on a march to Concord with the aim of seizing the local militia's weapons. This was a halting, ill-performed expedition against people who had been warned of the soldiers' impending arrival. When he realised that they were expected, Smith sent forward an advance-guard of six light infantry companies under Major John Pitcairn to secure the bridges at Concord; at the same time he sent a message back to Gage requesting reinforcements. It was known that a large quantity of the weapons and stores to be taken were secreted in the farm buildings of Colonel James Barrett, commander of the Concord militia, which lay about two miles beyond the North Bridge over the River Concord.

Arriving at the village of Lexington, about six miles short of the bridge, Pitcairn's men encountered a force of about 77 American militiamen, under Captain John Parker, drawn up on Lexington Common. Outnumbered, the militia were slowly and reluctantly withdrawing when a shot was fired, followed by a volley from the redcoats, bringing down eight colonials. The shots that had been fired were to echo around the world. As the news spread, local militia, called out by bells, musket-shots and messengers, grabbed muskets and powder-horns, streaming towards Concord.

By the time the skirmish at Lexington had ended, Smith's main body had closed up on Pitcairn's advance-guard, and the force began their march onward to Concord. The town was reached at about 7 a.m., at which point the American militia commander, Colonel Barrett, ordered his men to withdraw across North Bridge to Punkatasset Hill, just west of the bridge and overlooking it, to await reinforcements. Smith then ordered Captain Lawrence Parsons of the 10th Regiment to the North Bridge with seven companies of light infantry, while Captain Munday Pole took another company to secure the South Bridge. Meanwhile the rest of the force systematically searched the town. Two companies remained at the North Bridge while the rest set out for Barrett's farm, led by Captain Parsons; then another company left the bridge to join Parsons, so that only the light company of the 43rd, under Captain Walter Sloane Laurie, remained to hold it.

Meanwhile, the militia force on the hill had steadily grown until about 400 minutemen, militiamen and unorganised men and boys were angrily watching the flames and smoke of burning military supplies rising above the town below, fearing their homes were being torched. Although there were more than 700 British troops in and around Concord itself, it was Laurie's company of some thirty men, pushed forward about half-a-mile beyond the town, who alone faced the enemy. Eventually Colonel Barratt gave the order that sent the militia striding resolutely forward, led by a pair of fifers playing 'The White Cockade', after being warned by their commander not to be the first to fire. They were formed in column of twos, under command of Major John Buttrick, with Captain Davis and Colonel John Robinson at their head; Colonel Barratt remained on the crest of the hill. As they neared the British outpost, the light company of the 4th Regiment, posted on a nearby height, withdrew and joined the men on the bridge, along with the light company of the 10th Regiment, so that three British companies were facing the Americans.

Coming onto the heights just vacated by the light company of the 4th Regiment, they halted, overlooking the 'rude bridge that arched the flood', before moving again down the path from the hill that met at right-angles the road leading to the bridge. They formed up on the causeway leading over grassland to the crossing; then Major Buttrick led his irregulars forward against 'the flower of the King's Army' as the flank companies were known. By now these redcoats had recrossed the bridge and were lining the opposite side of the river, with one company flanking the other two; a small detail had been left behind by Laurie and were endeavouring to pull up the planks of the bridge.

Already 'blooded' at Lexington, the redcoats had no hesitation in firing first, but to poor effect, for they were so formed up that only one company could bring its muskets to bear. Then Major Buttrick gave the order, 'Fire, fellow soldiers, for God's sake, fire!', and for the first time Americans fired a volley of musketry into British ranks. This return fire drove the redcoats from their position, having had three regulars killed, and four officers with four private soldiers wounded; in the three-minute exchange, the Americans lost two killed (one of whom was Captain Davis) and three wounded.

Laurie's force retreated to the centre of the town in some disorder, colliding with two companies of reinforcements belatedly ordered forward by Colonel Smith, who made no attempt to retake the bridge to cover the return from Barrett's farm of Parsons's force. However, the Americans did not continue their pursuit or attempt to cut Parsons off, so they were able to recross the bridge without interference. As they crossed, Parsons's troops came upon a wounded British soldier who appeared to have been mutilated, giving rise to later reports that the Americans had been guilty of atrocities, scalping and cutting off ears. Later it transpired that a sixteen-year-old boy, claimed to be half-witted, crossing the bridge after the skirmish, had struck a seriously wounded British redcoat in the head with an axe.

Pausing to regroup his troops and feed them, Colonel Smith delayed two hours or so in Concord before beginning what was going to become an ordeal by fire, as increasing numbers of Americans subjected the column to a galling and demoralising fire. At Meriam's Corner, where the ridge ended, the Regulars had to crowd together to cross a narrow bridge, coming under fire at less than 150 yards from front, flanks and rear. The British reached Boston that night, having covered 16 miles in the most painful fashion, suffering casualties of about 273 men to the American's losses of 95.

Moore's Creek Bridge, North Carolina, 27 February 1776

The flames of revolution were fanned in Carolina by stirring reports from Lexington and Concord which eventually caused the royal governor Joseph Martin to flee, a Provincial Congress to be organised, and American patriots to prepare for war. Subsequently, Martin convinced the British that, with the help of a few British regiments he could raise a force of Loyalists large enough to quell the rebellion in North Carolina, aiding the capture of South Carolina and Georgia. Martin's hopes were based on persuading a relatively new group of immigrants, the Highland Scots, who had fought for the Stuarts in the '45 rebellion and had fled to the New World after the bloody defeat at Culloden, to throw in their lot with the British. Strange as this might seem, considering their obvious lack of love for the Hanoverian King George III, they had still less affection for their neighbours, many of whom were Lowland, or Scottish-Irish immigrants. Learning that an expedition from Ireland was to link up with a force under Clinton from New York, Martin began raising an army intended for a co-ordinated uprising of Loyalists, when the expedition arrived. From Boston, General Gage sent eighty-year-old Donald McDonald, an experienced soldier, and Donald McLeod to lead the enterprise.

McDonald raised the royal standard at Cross Creek (later to become the town of Fayetteville), calling for an assembly of armed supporters, relying on his reputation as a veteran of Culloden. Soon, the clans were astir, marching out of their settlements to the stirring sounds of bagpipes and drums, bearing claymores and dirks, some wearing kilts and tartans, just as they had set out for Glencoe, Prestonpans and Culloden. By 18 February, the numbers had reached 700–1,000 Highland Scots and about 800 other Loyalists, some being Regulars. Their intention was to make contact with the king's troops who were expected to land on the North Carolina coast, confidently planning to rout a rebel force they believed to be marching north-west towards them.

As word of the Loyalist activities leaked out, the Patriots began muster-ing their forces under the command of Colonel James Moore of the 1st North Carolina Continentals, who raised about 650 men and five guns and marched out from Wilmington. On 15 February, camped at Rockfish Creek some twelve miles south of Cross Creek, they were joined by Colonel John Alexander Lillington's 150 minutemen, 200 men under Colonel Kennon, and 100 volunteer rangers under Colonel John Ashe.

Realising that the enemy were gathering around him, McDonald decided to avoid a general engagement and march to the coast to join the expected British expedition, heading generally east across the Cape Fear and South Rivers, then south-east towards Wilmington. It was a colourful affair. Pipes playing, kilts swinging, out marched McDonalds, Camerons, McCraes, Mackenzies, McLeods and other Scots clansmen. Moore, the American commander, hoped to intercept their march by withdrawing along the Cape Fear River, when he received news from Colonel Richard Caswell, commander of North Carolina Partisan Rangers Militia, that he was between Black River and Moore's Creek, and that the enemy had crossed the former. Asking Caswell to meet him there if possible, Moore said he would attempt to stop McDonald's army at Moore's Creek Bridge, about eighteen miles above Wilmington. Lillington and Ashe reached the creek on 25 February, and Caswell arrived next day. Moore was not with them, remaining at Elizabethtown to block the enemy route to Cape Fear; he did not join them until the day after the action.

Lillington's men prepared a defensive position, digging trenches and erecting earthworks among the myrtles, with the river between them and the advancing Scots. Caswell's force arrived and began digging in on the far bank, beyond the bridge, until he realised that it was not sound military practice to position himself with a river behind him! Abandoning the half-dug works, his men joined Lillington's force on the far bank. With no signs of the Loyalists, the Patriot soldiers had time partly to dismantle the bridge, removing flooring so that the Loyalists would have to cross on the log stringers, which had been greased.

After marching for three days through rough terrain, the Loyalists halted late on 26 February and pitched camp six miles from the bridge. When scouts returned to report the Rebels positioned around the bridge, the Loy-alists gathered themselves and resumed their advance at about 1 a.m. on the 27th. Their leader Donald McDonald had been taken ill during the night, so that command passed to Captain John Campbell. Eighty selected clay-more-armed men formed the advance-guard, 1,000 men made up the main body, and 300 riflemen brought up the rear. They heralded their approach with skirling bagpipes and beating drums, so that when they approached the creek at dawn the Patriots were ready for them. It was between dawn and sunrise on a soft February day that they came up to the abandoned works on their side of the creek, which caused them to believe that crossing the bridge would be unopposed.

The Highland Scots, many dressed in plaids and kilts, their claymores glinting in the early sunlight, rushed onto the bridge shouting 'King George and Broadswords!' They were met by a withering hail of fire from muskets and two artillery pieces, pouring out from behind breastworks only thirty yards away to cut down the advance-guard almost to a man, with both McLeod and Campbell killed. Some men slumped forward, others sprawled back, many losing their balance and falling into the stream below, to drown. It was all over in less than five minutes. Rushing from their cover, rebel troops counter-attacked, some replacing planking as others clambered over heaps of kilted dead to pursue fleeing, panic-stricken survivors. Fording the creek with a few men, Slocum forced his way through the swamp on the west bank, cutting off many of the fugitives. About thirty Loyalists were actually killed or wounded in the brief action on the bridge; total casualties were about seventy, The Patriots had only two casualties, one of whom died later.

Moore's foresight in posting the 2nd and 4th North Carolina Regiments at Cross Creek paid off. He took an estimated 850 prisoners on 28 February, including General McDonald and several other Loyalist officers, as well as £15,000 in specie, 1,500 rifles, 350 muskets and 150 swords and dirks. Thus the whole Loyalist army was destroyed and prevented from linking up with the British expedition, the spirit was drained from their sympathisers, and – most importantly – the flames of revolutionary ardour were fanned to the extent that North Carolina became the first of all the colonies to vote for independence.

Before the fateful day had ended at Moore's Creek Bridge, an unknown correspondent had written an eye-witness account of the action. This is quoted in Frank Moore's A Diary of the American Revolution (1860):

This morning, the North Carolina minutemen and militia ... had an engagement with the Tories at Widow Moore's Creek bridge. At the break of day an alarm gun was fired, immediately after which, scarcely leaving the Americans a moment to prepare, the Tory army with Captain (Donald) McLeod at their head made their attack on Colonels Caswell and Lillington, posted near the bridge and, finding a small entrenchment vacant, concluded that the Americans had abandoned their post. With this supposition, they advanced in a most furious manner over the bridge. Colonel Caswell had very wisely ordered the planks to be taken up, so that in passing they met with many difficulties. On reaching a point within thirty paces of the breastworks they were received with a very heavy fire, which did great execution. Captains

McLeod and (Farquard) Campbell were instantly killed, the former having nine bullets and twenty-four swan shot through and into his body. The insurgents retreated with the greatest precipitation, leaving behind them some of their wagons, etc. They cut their horses out of the wagons and mounted three upon a horse. Many of them fell into the creek and were drowned. Tom Rutherford ran like a lusty fellow: both he and Felix Keenan were in arms against the Carolinians, and they by this time are prisoners, as is Lieutenant Colonel (James) Cotton, who ran at the first fire.

The battle lasted three minutes. Twenty-eight of the Tories, besides the two captains, are killed or mortally wounded, and between twenty and thirty taken prisoners, among whom is His Excellency General Donald Macdonald (the ageing commander-in-chief of the Tories, who had remained in the Tory camp too ill to lead the assault. This, we think, will effectually put a stop to Toryism in North Carolina.

Throg's Neck, New York, 18 October 1776

During his New York campaign of autumn 1776, the British commander General Howe planned an amphibious operation with the intention of avoiding Washington's strong defences on Harlem Heights. On the morning of 12 October he embarked the greater part of his force in eighty vessels, passing up the East River under cover of a warm, heavy fog, to begin landing his 4,000 men at about 9 a.m. on a peninsula jutting two miles into Long Island Sound, known as Throg's Neck, to the left and rear of Washington's line which ran directly from the Neck to King's Bridge (see below).

Washington immediately realised that it was Howe's intention to work round to the rear of his position; indeed, if Howe's force had been able to push across the creek at Throg's Neck, they would have cut off the Americans' only line of retreat and smashed them between two strong forces. Evidence exists to indicate the fact that Washington at first believed the ground he was holding between the Neck and King's Bridge was defensible, but a subsequent Council of Generals decided that Manhattan Island could be held no longer, and that the time had come to move, unless having to fight on ground of Howe's choosing. The British commander had repeatedly shown he could land troops in the American rear while turning their flank with his main body, advancing from Throg's Neck.

In the event, however, things did not turn out as expected. The British troops, as soon as they were ashore and started inland, discovered that the Neck was separated from the mainland by a creek with marshy borders, that could only be crossed in two places – a causeway and wooden bridge at the lower end, and a ford at the upper – and both were guarded.

Reconnoitring the area a few days previously, the American General William Heath recognised the tactical importance of the bridge over the mill dam at Westchester village; also, he noticed a huge pile of cord wood occupying an area on the west side of the creek. So, on 12 October, he had Colonel Edward Hand's thirty-man guard from the 1st Pennsylvania Rifle Regiment of his A Division, snugly lying in its shelter, with another detail at the ford. The riflemen halted the redcoats in their tracks – all 4,000 of them, with field pieces – for several hours, until more than 1,000 reinforcements arrived to bottle up Howe's forces. The new arrivals were Prescott's Massachusetts Continental Regiment, with a 3-pounder gun at the causeway, and Graham's New York Continental Regiment, with a 6-pounder gun, at the ford.

Frustrated, Howe's force remained in the area for some days, ruminating on what they could have done had they been able to force their way past the thirty riflemen, and moved to King's Bridge, eight miles away.

In his Memoirs (published in New York in 1901), General William Heath described the events in his own words:

The troops landed at Frog's Neck and their advance pushed towards the causeway and the bridge at Westchester Mill. Colonel (Edward) Hand's (thirty) riflemen took up the planks of the bridge as had been directed and commenced a firing with their rifles.

The British moved towards the head of the creek, but found here also the Americans in possession of the pass. Our General (Heath) immediately (as he had assured Colonel Hand he would do) ordered up Colonel (William) Prescott, the hero of Bunker Hill, with his regiment and Captain (David) Bryant of the Artillery with a three-pounder to reinforce the riflemen at Westchester causeway, and Colonel (John) Graham of the New York Line with his regiment and Lieutenant (Daniel) Jackson of the Artillery with a six-pounder to reinforce at the head of the creek – all of which was promptly done to the check and disappointment of the enemy.

The British encamped on the Neck. The riflemen and (Hessian) jägers kept up a scattering popping at each other across the marsh, and the Americans on their side and the British on the other threw up a work at the end of the causeway, Captain Bryant, now and then, when there was an object, saluted the British with a field piece.

In the afternoon, forty or fifty sail of vessels passed up and came to anchor off Frog's Point. The same evening General (Alexander) McDougall's Brigade joined our General's (Heath's) division.

Still known today as Throg's Point or Neck, it is now Fort Schuyler Park, in the south-east corner of the Bronx.

King's Bridge marked the point where the Post Road crossed Spuyten Duyvil Creek, separating Manhattan from the Bronx. It was strategically important in the New York campaign of 1776, and later in the British defence of the colony of New York. In July 1781, it was an objective of American forces under General Benjamin Lincoln operating against Manhattan at the start of the Yorktown campaign.

Stony Brook Bridge, 1777

During the first two or three days of January 1777, the British commander Cornwallis was marching with superior forces against Washington in the Trenton-Princeton area. The American leader planned to slip from his camp under cover of night, and strike Princeton and Brunswick. By 3 a.m. on 3 January, the muffled wheels of the guns and the tired feet of the half-frozen exhausted Americans were crossing Stony Brook, only two miles from Princeton.

When Cornwallis marched for Trenton on 1 January he left behind in Princeton Lieutenant-Colonel Charles Marwood with a rearguard of 1,200 troops. At dawn on the following day Marwood marched from the town with the 17th and 55th Foot en route to Trenton, leaving the 40th Foot in Princeton to guard supplies. This force, with a troop of the 16th Light Dragoons, were crossing Stony Brook Bridge when they saw behind them a column of marching men, whom initially they mistook for Hessians. In fact, they were a force of 350 Americans, led by General Mercer, sent by Washington to defend and/or destroy the bridge so as to prevent pursuit by Cornwallis and cut off escape from Princeton. It was about 8 a.m. when the meeting occurred and Marwood, recovering from his surprise, about-faced his force and doubled them back over the bridge towards a hill on the east side of the brook. At the same time, Mercer's force dashed for the same site – the two forces meeting headlong in Clark's Orchard, where the British bayonets routed the Americans, killing General Mercer. In pursuit of the fleeing enemy, the British also routed another small force under General Cadwallader.

Led by Washington, showing utter disregard for his own safety, American troops, heavily outnumbering Marwood's force, compelled him to abandon his guns. The latter charged with his men through the American ranks, then turned and regained the road to Trenton. From start to finish, the action had lasted just fifteen minutes.

Pushing on to Princeton, Washington took the town when the small British garrison surrendered; unable, however, to risk a pitched battle with Cornwallis's relatively fresh troops, he headed for Morristown. Moving with the utmost speed, Cornwallis urged his men forward. Reaching Stony Brook Bridge, which the Americans had destroyed, he drove on his soldiers into the icy water and to the far bank. The British reached Princeton just as the last American regiment was marching out.

Bennington, 16 August 1777

Seeking supplies, the British commander, General Burgoyne, authorised a raid into the New Hampshire Grants (later Vermont) by a force of about 800, comprised of about 300 German dragoons, the same number of Tories, a small number of British light infantry plus a hundred or so Indian scouts – all under command of German Lieutenant-Colonel Friedrich Baum. Reaching the Bennington area on 14 August, the first contact was made, although the raiders were delayed by a burned St Luke's Bridge. This necessitated a détour of about one and three-quarter miles to a bridge or ford on the Walloomsac River, about four miles from Bennington, where American General Stark waited with his force. Realising the possible importance of the bridge, Baum placed there half his small force of British riflemen, all the Canadians, half his Brunswick Grenadiers and one gun (about seventy-five men in all). On the American enemy side of the river he placed about 150 men (mostly Tories) in an improvised entrenchment, later known as the Tory Redoubt; but he made his main position on a hill overlooking the right bank, called the Dragoon Redoubt, which held about 200 men and a 3-pounder gun.

The Tory Redoubt was easily taken when the inexperienced defenders all fired together and were overwhelmed while reloading. The attack on the bridge was equally successful, as the Canadian defenders were first to flee, followed by the English light infantry and the Brunswick Grenadiers, abandoning the gun. The dragoons held out longer, until an ammunition cart within the entrenchment exploded and the attackers entered during the confusion. Few of Baum's men escaped, other than the Indians who had run away before the action began.

Matson's Ford, Pennsylvania, 11 December 1777

Cornwallis advanced from Philadelphia on the night of 10–11 December, with 3,000 men plus almost the entire force of Howe's dragoons and mounted jägers, to forage along the south bank of the River Schuykill. By a coincidence, Washington left for his winter quarters at Valley Forge, and his advance parties met up with Cornwallis's party at Matson's Ford (now West Conshoboken, Penn.). After destroying the makeshift bridge they had built of wagons and planks, the Americans withdrew. The raiders returned to Philadelphia on the evening of 12 December with about 2,000 sheep and cattle.

Quintan's Bridge, New Jersey, 18 March 1778

American Colonel Asher Holmes, whose men were foraging in the area, had taken a position to cover Quintan's Bridge on Alloway Creek, with 300 militia. At dawn on 18 March, British Colonel Marwood, leading a force of British Regulars and Sincoe's Rangers, concealed a number of detachments on that side of the creek opposite the rebels' position, posting seventy men of the 17th Regiment plus three separate groups of rangers in Wetherby's Tavern and behind a force to its rear. When men of the 17th Regiment were seen by American Captain Smith moving about near the tavern, he had bridge planks replaced and led 200 men over in pursuit, leaving 100 men on high ground by the creek. As the Americans made contact with the decoy group, Captain Saunders emerged from the house to their rear, cutting off Smith's retreat to the bridge and driving his men in confusion towards another crossing of the creek. The pursuit was conducted by Saunders's party and thirty mounted rangers, and in due course by Marwood's entire force.

In the nick of time, Colonel Hands arrived with his Cumberland Militia and two guns; they occupied the Americans' original position to prevent the British crossing the bridge and completely wiping out Holmes's force. As it was the rebels lost thirty or forty men, most of whom were drowned; the British lost one man.

Quinby Bridge, South Carolina, 17 July 1781

Driven from one position to another by stronger forces of American commanders Sumter, Henry Lee and Marion, British Colonel John Coates withdrew down the Cooper River, towards Charleston, to Quinby Bridge. Here his small force of the unseasoned 19th Regiment and some mounted South Carolina Rangers took up a strong position along the creek, and was awaiting his rearguard and baggage to withdraw across the bridge before removing the planking. Coates was unaware that Lee had destroyed his rearguard and was taken completely by surprise when rebel Captain Armstrong, closely followed by Lieutenant Carrington and their cavalry, charged across the bridge. This sudden onslaught drove off all the British, except their commander and a few men who rallied around him, who put up a strong resistance. The third American cavalry section, under Captain O'Neal, could not get across the bridge to help, because the preceding horsemen had dislodged the planks to create an impassable gap, and the muddy banks of the creek made it unfordable.

After fierce fighting, Armstrong and Carrington were forced to retreat, in various directions because of the impassable bridge, and the action petered out.

THE WAR OF 1812 (1812–15)

The War of 1812 between Britain and America was caused by long-standing disputes dating back to the American Revolution, 30 years earlier. It was marked by the American desire to annex Canada and increased by tensions arising from British encroachments upon American neutrality brought about by the ensuing Napoleonic Wars. Beginning with the defeat of an American force invading Canada in July 1812, it saw operations in the Niagara area, the destruction of some small coastal towns from Maine to Georgia, the burning of the White House in Washington and extensive minor naval engagements. It ended with a British defeat at New Orleans in January 1815.

Bladensburg, Maryland, 24 August 1814

In Washington itself were two bridges leading into Baltimore; both had been ordered to be destroyed to hinder a British advance, but, as with most things in Washington at that crucial time in American history, little had been done in the hot and sultry days of late August 1814. A working party of thirty men had been hanging around the lower bridge – the main one – for nearly a week; they had no explosives, kindling or pitch, and their axes were inadequate to bring down what was a fairly substantial structure. The upper crossing, known as Stoddert's Bridge, was a much older and more rickety affair; it was quite capable of bearing traffic, but did not even have a guard placed on it.

When all this was discovered by General Winder, the local American commander, he posted a party of infantry across the river beside the lower bridge to prevent surprise. He tried to arrange for it to be blown if necessary, the Navy Yard being instructed to send a boatload of explosives. At the same time, he ordered the upper bridge to be burned, and soon the night sky was beaconed by flames arising from it.

The British commanders Ross and Cockburn assumed that Winder would destroy these bridges over the eastern branch of the Potomac River, and decided to make their crossing at Bladensburg, where they knew there was another bridge.

The pretty town of Bladensburg, nestling between rolling hills, lay on the east bank of the eastern branch of the Potomac River, with a bridge spanning the river directly west of the town. From the bridges to west and southwest, two roads branched off – one from Georgetown and the other the turnpike from Washington, gradually converging until they almost met at the bridge that crossed the river into the town. It was there that the road branched out again, now in three directions: the turnpike to Baltimore ran to the north, the direct route to Upper Marlboro led to the east, and another road, with some side-roads, ran south beside the river.

Bladensburg owed its existence to this convergence of roads, and in a sense played the role of a funnel through which everything bound for Washington invariably passed. This was entirely thanks to its bridge – a narrow wooden structure, 90 feet in length, standing on lateral supporting structures (abutments). Above the bridge, the Potomac's eastern branch soon became a fordable small stream; but the river was a barrier to the south, and to north and west was densely wooded.

One of the more far-seeing of the defenders, Colonel Wadsworth, threw up a primitive earthwork in the area of the bridge, aided by civilian volunteers. He built it facing the river, about 350 yards from the bridge. Behind it, Baltimore artillerymen positioned their six light cannon. The first defenders to arrive at the bridge, as early as 22 August, were Stansbury's Maryland militia brigade with their artillery, from Baltimore; they were posted west of the river, on a ridge commanding the Georgetown road and close to the river banks. Their positioning was faulty, however, in that the infantry regiments were separated by an open field and an orchard from the guns and riflemen they were intended to support.

To the left of the earthwork Stansbury placed two militia companies, with Major Pinckney's battalion of riflemen to the right, who were partly protected on the right by a rail fence and, to the left, by a barn. These placings, forming a line, covered both the bridge and the road fanning out from it. Stansbury's supports, Colonels Ragan's and Schutz's militia regiments, and Colonel Sterett's 5th Regiment were to the right and left respectively in an apple orchard some fifty yards behind the main defence line.

The potential efficiency of these troops was never to be revealed. Almost as soon as they had been placed, they were moved by James Monroe, officious Secretary of State from Washington, who ordered the two militia regiments out of the orchard and onto a hill further to the rear, more than 500 yards behind the front line and well out of supporting range. He also moved Sterett's 5th Regiment back to the same hill – leaving little if any support for the guns and infantry on and around the earthwork. Meanwhile, troops were arriving piecemeal from Washington, as well as guns, these being hurriedly (and usually inadequately) placed on the ground facing the direction from which the British were expected to arrive, to wait in some trepidation and apprehension. At one stage President James Madison himself, with his entourage, rode out from Washington and were cantering around the position when they were warned of the impending approach of the enemy!

Ross's British army arrived at the scene, after a tiring march of fifteen miles from Melwood, at about one o'clock; they came over Lowndes Hill and streamed into Bladensburg, finding no signs of life in the hushed L-shaped main street and its cluster of neat brick buildings and yards. But from a vantage-point, Ross could see the American preparations across the river – the earthwork with its guns, and swarms of troops milling about, some in uniforms, indicating that regulars were present. He was over-impressed by what he could see of the American defensive position, later writing: 'They were strongly posted on very commanding heights, formed in two lines, covered the bridge over the eastern branch, across which the British troops had to pass.' Seemingly, the American Secretary of War, riding with President Madison, was more of a realist, telling the President that 'it was between regulars and militia, and the militia would be beaten'.

Out of sight beyond the reverse slopes of Lowndes Hill, men were falling into columns, to the sounds of drums and bugles; the word of command to

146

advance was given, and they moved forward over the crest of the hill. Immediately a ripple of gun-flashes sparkled from the earthwork as the Baltimore artillery opened fire, causing casualties as the British column drew nearer to the bridge.

Concentrating their gunfire on the column, the American artillerymen did not notice groups of marines setting up cumbersome tripod devices in the area of a warehouse to the right of the bridge. Then came a series of frightening 'whooshes', immediately followed by streaks of smoke-tinged flame snaking low across the sky, causing militiamen to duck their heads.

Congreve's rockets had arrived on the American battlefield, to the consternation of the untried militia and other troops, who had no conception of what these frightening missiles were. Filled with gunpowder and capped with a warhead, the metal tubes were simple to fire and, with their tripods, light to carry; their simplicity was outweighed a thousand times by the uncomprehending fear they aroused, despite causing few casualties.

Thus the scene was dramatically set for the actors to come on stage, in the form of Colonel William Thornton's light brigade formed of the 85th Foot and light infantry companies. The colonel, on his grey horse, led his men in almost theatrical manner, sword flashing, galloping from cover and clattering onto the wooden span of the bridge. Miraculously, he survived the crashing salvo hurled out by the waiting artillery, emerging unscathed from the smoke as red-coated figures crashed to the ground. Encouraged by the demanding note of the bugles, the British poured across the bridge to fan out widely in the thick undergrowth on the American side of the river, before the artillery could load and fire again. The 1,000 or so British, outnumbering the Maryland defenders two-to-one, drove on, scrambling into woods and thickets to return fire, so that they quickly outflanked the guns and riflemen. All across the bridge by now, the light brigade edged towards Stansbury's right flank, on the Washington road, separating his troops from Winder's as the orchard trees masked the envelopment. Orders to fall back were given and initially obeyed in disciplined fashion; then it became a general retreat, dissolving into a disorganised rout, with no objective but to get away. Thus was achieved the battle's sad title of 'The Bladensburg Races'.

The Americans put onto the field 2,000 more men and nineteen more guns than the British, but were let down by their faulty dispositions, disorganised command-structure, and general lack of battle-experience on the part of their troops.

The action at Bladensburg stemmed from the British government's decision, in the summer of 1814, to send a force totalling 3,500 men, consisting of four regiments of Peninsular veteran regulars, a battalion of marines and a detachment of sailors dragging three small cannon, to invade the

United States of America. They landed in Chesapeake Bay on America's eastern coast in early August.

The story of the subsequent events is told by James Grant in British Battles on Land and Sea:

After our army under Wellington had crossed the Pyrenees in triumph, he was enabled to spare a force, consisting of the 4th, 44th and 85th Regiments, with some pieces of artillery, which were received on board a squadron at the mouth of the Gironde. The ships were the *Royal Oak*, 74 guns, carrying the flag of Rear-Admiral Pulteney Malcolm; the *Dictator* and *Diadem*, 64 guns; five frigates, two bomb-vessels, several brigs, store ships, and transports.

The troops were under the command of Major General Ross, and sailed for Bermuda, where, on 24 June, they joined Sir Alexander Cochrane, in the *Tonnant*, 80 guns, who was waiting to collect a fleet. On the 30th they were augmented by the arrival of the 21st Scotch Fusiliers, 900 strong. The 27th and 62nd Regiments also came – the two latter for Canada, the former as a reinforcement for General Ross, who, with 3,500 men, had orders to invade the United States of America.

These troops, badly provisioned, slenderly supplied even with ammunition, and, after their hardships in the Peninsula, many of them requiring repose and attendance in hospital, rather than exposure in battle, were landed on a morass at St Benedict's, on the left bank of the Patuxent, a river of Maryland, which throws itself by a large estuary into Chesapeake Bay, twenty-one miles north of the embouchure of the Potomac.

The disembarkation was unopposed. The expedition was supplied with artillery; but for want of horses to drag the guns, only one six-pounder and two small three-pounders were brought on shore; and except those belonging to General Ross and the staff-officers, there was not a single horse with the troops, whose strength does not permit them to be called an army, though Gleig states it at a thousand more than the number given, which we take from Brenton.

The rear-admiral and major-general resolved at once to advance upon Washington, the diplomatic capital of America, the former, with his boats and smaller craft, to follow the troops up the stream.

At four in the evening the bugles, that had been last heard by the legions of Napoleon in the south of France, sounded, and the regiments formed in marching order, and moved in the direction of Nottingham, a town situated on the Patuxent, where it was understood the flotilla was at anchor.

The march was conducted with caution and care. Three companies formed the advanced guard, preceded by a section of twenty files, marching a hundred yards in front; while beyond these were two solitary files to give warning the moment they saw a vestige of armed men. Parallel with the head of these three companies marched the flank patrols. These were parties of fifty men each, in extended order, sweeping the woods and fields to the extent of nearly half a mile. After the advanced guard, at the interval of 150 yards, came the light brigade, which also had some flankers to secure itself against ambuscades. Then came the 2nd brigade, marching steadily on, and next the artillery – the three toy guns already mentioned – drawn by seamen. Last of all came the 3rd brigade, having a guard in rear of the column, at the same distance that the advanced guard was in front.

Although our troops halted for the day at a point only six miles from St Benedict's, it is a remarkable fact that during this short march many soldiers dropped out of the ranks and fell behind from fatigue. This was caused by the men, though Peninsular veterans, having been so long confined in the transports, and unaccustomed to heavy marching order, that they were enervated to an unnatural degree. To add to this, the weather was excessively sultry.

For the night the troops halted, and rested as well as a tremendous storm of thunder and lightning together with a deluge of rain would permit them. Next day they moved to Nottingham, a port of entry on the Patuxent, that they might get in rear of the American flotilla of gun boats, commanded by Commodore Barney, on that river, and prevent it from retreating, while it should be assailed in front by the armed boats of Cochrane's fleet.

On the 22nd the troops were at Upper Marlborough, a few miles distant from Pig Point, on the Patuxent, where Admiral Cochrane, with Captains Barrie, of the *Dragon*, Gordon, of the *Barossa*, and Burdett, of the *Maidstone*, forced the Americans to destroy the whole flotilla.

'Having advanced to within fifteen miles of Washington,' says General Ross in his despatch, 'and having ascertained the force of the enemy to be such as might authorise an attempt at carrying his capital, I determined to make it, and accordingly put the troops in movement on the evening of the 23rd.' In this advance his only corps of cavalry, a force indispensable for an invading army, consisted of fifty artillery drivers, mounted on such horses as they could collect in the fields or stables on the march. As he proceeded, he received intelligence from various quarters that the Americans were concentrating their troops for the purpose of doing battle in front of the capital; but it was a fatal error on their part to suffer us to advance without making the slightest effort to arrest our progress.

After a halt of some hours, about noon on the 24th, the troops perceived a heavy cloud of dust, and on arriving at a turn of the road they discovered the Americans occupying a position of great strength and commanding attitude on a hill at Bladensburg, on the south-eastern branch of the Potomac, which runs past the lower part of the town.

They were formed in two lines, their advance occupying a fortified house which, with artillery, commanded the passage of the stream, which the British troops had to cross. From the bridge there a broad and straight road leads direct to Washington. It went through the enemy's position, and was carefully defended by artillery and riflemen, and 400 cavalry, the whole being under General Winder. The Americans were 9,000 strong, with twenty pieces of cannon, being more than double the number of our forces, now weakened by stragglers and sickness, and harassed by a hot and wearying march. The disposition for attack was speedily made, and commenced with so much impetuosity by the light brigade, consisting of all the light companies of the different regiments, and the gallant 85th, under Colonel Thornton, that the fortified house was stormed in a few minutes, the doors beaten down, and the defenders hunted out by the bayonet.

Startled by the rapidity with which all this was done, the enemy began to retire to higher ground, on which General Ross ordered Colonel Brooke's brigade, consisting of the 4th and 44th, to support Colonel Thornton. The latter regiment pressed the American left; the former assailed their right, and compelled them to abandon their guns.

Their first line gave way and recoiled in confusion on the second, which a well-directed shower of rockets, seconded by a bayonet charge, drove in confusion from the field. 'The rapid flight of the enemy,' says General Ross, 'and his knowledge of the country, precluded the possibility of many prisoners being taken, more particularly as the troops during the day had undergone considerable fatigue.'

Ten pieces of cannon fell into our hands, together with Commodore Barney, commanding that force, who was wounded and taken prisoner, a double mortification, after having been compelled to blow up his gunboats. The guns were at once destroyed. The position thus won, the road to Washington was open.

Our losses were, of all ranks, 64 killed and 185 wounded, with 18 horses. The march was resumed upon Washington; and by eight o'clock that evening the victorious little army was in front of it.

THE AMERICAN CIVIL WAR, 1861–4

Bull Run (First Manassas), 21 July 1861

Federal commander McDowell ordered a wide-turning movement against the Confederate left, by way of Sudley Springs Ford, a major crossing two miles upstream from the Stone Bridge. To divert Confederate attention from this, Tyler's First Division was to make a feint attack on Confederate Colonel 'Shank' Evans's position at the Stone Bridge. Tyler's force arrived before the Stone Bridge, took up positions at about 5.a.m. and about one and a half hours later fired the first shot with their huge 30-pounder Parrott gun.

Unable to match the range of this gun with his own smooth bore howitzers, Evans awaited the inevitable attack, confident that his two regiments of the 1,100-strong demi-brigade could hold a frontal attack over the narrow bridge. They waited two hours and nothing happened; then Captain Alexander's Confederate Signals Unit, eight miles away on Signal Hill, performed probably the first battlefield use of the wig-wag field service telegraph system, sending the message, 'Look out for your left ... you are turned.' Alexander had seen the glint of bayonets and musket barrels from the flanking column of the Federal force at Sudley. At once Evans abandoned his desultory fire-fight with Tyler, left the bridge and took up a position where his men were more needed.

In the later stages of the battle, the Stone Bridge provided a route of escape for fleeing Union troops.

Antietam, 17 September 1862

The fighting at the Lower Bridge (Burnside's Bridge) at Antietam was a key factor in Union commander McClellan's failure. The battlefield's best-known landmark, it is called 'Burnside's Bridge' after the Union general whose troops were held off for most of the day by a few hundred Georgia riflemen. It is noteworthy that Burnside and his staff appear to have had no idea of the terrain even on their own side of the bridge, and little if any reconnaissance was done prior to the major attacks beginning. They could have learned from locals that there was a usable ford downstream from the bridge, but seemingly no one was sent to locate that – or any other usable fords that might have obviated the need for so bloodily storming the bridge itself.

Restricting troop movement and hampering observation of the enemy's dispositions, Antietam Creek was more a nuisance to the Federals than a barrier, neither very wide nor deep, yet not to be crossed except by bridge. In fact, it was spanned by four arched bridges, all substantial stone structures. One was to the south at the mouth of the creek; then came the Rohrbach (Lower) Bridge on the Sharpsburg–Rohrersville road (later to be better known as the Burnside Bridge); the third, or Middle Bridge, was where the Boonsboro turnpike crossed the creek; and farthest to the north was the Upper Bridge, where a road from Keedysville to Williamsport crossed the stream.

McClellan, in his preliminary report on the campaign, written a month later, admitted that his 'design' was to throw the main weight of his attack against the Confederate left (northern) flank. He issued no written orders to this effect, nor called any order group of his commanders to let them know his intentions. It would seem that McClellan's original plan, therefore, did not entail a serious attack on the Lower Bridge. It could be construed as a desperate diversion to take weight off his right wing, hard-pressed by the Confederate left. Yet although McClellan's later detailed official report places little stress on the protracted attacks on this bridge, it is clear that during the battle McClellan was well aware of the need to relieve his right, manifested by his sending repeated orders, through Burnside, to make every effort, and at any cost, to take the Lower Bridge.

The Rohrbach or Lower Bridge was a triple-arched stone span 125 feet in length and 12 feet wide, situated at one of the most defensible spots on the battlefield, where the valley of the creek was narrow and flanked on both sides by steep hills.

There is no doubt that the topography of the area heavily favoured the defender and the terrain could not have served the Confederates better; the wooded heights west of the creek dropped steeply to the water's edge, with natural features on the hillside overlooking the bridge in the shape of a stone wall and an old quarry. These places were further strengthened by fallen trees and piled fence-rails; three artillery batteries were on higher ground to the rear, and on a plateau in front of Sharpsburg were two more batteries commanding the bridge area. If there was a weakness it consisted of the shortage of defending infantry, consisting of a few hundred Georgians under General Robert Toombs. The defence of the passage was the responsibility of D. R. Jones's division of four brigades, of which Toombs's brigade was placed forward of the others, covering the defences of the bridge and the wooded slopes above, supported by the other three brigades positioned on the ridges overlooking the valley. Toombs's force was as large as could be stationed at the bridgehead and, with its strong support, could handle the opposing force, constrained as it was by the lie of the land to form into a narrow column with a frontage of only eight men. Toombs's front, deployed behind his defences, was some 300–400 yards above and below the actual bridge. Of this, in his later report, Toombs wrote:

From the nature of the ground on the other side, the enemy were compelled to approach mainly by the road which led up the river for near three hundred paces parallel with my line of battle and distant therefrom from fifty to a hundred and fifty feet, thus exposing his flank to a destructive fire the most of that distance.

An attacking column at the bridge was vulnerable to fire of well-positioned defending infantry – at pistol-shot range – while the artillery batteries covering the bridge knew the exact range, so that a column reaching and try-ing to cross the narrow bridge, would have shrapnel fire ploughing through its length, its head melting away constantly to make it impossible for its front to be sufficiently strong to make any impression on enemy defences even if they were reached.

Later, experienced commanders present at the battle confirmed the view that the Confederate position was virtually invulnerable to direct attack over the bridge, basing their views on the fact that Union artillery could not reach the Confederate bridge defences, while the curve of the river valley allowed the bridge area to be perfectly enfiladed by their artillery.

Union forces began their assault on the bridge at about 9 a.m. and, one after another, their brave rushes forward were shattered by the Geor-gian riflemen's deadly short-range musketry. Came noon, as the bridge remained an unsurmountable obstacle, McClellan persisted in his queru-lous exhortations to get across at all costs. Each repeated wave of attack was a desperate, courageous combat in its own right. Stubbornly refusing to acknowledge defeat until it proved inevitable, the Federal troops utilised every stretch of wall, fence and tree as cover, from where they engaged in counter-fire with their hidden opponents. By one o'clock, the bitter, bloody battle had been running its remorseless course for more than three hours.

In the event, it was all so futile. With foresight it could have been delayed until the results were known of current attempts to find alternative crossings – General Isaac Rodman's Union division had been moving slowly down-stream from the bridge with this in mind. Nearly a mile south, rounding a sharp bend in the creek, his scouts came upon shallow water at Snavely's Ford, and crossed the stream late in the morning to drive against the flank of the Georgian defenders. At about the same time, Colonel George Crook's scouts discovered a ford only a few hundred yards above the bridge and his brigade began to cross, while Captain Seth Simond's battery took position to command the bridge area.

Then, just after one o'clock, the defenders detected a sudden move-ment across the creek, the sort of stir that had been an overture to yet another attack. And that was what it was: two infantry regiments (the 51st New York and the 51st Pennsylvania Regiments) in orderly ranks marched quickly from the cover afforded by the wooded hill, before breaking into a dash for the bridge, after forming into two columns. This time supported by their own converging artillery fire, they were over the bridge and among the defenders before their fire, or that of the Confederate artillery, could stop them. Almost at once the defence became split and a wide gap could be seen; Federal troops were now pouring across the bridge to gain the west side of the Creek, while simultaneously Rodman and Crook's men ham-mered the Confederate flanks.

General Sturgis commanded a division in the Ninth Corps and, in his subsequent report on the final attack on the bridge, tells how it happened:

Orders arrived from General Burnside to carry the bridge at all hazards.
I then selected the Fifty-first New York and the Fifty-first Pennsylvania
from the Second Brigade, and directed them to charge with the bayonet.
They started on their mission of death full of enthusiasm, and, taking a
route less exposed than the regiments (Second Maryland and Sixth New
Hampshire) which had made the effort before them, rushed at a double-
quick over the slope leading to the bridge and over the bridge itself,
with an impetuosity which the enemy could not resist; and the Stars and
Stripes were planted on the opposite bank at 1 o'clock p.m. amid the
most enthusiastic cheering from every part of the field from where they
could be seen.

Fredericksburg, 11 December 1862

Burnside, the Union commander, intended, in November 1863, to march
rapidly to Fredericksburg, then advance along the railway line to Richmond
before he could be intercepted by Lee, who would be cut off from his main
base. The Union advance forces reached the north bank of the Rappahannock on 17 November, well ahead of Lee, but delays in completing pontoon
bridges over the river allowed the Confederate forces to reach high ground
on the south side. Subsequently, Burnside determined to cross the river at
Fredericksburg and attack Maryes Heights, a prominent ridge about a mile
from the river, on which Longstreet's force was positioned. The crossing
was to be made over a series of pontoon bridges – two at Fredericksburg,
one south of an old canal boat bridge, and three more at the mouth of Deep
Runs – simultaneously on the night of 11 December. Union engineers
began their work at daybreak on that day, greatly harassed by Confederate
sharpshooters well aware that the work was to be done, having been
warned at other sites by noise of planks being unloaded, timbers creaking,
hammering and bolts being tightened, along with loud cursing as bridge-
layers smashed chilled fingers. At first, fog shielded the workers, but the
sharpshooters, notably Barksdale's Mississippi Brigade, fired at sounds,
then as the work reached midstream and the fog lifted, their firing became
deadly, with the pontoniers, unarmed and exposed, being repeatedly
forced back to the bank, then bravely trying again, coming forward over the
half constructed structures.

By 9 a.m. two bridges had been completed and Confederate sharpshooters driven from the far bank, more Federal troops came into action
and slowly other bridges were finished,and by mid-afternoon, the Southern
troops had been forced back several hundred yards. But they had delayed
Burnside's Northern Wing for more than twelve hours.

Carter's raid into East Tennessee, 26 December 1862

On 26 December Federal General S. P. Carter's small cavalry brigade, composed of 7th Ohio and 9th Pennsylvania Cavalry, left Manchester, Kentucky, and crossed the mountains east of the Cumberland Gap to enter the Upper Tennessee Valley. In what was described as 'the first successful Union cavalry operation in the West, although unimportant in its results', he destroyed two important railroad bridges at Wautauga Bridge and Carter's Station, south-east of Blountsville. In the course of the operations the Federals lost only three men while inflicting 292 Confederate casualties.

Chancellorsville, 4 May 1863

The uncoordinated Confederate attacks of 4 May cut Sedgwick off from Gibbon at Fredericksburg, but otherwise caused no appreciable damage. That night a thick fog rolled in from the river, under cover of which XI Corps fell back to a pontoon bridge hurriedly set up by engineers of General Benham's force, and by dawn were north of the river. From the river bank Confederate scouts fired signal rockets to indicate targets to their artillery, but the indirect fire had little effect on the withdrawal. Robbed of his target, Lee now decided to attack Hooker on 6 May, but the latter did not wait, using the stormy weather to mask his retreat, although almost wrecking the pontoon bridges. So, on the morning of 6 May only empty trenches and deserted camp-sites presented themselves to the Confederate leader.

Big Black River (Vicksburg campaign), 17 May 1863

Confederate General Pemberton tried to defend the crossing of the Big Black River by digging a trench across the mile-wide neck of the horseshoe band directly on Grant's route. In the resulting hour-long battle, Confederate General Bowen's 4,000 men were routed with great loss by the 10,000 strong Federal army. The pursuit that followed was delayed a little by Pemberton's forces destroying the bridges, but next morning Grant's army crossed the river, using their own engineer-constructed bridges.

South Anna River (Gettysburg campaign), 23–28 June 1863

Union General Getty, leading a force of 10,000, marched up the north bank of the Pamunkey River on an expedition to destroy the railroad bridge across the South Anna, and cutting the railroads north of Richmond. Defeated in his objective by the defending presence of a Confederate brigade, he contented himself by destroying some smaller bridges between the South Anna and the Chickahominy.

Elk River bridge (Tullahoma campaign), 30 June 1863

Federal General Rosecrans, in mid-June, performed a skilful manoeuvre that forced Confederate General Bragg to withdraw south of the Tennessee

River, using a bridge across the Elk River from Tullahoma to Decherd. Wilder's mounted infantry were sent to destroy the bridge, but were denied by Forrest's cavalry. Bragg retreated across the Elk River on 30 June, destroying the bridges over the flooded river so that he was able to retreat behind the Tennessee River without loss.

James River bridge (Petersburg campaign), 14 June 1864

To facilitate movement of the Army of the Potomac across the James River there was built what was claimed to be 'the longest continuous pontoon bridge ever used in war'. Working from both sides of the river, 450 Federal engineers completed it in eight hours in an area between Windmill Point and Fort Powhatan. The river was between 2,000 and 2,200 feet wide, up to 15 fathoms deep in mid-channel; it had a tidal range of 4 feet and a strong tidal current. The engineers had to use 101 pontoons and three schooners. When the troops and equipment had all crossed, by 7 p.m. on the 18th, the bridge was broken into three rafts and floated to City Point.

Chattahoochee River (Atlanta campaign), 4–9 July 1864

At 3 p.m. on 8 July, a surprise crossing of the Chattahoochee River was made by the 12th Kentucky Regiment, using a score of pontoons that had been hidden in Soap Creek. The operation was covered by fire from the Federal side of the river by Byrd's brigade, while Cameron's brigade hastily set up a 'fish-dam' about a mile above the mouth of Fish Creek. The crossing was unsuccessfully opposed by a small Confederate cavalry force and a single gun. Byrd's brigade laid a pontoon bridge after being ferried across, to establish a strong bridgehead by daylight on the following day.

High Bridge (Appamattox campaign), 7 April 1865

In the last days of the Confederacy, Longstreet was retreating towards Farmville, and Gordon, commanding what was left of Ewell's and Anderson's corps, crossed the Appamattox over a wagon bridge that ran under and alongside High Bridge. But Mahone, who was covering Gordon's movements, did not order the bridges to be burned in time, allowing pursuers – Barlow's Union division – to seize the bridge and, despite opposition from confederate skirmishers trying to fire the structure, cross the river. A party of Federal pioneers put out the High Bridge fires, at the same time as the skirmishers were fighting below the open deck on which they were working.

High Bridge gained its name by being built on 60 foot-high piers where the river was narrow, and a lengthy northern approach over low ground.

7. MID-NINETEENTH-CENTURY EUROPEAN WARS

THE CRIMEAN WAR (1853–6)

Initially between Russia and Turkey, this was later to involve Britain, France and Sardinia as allies of Turkey when the war became a prolonged siege of the Russian naval port of Sevastopol on the Crimean peninsula. Major battles were fought also at the Alma, Balaclava and Inkerman. The siege of strongly defended Sevastopol lasted from October 1854 until September 1855.

The Traktir Bridge, 16 August 1855

The following account is from British Battles on Land and Sea, ed. Field Marshal Sir Evelyn Wood (1915):

The battle of the Chernaya, or of Traktir Bridge, was a despairing but vigorous attack upon the French right flank, where our newly arrived Sardinian allies were posted. Thirty thousand Russians, under Generals Read and Liprandi, with a reserve of 19,000 more infantry, the whole supported by cavalry and a numerous artillery, advanced at daylight, but attacked too soon the heights held in force by the French, and were driven back with great slaughter.

The final assault was still delayed, but all hope of holding Sevastopol was at an end. Since the commencement of the Crimean campaign, the Russians had lost hundreds of thousands of men in the fortress and in the field, and their condition was desperate. Preparations to evacuate the city were at last begun – the bridge of boats across the harbour, barricades and obstacles in the streets and approaches. Yet Prince Gorchakov still hesitated, and wished at the eleventh hour to prolong the defence in spite of the sacrifices it would entail.

The Russian General Gorchakov threw two corps against about 37,000 French and Sardinian troops on the height above the Chernaya River. The combat lasted five hours and was marked by dogged determination of the Russian infantry, although thrown back and defeated with about 8,000 casualties. The Allies lost 1,700 killed and wounded.

The passage that follows is taken from William Cooke Stafford's England's Battles on Land and Sea (1859):

About that time, the English noticed the arrival of fresh troops from the north, at Sevastopol. After he received these reinforcements, consisting

157

of the 4th and 5th divisions of infantry, Prince Gorchakov 'considered it indispensable to execute a movement on the Chernaya, in order to reconnoitre the position of the enemy's troops covering the siege of Sevastopol, and, if possible, drive them from the Chernaya to Mount Sapoune'. This movement was made on the night of the 15th, and the morning of the 16th of August, upon the French and Sardinian armies posted in the neighbourhood of the Chernaya, in a position described as 'picturesque and romantic'. The Chernaya, in its course from the valley of Baidar to the harbour of Sevastopol, runs between two ranges of hills – those on the west 'dividing that part of the broad valley, extending from the harbour of Sevastopol to that of Balaklava, into two defiles'. These hills, called the Fediukine Heights, were occupied by the French divisions of Generals Herbillon, Camou and Faucheux, the last named officer having succeeded General Mayran, who was killed on the 18th of June.

From General Sir Edward Hamley's book comes the following:

These heights, lower than the plateaux, and of insignificant elevation compared with the surrounding mountain ranges, are ascended by easy slopes, are smooth and grassy at the top, and are furrowed by deep chasms, in one of which lies the road to the Traktir bridge, over the Chernaya; which bridge the French had fortified. Other and more abrupt hills rise to the right, on both sides of the river; but in front of the French, the ground, beyond the Chernaya, extended in level meadows to the wide plain, which winds round the base of the great plateau of Inkerman.

And from Lieutenant-Colonel Calthorpe, an officer with the British army:

A canal on the right bank receives the waters of the Chernaya and of the Souhaia: it crosses the river by an aqueduct, and falls into a small lake at the foot of Mount Sapoune. There is a bridge over this canal, by which the road passes to the Mackenzie Heights. The valley of the Souhaia is overlooked by elevated and undulating hills, on which the advanced posts of the Sardinian army were stationed. The Sardinians also occupied the high ground on the left bank on the river, nearer Balaklava, and to the north of Kamara, called the Heights of Hasfort. There the greater part of their army was posted, amounting to about 12,000 men, with four batteries of artillery. Beyond them, to the east, was a portion of the Turkish troops.

In the valley of Baidar was also stationed a mixed force of French and English cavalry and Turkish infantry, under General d'Allonville. The

French had in reserve four regiments of Chasseurs d'Afrique, and five troops of horse artillery, under the command of General Morris, stationed in rear of the Fediukine Heights. The larger portion of the English cavalry, under the command of Lieutenant-General the Hon. Sir James Scarlett, still occupied the valleys of Kadikoi and Kamara.

In the evening of 15 August, General Herbillon (who held the command of the French troops by the Chernaya, being the senior officer on that position) received a despatch from General d'Allonville, informing him, that, all the previous day, the Russian troops in that neighbourhood had been marching in the direction of the Mackenzie Heights: 'but his attitude imposed on that side, and dared not attack him'. The French general does not appear to have taken any additional precautions himself in consequence of this information; but he apprised the Sardinian chief, who kept his army under arms most part of that night. Before morning, large masses of the Russian troops had descended from the Mackenzie Heights, or debouched by Aitodor, to the plain on the right bank of the Chernaya, in front of the French divisions. This force was composed of 6,000 cavalry, five divisions of infantry, cavalry, and artillery – being upwards of 55,000. They were divided into two columns, and a reserve of cavalry, of about 15,000 men. One column was commanded by General Liprandi; the other by General Read: Prince Gorchakov took the command of the whole.

About one or two o'clock in the morning of the 16th, the Hon. Captain Keane, RE, had his attention attracted by a number of lights which were displayed from various parts of the English camp. It was known that the Russians had spies amongst the troops, and he had no doubt that these were signals to intimate that all was right, and that they might make the attack which the allied commanders had been informed they were preparing for. That officer acted promptly. He sent a messenger to General Jones, and rode off himself to General Scarlett's quarters, whom he roused; and informing him of his suspicions, that officer despatched an orderly to warn General Marmora. The Sardinian troops on the west side of the Chernaya were immediately on the alert; but in the meantime, the Russians (whose movements were obscured by a thick mist) opened their fire upon the Sardinian advanced posts on the east side of the river. The men stationed there were obliged to retire, and the enemy placed a field battery on the hill they left: it was commanded by some French guns in position, from which a fire was soon opened on the enemy. The Russian infantry then advanced to the Chernaya in columns. One forced its way by the bridge over the canal; another attacked the tête-du-pont, by which the Traktir bridge was defended. General de Failly, who commanded there, was unable to maintain his post with the few men at his disposal. 'The enemy rushed upon the bridge like an avalanche driven by storms from the summits of the mountains. By the aid of ladders, flying bridges, and heavy planks, they crossed the Chernaya, under the protection of the fire of their artillery, and the thickness of the mist.' Despite the continued discharge of musketry from some battalions that had come to support the French advanced posts, they kept on their way.

When the Russians reached the west side of the river, they re-formed, and the column under General Read attacked the heights occupied by the French – too suddenly it appears, and in anticipation of the orders to have been given by Prince Gorchakov, who never learnt the reason of this disobedience; General Read, and Major-General de Weimarn, the chief of his staff, being killed soon after the firing on that side of the river commenced. When the heights were attacked, the French divisions had struck their tents, taken their arms, and occupied the positions which had been previously assigned to them. Some heavy guns were also brought up, and a heavy fire of cannon and musketry was kept up for upwards of half-an-hour, with great loss on both sides.

THE FRANCO–PRUSSIAN WAR, 1870–1
Passage of the Rhine at Chalampé, 1870

During the Franco–Prussian War, the French employed irregular troops known as Franc-Tireurs, four groups of which had been formed in 1868, when war with Germany seemed likely, although they only numbered about 800 men. At the outbreak of war on 18 July 1870, the Franc-Tireurs were mobilised and became part of the Garde Mobile III Corps, based at Nancy, but seemingly played only a nebulous part in military operations.

However, as a result of information that the Prussians were preparing to construct a bridge of boats across the Rhine near Chalampé, in order to improve their lines of communication, a reconnaissance was carried out along the French bank of that river. It was led by Lieutenant-Colonel Lostie de Kerhor, commander of the fortress at Neuf-Brisach, and consisted of the Neuf-Brisach company of Francs-Tireurs, plus Lieutenant Koenig's Colmar company of fifty men. Aided by heavy mist, at dawn the French, in boats belonging to the local customs office, silently crossed the river to the German side. Here they moved quickly to the Bellingen railway station, on the main Bâle-Freiburg line, where they took advantage of the complete lack of opposition or resistance, to tear up railway lines and cut telegraph wires.

Returning back across the Rhine, they took with them seven pontoons intended for the intended bridge of boats, sinking them on the French side of the river. Although only a small action, the event was significant in being the only occasion throughout the war when French troops actually stood on German soil.

The bridges at Villersexel, 9 January 1871

Advancing Prussian troops reached the town of Villersexel on the morning of 9 January 1871 to find it in French hands, although only 200 men of 20 Corps advance-guard, who set about preparing what should have been excellent defensive positions. The town, standing high on the left bank of the River Ognon, effectively barred the passage of the river, which at this point divided into a maze of channels. In addition, the château of the Marquis de Grammont, situated in wooded grounds west of the town, sloping sharply down to the river bank, commanded the main bridge over the Ognon, which was barricaded by townsfolk. Taking up positions in the park – shown them by the marquis himself – the troops felt confident as the only other means of crossing was a shaky rope bridge and a lock at the eastern end of the park, also commanded from French defences.

But, like so many other French hopes and aspirations in this war, they were to suffer disappointment, for the German troops quickly discovered a way of crossing the lock and the rope-bridge, taking the defenders of the main bridge in the rear and scattering them. By noon, when the main body of the French 20 Corps arrived on the scene, the Prussians were firmly in command of the château and town.

Passage of the Danube, 26–27 June, 1877

On 24 April 1877, Russia invaded European Turkey, precipitating a war that lasted more than ten months. Major Eady, in his Historical Illustrations, includes the following passage relating to the Russian army and its campaigns in Turkey:

On the 26th (June), the detachment of General Dragomiroff, consisting of the 14th division and the troops attached to it, arrived at Zimnitza. At dark that evening the pontoons were launched in the creek which runs past the village of Zimnitza, and were then hauled out into the main river and down to the point of embarkation. There were 104 boats of the regular pontoon train, 100 boats and rafts which had been constructed in the neighbourhood, and four battalions of pontoniers to manoeuvre them. The troops numbered in all about 15,000 men, and were divided into six detachments of 2,500 men each, the plan being to cross by detachments in a body; but after the first detachment had crossed, this was found to take too much time, and as soon as enough boats returned to take one company they were immediately loaded and sent back.

While the boats were being launched, five batteries (forty guns) of nine pounders, supported by regiment No. 35 (of the 9th division), were established on the northern bank of the main river, to cover the passage, and silence the enemy's batteries on the south bank, as well as the

161

monitors, should they venture down from Nikopolis. The troops began embarking at midnight, and about one o'clock in the morning they put out from the shore and began rowing towards the Turkish bank, aiming to reach it at a point about three miles below Sistova, at the mouth of a small stream known as the Tekir-Dere. Just as they were approaching the shore they were discovered by the Turkish outposts who opened fire upon them and gave the alarm; but the boats, although somewhat dispersed by the wind, reached the shore and landed their men in the vicinity of the point designated. The twelve companies composing the first detachment formed on the bank and climbed up the steep bluff, driving before them the line of Turkish skirmishers. By two o'clock they had gained possession of the banks of this little stream, and of a neighbouring hill, about three-quarters of a mile from the shore and east of Tekir-Dere. Soon after this, the day began to dawn, and the Turks were thoroughly roused by the noise. It was, however, too late. The Russians had gained too firm a hold of the Turkish bank to be driven off before their supports could be brought up, and the natural bulwark of Turkey against Russia had been lost.

8. BRITISH COLONIAL WARS

THE INDIAN MUTINY, 1957–8

The dramatic events of the Indian Mutiny, a protest of a section of the Bengal army which developed into a widespread revolt against British rule, are described in many books published in the fifty or so years following the uprising. Inevitably such accounts focus special attention upon the siege and relief of Lucknow. The following passage from a Calcutta Review article is contained in G. W. Forrest's A History of the Indian Mutiny:

On 6 August, the day after the second battle of Busherutgunge, Havelock telegraphed to the Commander-in-Chief: 'I must prepare Your Excellency for my abandonment, with great grief and reluctance, of the hope of relieving Lucknow. The only three staff officers in my force whom I ever consult confidentially, but in whom I entirely confide, are unanimously of opinion that an advance to the walls of Lucknow involves the loss of this force. In this I concur. The only military question that remains, therefore, is whether that, or the unaided destruction of the British garrison at Lucknow, would be the greatest calamity to the State in this crisis. The loss of this force in a fruitless attempt to relieve Colonel Inglis would, of course, involve his fall. I will remain, however, till the latest moment in this position, strengthening it, and hourly improving my bridge-communication with Cawnpore, in the hope that some error of the enemy may enable me to strike a blow against them, and give the garrison an opportunity of blowing up their works and cutting their way out.'

Day and night, in sun and in rain, the general, his staff, and engineers were employed in improving his bridge communication with Cawnpore. The river had sunk, and Lieutenant Moorsom with a large gang of men was busy constructing a road across the islands and swamps and connecting them by a bridge of boats. Four boats lashed together and covered with planks formed a floating platform capable of holding a battery and intended to be towed across the main channel by the steamer. The whole work was under the supervision of Captain Crommelin of the Engineers, who had designed and started it in opposition to the views, as regards practicability and success, of nearly every officer of the force. Mainly owing to his indomitable energy, it was completed in the face of all difficulties on 11 August.

The construction of this causeway, over a width of upwards of a mile of this inundated shore of the Ganges, bridged the narrower and deeper parts. The portion of the river which had to be forced was thus reduced to nearly 700 yards, about a quarter of the original distance.

From British Battles on Land and Sea (ed. Sir Evelyn Wood) comes this account of the attack on the Charbagh Bridge:

Havelock was now in actual contact with the assailants of the garrison in Lucknow. To defeat the enemy in the open field had been comparatively easy. The task of breaking into Lucknow, through its tortuous lanes and massive buildings, was more arduous.

The general, after considering carefully all possible lines of attack, decided to carry the Charbagh bridge, and then, wheeling to the right, to fight his way into the Residence through the palaces and large houses lying to the east of the enclosure. Everything being ready for the advance, the troops paraded early on the morning of 25 September, and between eight and nine o'clock the 5th (Northumberland) Fusiliers took the lead, followed by Major Maude's battery.

The enemy, to defend the bridge, had a battery of six guns in position and had occupied the neighbouring houses with infantry. Meeting a storm of shot at a turn in the road, the British troops were ordered to lie down until the guns could come into action. The narrowness of the road made it impossible for more than two to be unlimbered and with these Maude had to contend against the enemy's six.

For a long while the unequal fight continued. Gunners fell rapidly. Infantry soldiers replaced them; still no impression could be made on the enemy. Then Maude turned to Lieutenant Havelock, the general's aide-de-camp, and called out: 'For Heaven's sake do something!'

Young Havelock, mounting his horse, rode through a tempest of shot back to General Neill, and urged him immediately to rush the bridge. Neill declined to advance without orders. Havelock then rode away; but, having rounded a bend in the road, waited a minute and then came back at a gallop. Pulling up his horse on its haunches, he saluted Neill and said, as though bringing an order from his father: 'You are to carry the bridge at once, sir.'

Immediately the order was given, Lieutenant Arnold and a few of the Madras (Royal Dublin) Fusiliers charged forward on to the bridge, accompanied by Colonel Tytler and Lieutenant Havelock.

The first blast of the enemy's grape swept down all the officers, Havelock excepted, and he, with Corporal Jacques, were the only two effectives on the bridge, but Havelock, waving his sword, called on the Fusiliers to follow him. The men responded nobly, and, dashing forward, carried the bridge, bayonetting the gunners before they had time to reload. The entire British force then crossed, and the 78th (2nd

Seaforth) Highlanders having been left to hold the bridge until the rear-guard had passed, the column swung round to the right and pushed on through the narrow lane that ran parallel to the canal.

The rearguard passed, and the Highlanders were heaving over into the canal the guns which had been captured on the bridge when suddenly the enemy fell on them in great force.

It was only with difficulty that the attack was repulsed, the Highlanders being engaged for three hours in a fierce and bloody conflict.

The same action is described in Cassell's Illustrated History of India by James Grant:

On the 25th, between the Alum Bagh and Lucknow, there was fighting nearly every inch of the way. The troops got fairly into action about a quarter of a mile from the camp, and shot passed over and about them in a perfect hum or scream. On every side men fell; the enemy firing from a garden or compound with their artillery, and from the houses of a village with their musketry. The 5th, which were in advance, were ordered to lie down, while the artillery silenced the guns. As this was not done soon enough, the 5th were ordered to charge and take them. This was bravely done; but it was still slow work clearing the villages and making their way round the city to the Residency, the small army of 3,000 men having, at the very lowest calculation, 90,000 men to contend with, who were fighting behind houses or loopholed walls, whilst the British were exposed in the streets. At the outskirts of Lucknow, at the bridge of the Charbagh ('four gardens'), thrown over the canal that encircles the south side of the city, the rebels had a number of guns planted behind a strong palisade. They did dreadful execution; but, nothing daunted at the lanes of death constantly opened in their ranks, Sir James Outram himself, with Brigadier (late Colonel) Neill and his gallant Madras regiment, and the men of the 5th, 64th and 84th regiments, advanced and surmounted every obstacle, took the guns at the point of the bayonet, cutting down the gunners, or putting them to flight. General Havelock, with the brave 78th and 90th, dashed in after them. They had to fight for each inch of ground; but they successfully drove the enemy from one enclosure and the other, from garden to garden.

The ensuing account of Havelock's march towards Lucknow comes from The History of the British Empire in India and the East by Dr E. H. Nolan:

With 2,500 men, Havelock in July 1857, during the hottest season of the year, marched 126 miles in nine days, from Allahabad to the relief of Lucknow.

165

It was on 7 July that Havelock mustered his little army at Allahabad; on the 12th he formed a junction with the advanced column, after a terrible march under the fierce sun of an Indian July. The main body of the enemy occupied strong posts at Futtehpore. The trunk road was alone available for the attacking party, the fields on each side being laid deep under water. The city of Futtehpore was only approachable through a fire directed under the cover of mango groves, enclosures, loopholed walls, and other defences. The British leader, having determined to give battle, fought to draw on the enemy to an imprudent onset against himself. He placed his eight guns across the road, protected by one hundred men of the 64th, armed with the Enfield rifles. The enemy paused; during the hesitation Havelock advanced, his infantry coming on at deploying distance, covered by rifle skirmishers, the few cavalry he possessed on the flanks. The 64th, his own regiment, formed his centre, the Highlanders his right, the 84th and the Sikhs his left. The enemy fled precipitately, awed by the range of the rifles, the rapidity of Captain Maude's guns, and the steady advance of the infantry. Their attempts to defend some hillocks, and high walls bounding garden enclosures, were defeated with the ease and skill characteristic of Havelock. He turned every defence with such celerity and prudence that he incurred hardly any loss in dispossessing the enemy of the strongest posts. Having driven them through the city, capturing their guns, Havelock hoped that the battle was won; but the enemy drew up beyond the city in a well chosen position. The English were nearly exhausted, and the irregular native cavalry showed symptoms of going over to the foe. The moment was critical, but Havelock was the man for a crisis. He again advanced, using his men cautiously, and throwing forward the skirmishers and guns; the enemy was again routed. Havelock congratulated himself that seldom was a success so great achieved with a loss so small. He did not lose a single European; six native soldiers were killed and three wounded. After alternate marching and repose, most skilfully and judiciously distributed, so as not to exhaust the men, and yet achieving celerity of advance, Havelock again came up with the foe on the 15th. They were posted at the village of Asang, some twenty miles from Cawnpore. The sepoys made little resistance, the fame of Havelock and his army of Persia had reached them, and the previous battle of Futtehpore dispirited them. They retreated precipitately before the advanced guard, under Colonel Tytler, leaving guns and baggage as trophies of the easy triumph.

The captured position was within five miles of another entrenched position, at the head of a bridge crossing the Nuddee. This was carried by Havelock in the most gallant style. The action was fought on the same day as that at the village. In both battles Havelock had only twenty-six men wounded, chiefly of the Madras Fusiliers; among the wounded was Major Renaud. One man was killed. The enemy suffered severely.

The second action – for the bridge over the Pandoo River at Nuddee – is described in greater detail by G. W. Forrest:

Authentic information reached Havelock that the bridge over the Pandoo River was not destroyed, but defended by entrenchments and two guns of garrison calibre. He also heard that the enemy intended, as a last resource, to blow it up, and, as the river was in flood, the destruction of the bridge would seriously retard his advance on Cawnpore. Not a moment was to be lost. The assembly again sounded: the soldiers resumed their arms, and a stirring British cheer marked their appreciation of their general, and his readiness again to engage the rebels. The heat was intense, but the excitement of battle kept them up. After marching two miles they suddenly, by a bend in the road, came in sight of the river, swollen by the rains, and still spanned by a narrow stone bridge. Two white puffs of smoke rose from a low ridge, loud report followed, and a couple of 24-pounder shot crashed right into the column. Another and another followed in rapid succession. Several fell wounded, and a stalwart Highlander was shot dead, 'half of his head having been taken off by a round-shot'.

Our dispositions were soon made. Fortunately the bridge was at a salient bend of the river in our direction, and Captain Maude at once suggested to the general his desire to envelop it with his artillery-fire, by placing three guns in the road and three on either flank. The whole of the Madras Fusiliers, being the most practised marksmen in the force, were extended as Enfield riflemen: they lined the banks of the stream and opened a biting fire. As the column marched along the road the enemy kept up a continuous and effective cannonade; and it being found impossible for the troops to preserve this formation, they deployed, and advanced with great steadiness, in parade order, in support of the guns and riflemen. Animated by his accustomed daring, Maude's battery moved resolutely up to within three hundred yards of the bridge, unlimbered, opened fire, and quickly silenced the heavy guns of the enemy. Then a vast cloud of smoke and dust rose from the bridge, and a loud crash, like the clatter of falling bricks, was heard. From the chief to the private soldier, all thought the bridge had fallen, and that they were baffled. But when the cloud rolled along the river they saw the parapet walls had gone, but the arch stood sound; and at this critical moment the right wing of the Fusiliers, suddenly closing, threw themselves upon the bridge, carried it, and captured both guns.

The day was won. Havelock pushed his force a mile beyond the bridge, a halt was made, and the men, utterly exhausted, threw themselves on the ground. During twelve hours our troops had been under arms and twice engaged, and their endurance tested to the uttermost. The scorching sun glared down its unpitying rays upon their arms, which glittered with intolerable radiance, till the brain reeled and eyeballs ached with the intensity of that dazzling sheen.

Yet their indomitable energy rose superior to every trial: instinct with the dignity of manhood, they uttered no complaint, but bore on nobly. Night had again closed when their long fast was terminated by a meal.

The following extracts also come from James Grant's book:

When, on 1 March, Sir Colin Campbell was within a few miles of Lucknow, in his camp at Buntara, he fully considered all the information obtainable up to that time concerning the defences of the city. One result of the inquiry was to convince him that a necessity would arise for operating from both sides of the Goomtee River, whenever the actual assault should take place. This would be necessary, or at least desirable, because such a course would enable him to enfilade (that is, attack laterally or at the extremities) many of the enemy's newly constructed works; and because he would thus be able to cut off the enemy from their external sources of supply. It is true that he could not hope wholly to surround a city which, with its fortified suburbs, had a circuit of little less than twenty miles; still he would make an important approach towards that condition by cannonading from both sides of the river. One of his earliest preparations, therefore, had relation to the means of crossing the river; and to this end his engineers were busily engaged in fitting casks so that they might be placed across the river as a floating-bridge. The former bridge of boats, opposite some of the palaces, had been removed by the insurgents; while the iron and stone bridges were well watched by them.

Grant underlines the importance of these bridges by detailing the immense size of the siege-trains employed in these operations:

On the 2nd, Sir Colin marched at daybreak from his camp at Buntara, diverged from the road to the Alum Bagh, and took that which went near the Jelalabad fort towards the eastern margin of the suburbs. With a portion only of his army, he advanced to the Dil Koosha, the palace and park at the easternmost extremity of the city. The chief officers with him at the time of this advance were Generals Lugaard, Adrian

Hope, Hope Grant, Little and Archdale Wilson. His main object at first, with a force of five or six thousand men, was to march to such a spot, near the Dil Koosha, as would enable him to form a camp just beyond reach of the enemy's guns; and to protect his enormous siege-train, as it gradually arrived, until the time was come for commencing active operations. Not only the siege-train, but the countless appendages of an Indian army, would equally require protection during its passage from Buntara to the Dil Koosha. Mr Russell, who accompanied this expedition in person, says that no language can correctly convey an idea of the vastness in the number of elephants, camels, oxen, horses, camp-followers and vehicles that daily demanded the commander-in-chief's attention at this period. 'Who really can bring before his mind's eye a train of baggage-animals twenty-five miles long, a string of sixteen thousand camels, a siege-train park covering a space of four hundred by four hundred yards, with twelve thousand oxen attached to it, and a following of sixty thousand non-combatants?' Even the doolies or litter carriages for wounded men constituted a formidable item. To each company of a regiment there were ten doolies, and to each dooly were six coolies or native porters: thus there were nearly five hundred dooly-carriers for each average regiment; and even with this large supply, if the sick and wounded in any one regiment exceeded eighty men, there would be more than the coolies could properly attend to.

When Sir Colin came to reconnoitre the enemy's position, he found that the new lines of defence, constructed since November, were vast and well planned. He further saw that no immediate attack could be successfully made upon them by infantry, without such a sacrifice of life as he had determined if possible to avoid. To fight with artillery, before sending in his foot-soldiers to fight, was his plan; and he now at once sent back a messenger to the camp at Buntara, for the rest of the troops and heavy siege-artillery to advance without delay. All during the following night was the road from Buntara to the Dil Koosha filled with an apparently endless train of soldiers, guns, commissariat-carts, beasts of burden and of draught, and camp-followers – ready to swell the large number already at the last-named place. This train was protected on either side by cavalry and horse-artillery, ready to dash out against any of the enemy that should threaten interruption. It was a formidable burden for the bridges to bear, comprising, besides the infantry and cavalry, thirty guns, and a large train of baggage and ammunition animals; nevertheless the floating fabrics bore up well, and fully answered their intended purpose. English troops of the line, Highlanders, lancers, hussars, dragoons, artillery, engineers, commissariat, horses, oxen, camels, elephants – all passed safely over, and speedily fell into orderly array on the other side of the river. This was, of course, not done without a little fighting. The enemy could not be blind to the proceeding, nor to the consequences likely to result from it.

The portion of the siege-plan connected with the left bank of the river had never been lost sight of during the preparatory operations on the right. While the infantry, cavalry, artillery and commissariat were busily engaged in camping near the Dil Koosha, the engineers were collecting the casks, fascines of fagots, ropes, and timbers, necessary for forming a bridge, or rather two bridges, across the Goomtee, at some point below where the enemy were in greatest force. The spot selected was near headquarters at Bibiapore, where the river was about forty yards wide. The enemy, uneasy at the proceedings of the engineers, gradually assembled in considerable numbers on the opposite bank; but as the British brought up guns to oppose them, the engineering works proceeded without much molestation. These bridges exemplified some of the contrivances which military commanders are accustomed to adopt, in the course of their onerous duties. The groundwork of each was a collection of empty beer-casks, lashed by ropes to timber cross-pieces, and floated off one by one to their positions; a firm roadway of planking was afterwards fixed on the top of the whole range from end to end. Firm indeed must the construction necessarily have been; for troopers on their horses, heavy guns and mortars, ammunition-wagons, and commissariat carts, all would have to pass over these bridges, secure so far as possible from accident to man or beast.

To Sir James Outram was entrusted the command of that portion of the army which was to cross by these bridges of casks, and operate against the city from the left bank of the Goomtee. This gallant officer had been in and near the Alum Bagh for a period of just one hundred days, from November to March, defending himself successfully against numerous attacks made on him by the enemy, as narrated in former chapters. It was right that he should now have the most important command under Sir Colin.

While Outram was thus crossing the river on the 6th, Sir Colin remained simply on the defensive near the Dil Koosha, deferring all active operations until the subsidiary force had got into fighting order on the left bank. The enemy maintained a continuous fire from the Martinière; but the gunnery was not good, and very little mischief was occasioned. One of the most striking circumstances connected with the position and proceedings of the commander-in-chief was that he carried the electric telegraph with him from camp to camp, from post to post. Chiefly through the energy of Lieutenant Patrick Stewart, poles were set up and wires extended wherever Sir Colin went. Calcutta, Allahabad, Cawnpore, Buntara and the Alum Bagh, could all communicate instantly; and now a wire made its appearance through a drawing-room window at the Dil Koosha itself, being stretched over a row of poles along the line of route which the commander-in-chief and his troops had followed. The wires even followed Outram over the river, and made their appearance – for the first time in the history of Oude – on the left bank. No sooner did Sir Colin advance a few miles, than Stewart followed him with poles and wires, galvanic batteries and signalling apparatus – daring all dangers, conquering all difficulties, and setting up a talking machine close to the very enemy themselves. It may almost literally be said that, wherever he laid down his head at night, Sir Colin could touch a handle, and converse with Lord Canning at Allahabad before he went to sleep. The value of the electric telegraph was quite beyond all estimate during these wars and movements: it was worth a large army in itself.

On the 10th, while Outram was engaged in strengthening the position which he had taken up, he sent Hope Grant with the cavalry of the division to patrol over the whole of the country between the left bank of the Goomtee and the old cantonment. This was done with the view of preventing any surprise by the approach of bodies of the rebels in that quarter. An extensive system of patrolling or reconnaissance had formed from the first a part of Sir Colin's plan for the tactics of the siege. Outram on this day brought his heavy guns into a position to rake the enemy's lines, to annoy the Kaiser Bagh with a vertical and direct fire, to attack the suburbs in the vicinity of the iron and stone bridges, and to command the iron bridge from the left bank; all of which operations he carried out with great success. The enemy, however, still held the right end of the iron bridge so pertinaciously, that it was not until after a very heavy cannonading that the conquest was effected.

He obtained possession of the iron bridge, leading over the river from every part of the left bank of the river between that bridge and the Padishah Bagh; thus leaving him in a position to enfilade the central and inner lines of defence established by the enemy among the palaces.

On the 16th Sir James Outram, after ten days of active operation on the left bank of the Goomtee, crossed over by a bridge of casks opposite the Secunder Bagh; and then he advanced through the Chuttur Munzil towards the Residency. To lessen the chance of the enemy's retreat as much as possible, he marched right through the city, not only to the iron bridge near the Residency, but to the stone bridge near the Muchee Bhowan. All this was an enterprise of remarkable boldness, for the buildings to be successively conquered and entered were very numerous. Up to this Outram's march of the 16th through the city had been almost unopposed; but he now ascertained that the houses and palaces between the iron and stone bridges were occupied by the enemy in considerable force. Hard fighting at once commenced here, in which the

171

20th, 23rd and 79th regiments were actively engaged. They advanced at a rapid pace from the Residency towards the iron bridge. A 9-pounder, planted to command a road by the way, fired grape into them; but it was speedily captured. By that time the large guns were brought into position, to play upon the stone bridge, the Emanbarra of Azof-u-Dowlah, and other structures north-west of the iron bridge. At that time Grant and his troopers were near the stone bridge on the left side of the river, while Outram's guns were firing on it from the right bank; as a consequence, no more escape was permitted by that channel; and the fugitives therefore ran along the right bank of the river, to a part of the open country north-west of Lucknow, not yet controlled by the English.

It would seem doubtful that the successes of Havelock's first relief of Lucknow, July to September 1857, and the second relief in March 1858., would have been possible had it not been for the sterling work of his Engineers, particularly in the building of bridges. The following accounts give an indication of what transpired, and are taken from Lieutenant-Colonel E. W. C. Sandes book The Military Engineer in India.

1st Relief of Lucknow, Jul to September 1857

It was evident to Havelock that to keep in close touch with Neill he must bridge the Ganges but this would require time, and meanwhile some improved means of crossing must be provided. Colonel Tytler, his Quartermaster General, came forward with a scheme for a causeway more than a mile long over inundated land, three small floating bridges and a trestle bridge to lead up to the main channel. The work began on 3 August under Crommelin and Lieutenant G. E. Watson, who assisted him, and was pushed on so rapidly that the main channel was reached on the 12th, when Havelock had fought a third battle at Bashiratganj. As Neill was in grave danger from the rebels at Bithur, Havelock wished to cross at once to his assistance. Crommelin did not fail him. Sixty boats, 300 boatmen, and a small steamer with a lighter attached to her were ready at the pierhead at the end of the causeway early on 13 August, and the whole force except the rearguard was ferried across to Cawnpore in five and a half hours. 'I never worked harder in my life,' wrote Crommelin, 'and whilst paddling in the water I drank freely of beer and brandy and water.'

This crossing by causeway and ferry enabled Havelock to defeat the mutineers heavily at Bithur on 16 August, but it was clear that the Ganges should be bridged for a rapid advance when reinforcements arrived. Accordingly Crommelin and Watson began to prepare materials and collect boats. On 15 September they started their great work, and toiling night and day, spanned the Ganges in less than four days by a bridge 700 yards in length and containing upwards of 70 large boats. Major-General Sir James Outram and some reinforcements had arrived in Cawnpore on the 15th; and Havelock, Outram and 3,000 men crossed the bridge on 19 and 20 September to begin their advance on Lucknow. Brushing aside all resistance, Havelock was within sixteen miles of Lucknow on the 22nd.

From James Grant's Cassell's Illustrated History of India comes the following:

It was on 19 September that the two generals crossed with this army into Oude, making use for that purpose of a bridge of boats over the Ganges, most laboriously constructed by Captain Crommelin. The enemy, assembled near the banks, retired after a nominal resistance to Mungulwar. The heavy guns and the baggage were crossed over on the 20th. On the 21st the British again came up with the enemy, turned their right flank, drove them from their position, inflicted on them a severe loss, and captured four guns. With the heroism of a true soldier, Sir James Outram headed one of the charges that brought about this victory; serving as a volunteer under Havelock. The enemy were not permitted to destroy the Bunnee bridge over the Sye; and thus the victors were enabled to pursue their route towards Lucknow.

The River Prah, 1874

The following action which occurred during the Ashanti War of 1873–4 is mentioned by James Grant in British Battles on Land and Sea:

While our troops were being massed upon the Prah early on the morning of the 6th, our organised body of scouts, under the gallant Lieutenant Lord Gifford, crossed in canoes, and explored the country along both sides of the road. The whole of Russell's Regiment followed by companies in boats and rafts. These pushed on to Atobiassie, where they encamped for the night.

Lord Gifford's party, which consisted of fifty bayonets – men of the West India Regiment, Houssas, Kossos and Bonny natives – kept five miles in advance, and reached a place called Essiaman, and found it occupied by an Ashanti outpost. As he approached the village, he was fired on by a small party of Ashantis. He returned their fire, and they at once evacuated the place, leaving one of their number dead behind them. Only one of Lord Gifford's men was wounded, but that severely.

The bridge now formed across the Prah was a solid structure, capable of supporting the weight that was likely to be put on it. Built on the principle known in America as 'cribbing', it was made of logs some six inches in diameter, cut into lengths of about six and four feet. The longest logs were first taken, and after being squared at the ends, so as to lie flat on each other, at the point of contact holes were bored by augers. The four longest logs were then taken and laid in a square, two resting upon two. Other logs were then laid on, and the result was a species of cage or pier, tapering upwards from six feet square at the base, to four feet at the top, ropes holding the whole together; and it was sunk by sand-bags to the depth required. Seven of these piers were required.

Every morning, at half-past six, the sailors crossed the bridge to clear the bush with axe and cutlass for our *tête-du-pont*.

Operations against the Chins and Lushais, North-West Frontier, 1889–90

The following passage is taken from Colonel Sandes's book:

The Northern Column from Burma set out at he end of November, 1889, and by the close of the year had established several posts for the protection of the frontier from Chin raids; but the Southern Column, delayed by the extraordinary difficulties of the country, took 66 days to reach Haka from Kan instead of 12 as had been estimated. Not only the sappers, but almost every man in the force had to be employed on road making, although the route was only 64 miles in length. The same difficulty confronted General Tredegar who did not finish his road to Haka from the west until 13 April, 1890. But meanwhile the advance parties from east and west had met on 26 February at Tao, 52 miles by road from Haka and midway between that place and Lungleh, and after some punitive operations the campaign came to an end in May. The last of the regular troops then marched out of the Chin and Lushai countries, leaving the newly established posts to be garrisoned by detachments of the Burma Police. Every unit had suffered terribly from malaria. Of 69 British officers with the Burma Southern Force only seven escaped infection, one died, and 26 were invalided. The enemy had made elaborate defences in several places – notably at Falam, north of Haka, where they erected innumerable stockades and obstructions extending over nine miles of country – but they lacked the courage to defend them. There was, indeed, very little serious fighting against the head-hunting Chins and Lushais in 1889 and 1890, but an immense amount of laborious engineering.

The work was chiefly road construction; but there was also much bridging, and many rafts were made for river transport. Fort Tredegar was built near Fort Lungleh, and several other posts on neighbouring ridges. The difficulties in linking up these posts were stupendous. The jungle was so dense that the limit of vision was less than a dozen yards, and great masses of rock were continually encountered which had to be removed by blasting. Enormous trees also had to be cut by explosives and their roots dug up. There was not a single open space between Lungleh and Haka, 55 miles apart as the crow flies and twice that distance by road; and if the jungle was not of trees matted together with thick creepers, it was of stout bamboos or elephant grass up to 20 feet high In places a gradient of one in five was necessary, and the track had sometimes to be blasted out of solid rock. Every valley demanded a bridge. The Chittagong Column alone constructed seven bridges of 48 feet span,or more, the largest being a crate and trestle bridge of 17 spans and 101 yards in length. Suspension bridges of telegraph-wire rope were erected also when a clear waterway was essential. Weakened by fever, soaked by torrential rain, and bitten by leeches and mosquitoes, the engineers and sappers and miners were glad to leave the dense forests of the Lushais and Chins in March and April, to return to the plains of India or the valley of the Irawaddy.

The Hunza Nagar Expedition, 1891

Colonel Sandes also describes another expedition on the North-West Frontier:

A small guard of infantry had been established already at Gilgit, where there was a British Agency, and in September the government decided to place a garrison at Chalt, and to improve the road from Gilgit to that place. The garrison at Gilgit was strengthened, and a force under Lieutenant-Colonel A. G. A. Durand then moved up to Chalt.

Less than 1,200 men were available for an advance from Chalt, and of these one-half were Kashmir State troops. The only regulars were 200 men of the 5th Gurkha Rifles, a small detachment of the 20th Punjab Infantry with a Gatling gun, some 80 men of No. 4 (Hazara) Mountain Battery with two 7-pounder muzzle loading guns, a few signallers, and six men of the 4th Company, Bengal Sappers and Miners, under Captain F. J. Aylmer, a company of Kashmir Sappers at Gilgit, but the men were of little value and were not sent forward to Chalt. Aylmer had set out from Rawalpindi on September 19th with 12 sappers and some equipment, including explosives and a long wire rope and traveller for a flying bridge (a ferry-boat or raft operated by cable) at Bunji. He accompanied Durand and other officers over the difficult Burzil Pass, constructed a new bridge at Ramghat, and arrived in Bunji where he completed a flying bridge of 500 feet span in about ten days. None of the inhabitants would believe that a flying bridge could actually transport people across a river, but when a few had tried it they clamoured for another trip. At Gilgit, Aylmer found that a bridge was required at once to span the deep and rapid river, so, as skilled labour and materials were scarce, he decided to make one with a number of rough stone piers. His workmen were the soldiers of one of the Kashmir regiments, and his method of construction was as follows. From a shore pier a cantilever platform was pushed forward on which two strong men stood as far out as possible. They were kept supplied with boulders which they hurled forward into the torrent as far as they could, thus gradually forming a second pier. When this pier showed above water-level, a temporary way was made to it and it was built up readily to the proper height and the bay completed. The cantilever platform was then transferred to the new pier, and the work proceeded. By these means the river was spanned successfully in five days. Aylmer then went on with some of his sappers to Chalt, improving the track as he passed along it, and on arrival bridged the Hunza River above Chalt. A gang of 200 wild Pathan road-coolies, who had been working on the road under Mr Charles Spedding, joined the force at Chalt as an 'Engineer Corps'.

Mission to Tibet, 1904
The next extract is likewise from Sandes's book:

We now pass to another 'Engineer War' – the expedition into Tibet in 1904. This unique country falls into three great physical divisions. Firstly the remote, interminable and dreary plateau in the north, standing at an elevation of 15,000 feet or more above sea-level, swept incessantly by tearing winds, destitute of vegetation and dotted with hundreds of salt lakes. An early traveller in this ghastly land writes: 'Our journey through such infinite solitudes was one of inexpressible melancholy. Each day we traversed arid valleys, skirted blue lakes, and surmounted passes laden with snow. All nature was robed in silence except for the rushing of the wind which blew furiously as if it wished to roll aside the summits of the mountains.' To the east of this arctic region lies the province of Kham, a labyrinth of wild, rugged and almost unknown mountains. To its south is the more temperate and fertile valley of the Tsan-po or Brahmaputra, separated from India by the Himalayas and containing the wonderful city of Lhasa and its peculiar inhabitants. In the valley of the Tsan-po the bulk of the Tibetans dwell happily in the most rigid isolation, suspicious of foreign intrusion, well governed by the Dalai Lama and his national assembly, but oppressed by a monastic oligarchy, which has no counterpart in the world.

The Tibet Mission of 1904 must always rank high among military exploits. The operations during the advance of nearly 400 miles from Siliguri to Lhasa met with natural and climatic difficulties which have never been surpassed.

176

On the 16th the column reached Ralung, where General Macdonald learnt that the Karo La (16,600 feet) was strongly fortified by sangars and by a wall extending to vertical cliffs at the snow line, but the pass was forced, nevertheless, on 18 July with slight resistance. This engagement is remarkable. It was fought at an altitude of over 18,000 feet above sea-level; and when the Tibetans retreated over a glacier, some of the Gurkhas had to cut steps in the ice with their kukris to follow them. The advance continued: two Jongs were occupied, the expedition climbed over the Khamba La (16,400 feet) on the 24th and dropped down to Chak-sam on the broad Tsan-po more than 11,000 feet above the sea.

The crossing of the Tsan-po at Chaksam was a fine piece of engineering. The main stream was 140 yards wide: beyond it was a sandbank and then a subsidiary channel 25 yards in width. It was necessary to cross the main stream close below the junction of two channels where the force of the current was more than five miles per hour and there were many dangerous whirlpools. The stores available were four collapsible Berthon boats with superstructure to form two rafts, two large Tibetan ferry-boats captured at Chaksam, a few Tibetan skin boats, 200 yards of 1-inch steel cable and a traveller, and 640lb of 2-inch and 1½-inch manilla rope – a poor equipment for the transfer of 3,500 men, 3,500 animals and 350 tons of stores across a raging maelstrom. Yet Sheppard and his sappers, assisted by the pioneers, accomplished this feat in five and a half days. The crossing began on 25 July by rowing the Tibetan boats and Berthon boat rafts, but it was desperately slow work. The boats and rafts were carried far downstream at each trip and Major G. H. Bretherton of the Supply and Transport Corps was drowned. On the following day the river had risen, and only 14 boat-loads were across after 14 hours of toil. An attempt to get a line across the main stream had failed; but on the 27th, by mooring a Berthon boat far out from each shore, connecting the two boats by a line and taking other lines out to them, a complete line was linked up at last from bank to bank. A rope soon followed, and by it a steel cable was hauled across and fixed. A ferry was then established by using a traveller to carry one end of a rope across the stream and attaching the other end to a large Tibetan boat which could thus be swung and hauled to the far bank. When empty, the boat was towed upstream and then rowed across to be reloaded, the end of the rope being sent back by the traveller as before. An ordinary flying bridge served for the crossing of the narrow channel beyond the sandbank, and thus the obstacle of the Tsan-po was overcome.

Younghusband reached the holy and mysterious city of Lhasa, the goal of so many vain endeavours, on 3 August 1904, and marched with his escort through the gateway below the Potala Palace, a wonderful structure whose tiers of windows and golden roofs towered far above him. Long negotiations followed until a treaty was signed on 7 September in the throne room of the palace, which secured British influence in Tibet. Winter was approaching. It was necessary to return at once over the passes, so the sappers and miners set out on the 9th, with some infantry, to make arrangements for recrossing the Tsan-po at Chaksam. Additional engineering stores, however, had arrived at that place from India, and a better site for a ferry had been discovered at Partsi, 11 miles farther upstream, so all the gear was taken to Partsi and the work was begun. It progressed so rapidly that two steel-cable ferries, one of 105 yards' and the other of 140 yards' span, supplemented by a rowing ferry, were ready when the main body arrived from Lhasa on 27 September, and in another 48 hours every man and animal, and every ton of stores, had been transported to the southern bank. The return journey was uneventful. The mission and its escort entered Gyantse in two columns on 5-6 October and marched on in smaller columns to India, while Captains C. H. D. Ryder and H. Wood, RE, journeyed up the Tsan-po to examine Western Tibet as far as the sources of the Indus and Sutlej. Every kind of work fell to the lot of the Royal Engineers and their men in this campaign among the eternal snows, but they were equal to all demands on their resources. The venture into Tibet has rightly been described as a triumph of organisation and daring, and its story makes a fascinating interlude in the prosaic annals of the India that we know today.

THE BOER WAR, 1899–1902

On October 11 1899 began what was to prove the greatest struggle in which England had engaged since the peace that followed Waterloo. For, at 5 p.m. on that day, the forty-eight hours allowed by the Transvaal Government for a favourable answer to its ultimatum expired and the forces of the two Boer Republics put themselves in motion to carry out their favourite threat of sweeping the English from South Africa into the sea.

Thus began Chapter One of the first volume of a monumental illustrated literary work by H. W. Wilson entitled With the Flag to Pretoria and After Pretoria: the Guerrilla War. The extracts that follow reveal a systematic pattern of Boer destruction and British rebuilding of countless rail and road bridges throughout the theatre of war.

The Boers close in, 15–17 October 1899
On the 15th a brush between an armoured train with British troops on board and a small Boer force took place at Spytfontein, ten miles south

of Kimberley. Several of the enemy were killed and wounded without any British casualties. On the same day Vryburg, half-way between Kimberley and Mafeking, was evacuated by the Bechuanaland Police and seized by the enemy. On the 17th the Modder River bridge was destroyed with dynamite, a previous attempt to blow up the bridge-piers having failed. The Boers employed a number of 'skilled Continental engineers', whose whereabouts and nationality will have to be inquired into after the war, to accomplish the work. Finally, Belmont station, a few miles north of the Orange River, was occupied by a detachment and fortified, while demonstrations were actually made against Orange River station. Thus Kimberley was thoroughly isolated and cut off from the outer world.

Modder River, 28 November 1899

On the left several attempts had been made by the Ninth Brigade, splendidly led by General Pole-Carew, to cross the river, the approach to which had been secured by the Yorkshires and Lancashires. These two battalions stormed a farmhouse and a kraal just to the south of the dam, though the Boers were present in force. Several of the enemy were bayonetted in the mêlée about the house. Further to the left a line of low kopjes was captured at the point of the bayonet, and the British left was firmly based on the river.

The first attempt to cross was made by the Yorkshiremen, a few of whom pushed into the stream above the dam. They were led by Lord Methuen in person. But the fire was too hot for anything to live under it, and the detachment was driven back with heavy loss, Lord Methuen himself receiving a painful flesh wound which compelled him to hand over the command. Next, a company of the Highlanders forded or swam the river and reached the further bank, where, on the following day, five of the bravest were found dead in the enemy trenches. The others were driven back. Once more General Pole-Carew led the brave Yorkshiremen forward, this time to the dam that crossed the river. Here, under a heavy fire, the men one by one made their way along a rickety iron bar in the water just over the sluices, clinging to the uprights in which slid the sluice gates. One by one, in spite of the fire, they gained the other side, where gradually 400 men formed up – a band of heroes – and began to push forward along the north bank to take the enemy in the flank. General Pole-Carew sent for reinforcements. Colonel Northcott, of the staff, was directed by Lord Methuen to bring them up, but, before he could General Pole-Carew, fell back, mortally wounded by a shell splinter in the neck.

In justice to a much criticised general, it must be remembered that Lord Methuen on the afternoon of the 27th personally examined Modder River Bridge and rode to within 200 yards of what later proved to be the Boer position. The enemy did not stir or move; no shots were fired; and no sign whatever of the presence of 8,000 or 9,000 men could be detected. At Klekfontein Lord Methuen was reinforced by a fine Highland battalion, the 1st Argyll and Sutherlands. Deducting all losses, he had now 8,000 infantry, 400 cavalry and mounted infantry, and 300 artillery with twelve guns. At Belmont, in his rear, was the 62nd Field Battery with six more guns. It will be seen that the column still remained pitifully weak in two essential components of an army – cavalry and artillery.

At dawn of 28 November the division got under arms and cheerfully marched off to disperse the handful of demoralised fugitives who were, it was reported, all that would be encountered at Modder River. From the Modder it was to bend eastwards to Jacobsdal and come in upon the flank of the Boers at Spytfontein. The early morning air was clear and cold, but the breakfastless men marched joyously down the gentle slopes, eight miles long, towards the eagerly desired water. A few minutes of skirmishing was the most that anyone expected. Yet earlier in the morning – seemingly while the division was on the march – Lord Methuen received disquieting news. This was to the effect that the Boers were in great force at the Modder. Still he felt no great anxiety: he had been told that the Riet and Modder River were fordable everywhere, and therefore he thought that he could easily outflank the enemy and drive them from their positions. He does not appear to have communicated the news to his subordinate generals and battalion commanders. Indeed, so free from care was he that he gave his cook orders to get his breakfast ready as his line of men neared the Modder River. Still, the approach to the river was made in very open order and no reasonable precaution was neglected.

The disposition of the British troops was as follows. On the right was the Guards' Brigade, with the Scots Guards, Grenadiers, and 2nd Coldstreams in line from right to left, and the 1st Coldstreams following in support. On the left was the Ninth Brigade, under Major-General Pole-Carew, composed of the Northumberland Fusiliers, Yorkshires, and North Lancashires in line from right to left, with the Argyll and Sutherland Highlanders in support. The two field batteries were on the right, where also were the Lancers and mounted infantry. To the rear were the transport and ammunition wagons in charge of the Northamptons.

About the centre of the British front was the railway to Kimberley, which crosses the Modder upon an iron bridge. That bridge had been entirely destroyed by the Boers, and culverts on the line two miles to the south of the river had been blown up, thereby rendering it impossible for the armoured train with Lord Methuen's column to approach. Half-a-mile to the east of the railway bridge was the confluence of the Riet and Modder Rivers, the Riet coming in from the south-east and the Modder from the north-east.

The day after the battle the British column cleansed and occupied the Boer camp, and the engineers set to work to replace the railway bridge over the Modder. So seriously had the iron girders been damaged that it was necessary to build a new timber bridge, diverting the railway. The work was by no means easy, as the Modder is liable to rise eight feet in a few hours, after the heavy thunderstorms which prevail in the country, so that the new bridge had to be of great strength, while, as the river banks are high, deep cuttings had to be excavated on either side. Yet, so skilful and energetic were the railway engineers that by 7 December trains were able to cross to the British camp and tents, supplies and heavy baggage were sent forward to the troops. A pontoon bridge had been completed some days earlier, thus securing communications with the south.

The British advance begins

The Estcourt force pushed forward to Frere unopposed, but found that further progress was stopped by the destruction of the railway bridge over the Blaauwkrantz. The engineers at once went to work to build a trestle bridge. In the next two days the railway was repaired between Westcourt and Mooi River. On the 30th Lord Dundonald, who had arrived and taken over command of the mounted troops, pushed forward with 1,400 mounted infantry and a battery of artillery to Colenso, and drew a very heavy fire from the Boer positions. After reconnoitring these he fell back without the loss of a man. On the same day the railway bridge at Colenso was blown up by the Boers.

Colenso, 19 December 1899

In the days after the battle the Boers displayed their wonted inactivity. They made no attempt to annoy General Buller seriously, and were content with sending small parties of skirmishers south of the Tugela, who hung round the British camp at Chieveley, sniping water parties, patrols and outposts. On 19 December the naval guns opened a heavy fire on Colenso road-bridge, which was still standing, with the object of destroying it and cutting off the retreat of the Boers who were south of the river. The existence of a Boer bridge north of Hlangwane was not known at this date. After three hours of continuous shelling a projectile struck and exploded a Boer mine placed in the structure of the bridge, and a whole span was destroyed.

Springfield Bridge, 11 January 1900

On this occasion the average of the infantry was scarcely a mile an hour. At the start Sir Charles Warren's men had to ford the Blaauwkrantz in flood, and the drifts were choked with wagons, carts and refractory teams of oxen and mules. 'The passages through the spruits were nightmares,' says Mr Atkins, 'carts overturned in the water, wheels off, mules mixed up, fighting and knotted in their harness and half drowning, oxen with their heads borne down under water and heaving with all their mighty strength to the opposite bank, a gun or a wagon stuck, and the river of traffic looping round it as water flows round an island; spare teams of oxen moving about to help the unfortunate out of difficulties, a traction engine with one wheel almost buried in soft mud and two other engines pulling at it.' One ox-wagon which stuck close to Frere station could not be moved by eighty oxen, and must have been abandoned but for the traction engines, one of which was harnessed to it with a steel hawser, and hauled it triumphantly out of difficulties. The march, in consequence of these incidents, which, at first diverting enough, rapidly palled upon the men, was weary to a degree. Great caution had to be observed, for though the Tugela was in heavy flood and the Boer bridges broken, no one could be certain that the enemy had not some force south of the river carefully watching the British flanks and ready to cut off stragglers and vehicles in difficulty. The first halt for the infantry of the Second Division was to be made at Pretorius' Farm, six miles on the Frere side of Springfield and ten miles from Frere, and for the Fifth Division at Springfield itself; but that point was not reached by many of the men till long after midnight. At midnight the weather had broken once more and a terrific thunderstorm swept over the hills, drenching the tired men and inflicting upon them the misery of a sodden bivouac after their hard day's march. They slept as best they could, wrapped in their greatcoats and blankets, in the mud and slush. Hildyard's Brigade, with the two great 4.7s dismounted from their carriages and placed upon carts, had already struck into the column, half way to Pretorius' Farm, coming from Chieveley, so now the turning force was complete.

All the 10th and 11th the troops were on the march, streaming westwards in an unending column. On the 11th the cavalry under Lord Dundonald pushed forward, in advance of the army, to seize Springfield bridge – a long, wooden structure which spans the Little Tugela, and which, according to spies' accounts, had been left standing by the Boers.

Would it be so when Springfield bridge was reached, or must a battle be fought before the British could win possession of the Little Tugela?

At length the bridge came into sight. It was uninjured, and there was still no enemy. More than this, word came from the patrols in advance – Murray's Natal Mounted Scouts – that they had scoured the country beyond, up to Potgieter's Ford and the Big Tugela, and found it also empty. The bridge was crossed, and now it entered Lord Dundonald's head, in spite of his orders, which required him only to 'seize Springfield Bridge', to push on yet further, and endeavour to secure Potgieter's. The danger was that this ostentatious abandonment of the district by the Boers might mean some devilish trick – some ambush to which our army had now grown accustomed in South Africa. In that event no support would be at hand, for the infantry and artillery of the Fifth Division would be nine miles behind at Springfield. Yet, weighing the chances, Lord Dundonald dashingly determined to take the risk. He detached 300 men with two guns to hold the bridge; with the South African Light Horse – a splendid body of men – a company of mounted infantry, and four guns of the 78th Field artillery, he struck out resolutely for Potgieter's Drift and the great hill known as Spearman's Hill which commands it. At 6 p.m. the goal was reached. There was still no enemy; only half-a-dozen Boers could be seen, and these, wonderful to relate, were washing themselves in the river, and scuttled off like terrified insects when the cavalry came into view. The 700 British troopers started to climb the hill, dragging with them the guns, with inconceivable toil, and as night fell reached the summit. It was found to be fortified with trenches, laboriously excavated, and stone walls or schantzes raised by the enemy – evidence at once of Boer activity and insight. Messages were forthwith sent back to Pretorius' Farm to apprise General Buller of the success achieved, and to ask of him immediate support. For if the Boers should attack – and even with the Tugela in flood they might know of drifts or have bridges ready – Spearman's Hill could scarcely be held by this handful of men. The night was an anxious one, but it passed without incident. With day the real danger vanished, and all eyes could drink in the wonderful panorama that lay below.

Warren's divisions cross the Tugela, 17 January 1900

The West Yorkshires were the first to cross, ferries over in pontoons; the engineers set to work to build two bridges, both above the drift, the one of pontoons and the other of trestles. The first was completed in a couple of hours. The work was scarcely interrupted by the Boers. A handful of snipers fired a few shots at the British covering party of infantry and killed a soldier of the Devons, but beyond this the enemy showed no disposition to harass the attacking force, although there is little doubt that they could have inflicted considerable loss.

After the West Yorkshires and Devons, General Hart's Irish Brigade streamed across the river and marched to a bivouac on the further bank. The cavalry and mounted infantry had to use a difficult and dangerous ford, known as Wagon Drift, a mile lower down the stream. Owing to the swiftness of the current, which runs here at something like ten miles an hour, there were some misadventures; several men were swept away, and were with difficulty rescued by their comrades; one unfortunate trooper of the 13th Hussars was drowned although every effort was made to rescue him. It now only remained to pass the artillery, the transport, and the wagons of the column across, but this proved by far the most tedious and troublesome part of the operation.

Saving the Bethulie Bridge, February–March 1900

The enemy's force at Stormberg was greatly weakened by desertion and the despatch of detachments to other parts of the field of war at the end of February; finally on 4 March, the Boers abandoned the position which had been the scene of General Gatacre's defeat, and on the following day he occupied it without incident. He at once began the repair of the railway to the west, so as to open up through communication by land with Colesberg, Capetown and the west; at the same time he continued his advance northwards, and on 7 March occupied that great Mecca of rebels and the Afrikaner Bond – Burghersdorp. Four days later his outposts were a mile south of the Orange River and of the two important bridges, road and railway, which cross near Bethulie; on the 13th, the main British force neared the bridges, and skirmishing began. The Boers had taken the precaution of demolishing the railway bridge by blowing up with dynamite five of its spans; the piers, however, were left standing, and for their own purposes the enemy refrained from destroying the road bridge. They mined it in readiness, placing charges of dynamite and detonators at several points in holes cut in the stonework of the bridge; they also laid an electric cable from the bridge to their trenches on the Free State soil, but did not connect it with the charges. Finally, they placed several boxes of dynamite on the farther bank, under the last span of the bridge, in case of any failure in their other arrangements.

To save the bridge was a matter of extreme moment to the British. Late in the afternoon of the 13th a party of the 1st Sherwood Foresters crossed the bridge, and, unobserved, while the Boers, after their usual habit, were at tea, removed the cable and detonators. Then, under cover of night, Lieutenant Popham, with a little handful of men of the same battalion, stole across, got down under the bridge, and, finding no trace of a Boer sentry except a bandolier, removed the boxes of dynamite one by one to the roadway. The lieutenant, thinking that perhaps the enemy had retired, crept towards their trenches, when he trod by ill-luck upon a dog, and a hail of bullets speedily showed him that the Boers were there. Returning, he and his men boldly carried the boxes of explosives over the bridge to the British camp under a heavy fire. Fortune favoured them and no one was hit. There still remained a possibility that the enemy might succeed in exploding the charges next day by means of shell fire. To remove this source of peril Captain Grant of the Engineers crept over the bridge, and withdrawing the charges in succession from the holes in which they had been placed, flung them one after the other into the river. By this series of acts of superb gallantry the bridge was saved.

The relief of Ladysmith, February 1900

The construction of a new trestle bridge at Colenso, across which to carry the railway, was at once begun while all the material for the repair of the original bridge was hurried to the spot. On the 20th the Boers were thoroughly cleared out of the ground south of the river and Colonel Thorneycroft and his men crossed the Tugela at Colenso.

On 20 February General Clements had to repulse a last determined attempt by the enemy to work round his flank to the south, threatening the De Aar and Naauwpoort Railway. On the 23rd the Boers fell back to the positions near Rensburg, from which, weeks before, General French had dislodged them. Here they were attacked by General Clements next day, but without result. In view of his growing strength and of their increasing weakness, they retired farther before him, and on the 27th Rensburg was occupied by the British; on the 28th, Colesberg. The Boers in this quarter had apparently retired across the Orange River, for on 2 March the mounted infantry reconnoitred up to the road bridge without seeing the enemy, but the bridge was not immediately seized. At Norvals Pont it was ascertained by reconnaissance that the enemy was still in some strength. On 6 March they blew up the road-bridge there, as also the Colesberg road-bridge farther to the west; on the 8th General Clements reached Norvals Pont and made arrangements for bridging the river. The ferry was seized through the daring of a few Colonials, who crossed by a ford and threw up trenches. On the 15th a pontoon bridge was ready, and General Clements's column began its passage a few miles below Norvals Pont. There was no opposition, and he was able to push his outposts forward as far as Donkerspoort, where a day or two later General Pole-Carew met them. The repair of Norvals Pont Bridge was at once undertaken, but could not be completed for some weeks. Meantime, railway traffic between Cape Colony and Bloemfontein was carried on by means of a light line carried across Bethulie road-bridge. In this way the main army was kept supplied, though only with extreme difficulty.

The attack on Inniskilling Hill, 22–23 February 1900

Under General Hart the famous Irish Brigade marched out to storm Inniskilling and Railway Hills, by a frontal attack. Railway Hill was an eminence, steep in its upper slopes, rising gently from the Tugela in its lower slopes, along which the railway between Colenso and Pieters ran. It was boulder covered, strongly entrenched, and afforded the Boers admirable shelter. The spur, known as Inniskilling Hill, which ran out to the south-west of it, was virtually part of it, and in descriptions of the fight that followed is usually included with it under the one name of Railway Hill. To approach it, it was necessary for the British infantry to pass in single file under the fire of the Boer guns and rifles along the narrow iron railway bridge which crosses Langverwacht Spruit. Here there was no cover of any kind against the storm of shells and bullets; each man had to run the gauntlet without the faintest opportunity of replying to the enemy's fire. The passage of the 'bridge of death' by the Irishmen was an epic in itself, an epic of heroism and faithfulness unto the last. The men seemed one and all to be animated with a determination at all costs to fight their way through to Ladysmith, even though they left half their comrades on the road. The unending file of khaki-clad figures passed steadily over the bridge, while an equally unceasing train of 'Pom-Pom' shells flecked the permanent way with puffs of smoke and dust. Now and again would come the deadlier shrapnel, leaving in its wake a group of recumbent figures. But the line never paused or checked; the recumbent figures grew in number, yet the living passed eagerly on and gathered on the farther side, under the shelter of an embankment, for the assault.

9. WORLD WAR ONE

Mons, 23 August 1914

This famous battle, the first to involve British troops in World War One (1914–18), saw fighting shaped by the numerous bridges which dotted the field, with the Mons-Condé Canal, a perfectly straight waterway running directly on an east-west line, and along the front where the British Expeditionary Force fought. Set in a countryside marked by hamlets and houses, wandering water-courses and slag-heaps, the canal was about 20 metres wide, 2 metres deep and approximately 26 km long. It was crossed by eighteen bridges.

This lengthy front was manned by General Smith-Dorrien's 2nd Army Corps, facing north from the bridge at Le Petit Crépin in the west, to the bridge at Obourg, about 5 km east of the town of Mons. The canal ran round Mons into the River Sambre to form a salient north-east of it, which included the town bridges, the railway bridges to the north, plus a pair of significant bridges at Nimy and Obourg – all combining to form the most sensitive point of the British defences.

Securely dug in amid the buildings and the slag-heaps, the British infantry demonstrated for the first time their almost legendary accurate and rapid rifle-firing, decimating the solid blocks of advancing German infantry. Despite being troubled by massed German artillery fire, British rifles covered the bridges, but inevitably the superior numbers opposing them began to tell, as the Germans crossed the canal and infiltrated around flanks in the salient. The whole left of the British line began to withdraw west of Mons, where sappers of the Royal Engineers won two Victoria Crosses for their show of courageous persistence in blowing-up bridges. At the Mons bridges the Royal Fusiliers withdrew, covered by their machine-gun section, whose commander Lieutenant M. J. Dease won a posthumous VC while Private S. F. Godley was similarly rewarded, surviving the action although wounded and taken prisoner.

Major Eady, in his Historical Illustrations, writes of this period:

Most of the continental bridges are constructed with chambers specially made for containing demolitions, so that they can be easily destroyed; but in the German advance in 1914, no demolitions were really carried out, either because it was expected that the bridges and railways would be required for an advance later, or because they were loath to destroy their own property. It is of considerable interest to speculate what would have been the effect on the German advance of a systematic plan of destruction of means of communication, ruthlessly carried out.

A journey eastward on today's Route D925, along the attractive northern bank of the Aisne River on its northern side, takes one through the area held by the British Expeditionary Force in September 1914 and the point at which they crossed the river. From Soissons, one comes to Missy (10 km), Vailley (7 km) and Chavonne (4 km). At Pont Arcy (3 km) there remains an iron bridge similar to that blown by the Germans during World War One.

Royal Engineers in the Middle East, 1915–16
The following accounts of engineering operations in Egypt and Mesopotamia are given by Colonel Sandes:

In October 1915 Brigadier-General P. G. Grant, RE, was suddenly posted from France to Egypt, appointed Chief Engineer, Suez Canal Defences, under General Horne. Early in December, he rode out with Horne from various posts along the Suez Canal, and afterwards marked out the advanced line of defence with sand-pillars. In January 1916, he was directed to commence work. He was told in Cairo that he would be given Egyptian Army reservists as labourers, and was asked whether he could begin at once. Tools were deficient, plans incomplete, materials unknown and the promised labour untrained, but he promptly assented. Subsequently, when the reservists failed to arrive, other labour was obtained, and work was started under conditions which tested to the utmost the ingenuity and persistence of the Chief Engineer. 'We found that no material for revetting the trenches was available on the spot', writes Sir Philip Grant, 'so we had to make matting hurdles to prevent the sand from falling in. I secured two ship-loads of timber at Port Said and wired to Sir Reginald Wingate at Khartoum asking him to send all the available matting in the Sudan, which he kindly promised to do. Meeting Hawkins, of the Sudan Railways, in Port Said, I suggested that he should join the Royal Engineers and run a saw-mill in the docks. This he did; and Raikes, another temporary RE officer, who knew Egypt well, got the necessary saws. In a short time, Hawkins was sawing up timber and producing hundreds of hurdles which, with the necessary matting, were carried by a fleet of native sailing boats to various stations along the Canal. We made a bridge across the Canal with a number of peculiar native boats from Lake Manzala. It swung on a wooden hinge, and consequently opened and shut most correctly; and as the cables were fixed to a hawser, which lay across the bottom of the Canal when the bridge was open, there was no danger of, fouling the propellers of ships. Another bridge was made with casks.'

188

Crossing of the Tigris at Shumran, 23 February 1917

The Turks still clung to their left bank positions far down the Tigris and it was necessary to cross the river to cut their communications – an operation which was duly executed and involved the most brilliant exploit in which the sappers and miners were concerned in Mesopotamia. At this time there were 12 companies of Engineer troops on the Tigris front: with I Corps, the 1st, 3rd, 4th, 15th, 20th and 21st Companies, Sappers and Miners; and with III Corps the 71st, 72nd and 88th Companies, RE, and the 12th, 13th and 15th Companies, Sappers and Miners. There were also two Field Troops and two Bridging Trains at the front, one of the latter being a 'Mobile' Train under Captain F. V. B. Witts, RE.

Secret preparations were made by General Maude for crossing the Tigris upstream of Kut in the Shumran bend. There had been several feints at crossing below Kut, notably one on 20 December 1916, when Captain Witts led a party of 19 Bengal Sappers across the open and down to the bank, carrying a pontoon which was launched in full view of the Turks and loaded with British infantry. The enemy then opened fire, and, as most of the party were soon killed or wounded, the project was abandoned. The Shumran scheme was carefully rehearsed. The 37th Brigade of the 14th Indian Division (III Corps) was to be the first formation to cross; but the leading units, and those concerned in the ferrying operations, were to be the 2nd Norfolk Regiment, 2/9th Gurkhas, 1/2nd Gurkhas 12th and 13th Companies of the 1/4th Madras Sappers and Miners, a few Burma Sappers, and strong detachments of the three RE Companies, the 1/4th Hampshires and the 128th Pioneers. Artillery and trench mortars would cover the crossing, and No. 2 (Mobile) Bridging Train would be assisted by the 71st Field Company, RE, and some Welch Pioneers in making a bridge. It was decided to establish three ferries, each with 13 bi-partite pontoons, so three columns stole towards the river bank after dark on 22 February 1917, and launched their pontoons before dawn on the 23rd. The Tigris was nearly 300 yards wide, with a current running at five knots.

The Norfolks, crossing by a ferry immediately below the site selected for a bridge, caught the enemy by surprise. Others were not so fortunate. The 2/9th and 1/2nd Gurkhas in the second and third ferries, rowed by the Sappers of the 12th, 13th and Burma Companies and by some Hampshires, were met by a staggering fire. Many pontoons sank or drifted away, full of dead and dying, but the remainder made good. Ferrying continued steadily and by the afternoon the 37th Brigade was across. From 8.30 a.m. to 4.30 p.m., Witts and his Bengal Sappers of the Bridging Train, helped by the 71st Company, RE, and the Welch Pioneers, laboured under artillery fire to complete their bridge. At last it reached the left bank and the troops poured across in an unceasing stream. The remainder of the 14th Division, the 13th Division and the Cavalry Division were across during the night, driving the Turks slowly back and thereby forcing the Turkish Commander-in-Chief to evacuate all his positions below Kut. The enemy, fighting bravely, retreated on Baghdad. They attempted to dispute the passage of the Diyala River beyond Ctesiphon, but the British threw a bridge across the Tigris and enfiladed them so that III Corps (General Marshall) drove them out of their last position on 10 March. Sir Stanley Maude entered Baghdad on the following day, and his victorious troops completed the winter campaign by capturing Samarra on 23 April. The hot weather then prevented further large operations by either side.

Crossing of the Isonzo, 9 June 1917

The following version of the action between the Italians and the Austrians at the Isonzo River crossing comes from The War by Dr James Murphy in Masterpiece Library of War Short Stories (1920):

'You are now standing,' said the officer, 'on what must seem to you a very commonplace structure, a roughly built bridge spanning a river; but this strip of wood has a story which no other bridge in the world can tell. It was our forefathers who first taught the world how to build bridges. And I think it must have been a very early step in the development of their civilisation, for they enshrouded the process in a veil of religious mysticism. Even we still call our bishops *pontifici* – bridge-builders. But in our long history we never built a bridge which does us so much credit as this one. You must tell your people about it, for it is a story which deserves to rank among the great epics in the history of warfare.'

We were standing on the bridge near Sagrado, where the Italians first crossed the Isonzo and attacked the Austrian positions on the Carso. He had a habit of making neat little speeches, this officer and guide of mine. And in this instance his enthusiasm was fully justified, for the bridge at Sagrado is a more eloquent symbol of Latin prowess than all the great monuments which Italy has built to commemorate her achievement of national independence. Ever since I first stood on the spot and considered the difficulties under which the crossing of the Isonzo had been effected, I had no doubt or fear for the fate of Gorizia. Only a few thousand yards away it lies, now in Italian hands. Its conquest has placed the Italian army high in the world's estimate, but I think that the first crossing of the Isonzo was a deed of greater prowess.

Because of this conviction I gathered the details of the story from the lips of men whose souls were still aglow with the flame of battle and

190

whose bodies still bore the marks of the terrible fray. When I had collected a sheaf of notes, containing personal accounts in the picturesque Italian terms which I cannot hope to translate into English, I returned to my room at headquarters and wrote the story of the bridge.

At Sagrado the Isonzo is about four hundred yards in width, but a low island of gravel and sand stands in the centre of the stream. This was the point chosen for the Italian crossing. At half-past ten on the evening of 9 June the engineers began to construct the first span of the bridge, from the right bank to the island. While the work was in progress the troops of the advance-guard crossed the river in pontoon boats. They did not entrench or seek to establish themselves on strategic positions, but simply advanced point-blank against the enemy's lines. The night was utterly moonless, and the Austrians were taken unawares. The Italian advance guard entered Sagrado and captured some prisoners.

When morning broke, the first span of the bridge was almost complete. The first streaks of dawn were the signal for a tremendous rush on the part of the engineers and their helpers. Soldiers and officers from the infantry regiments, staff officers and drivers from the transport wagons, rushed to and fro in promiscuous procession, shouldered girders and piles and trestles, each man working in a fury of silent energy, as if the success of the whole project were dependent on him alone.

Before the last abutment was in place a cascade of shells thundered from the overhanging brow of the Carso, enveloping men and material in a vortex of flame and destruction. Shells burst along the girders and cross-beams, mercilessly massacring the engineers and hurling the dead and wounded into the stream. There was no cover. The great fortified bulk of the Carso, bristling with howitzers, machine guns and rifles, completely dominated the position. Under the terrific onslaught of artillery the Italians rolled backwards, seeking cover amid the wooded slopes of the right bank. Borne downwards by the foaming torrent, the wounded cried out piteously for help. Nets and life-belts were thrown to them, and Red Cross rescuers jumped headlong into the stream.

After a few hours the river had become deserted and the Austrian storm ceased. It was now possible to estimate the extent of the damage. Two-thirds of the bridge remained, badly gashed and splintered, but still well supported by the stout girders and piles. It was imperative to commence rebuilding immediately, for the advance-guard was isolated on the opposite bank, and about five hundred men were marooned on the island. These latter were in a worse plight than that of their companions, for the advance-guard was entrenched under the lee of a jut-

ting spur, on dead ground, so that while the Austrian fire swept harmlessly over their heads it mercilessly sprayed the island in the centre of
the stream. Once again the engineers set to work. Once again the Austrian artillery thundered. Like sailors on a doomed ship the Italians
clung to their structure, striving to staunch wounds and splice its broken ribs; but the enemy's fire was devastating. Within an hour the
greater part of the bridge was in ruins, and the engineers had suffered
terribly at the hands of hostile snipers. Owing to the hidden position of
the enemy's guns in the pits and caves of the Carso it was impossible
for the Italian artillery to reply effectively. For the moment no other
choice offered itself save that of abandoning the project and awaiting
the cover of night.

One can well understand the anxiety which now reigned in the minds
of the Latin troops. Their comrades cried to them from beyond the
river. The men on the island lay motionless on the bare sand. It was
impossible to distinguish between the dead and wounded. No succour
could be sent, no relieving troops, no food, no medical aid, not even a
message of encouragement. Worse than all, such quantities of bridging
material had been destroyed that the supply was now running short,
and the enemy's long-range guns pounded the roads by which the transport of supplies approached the right bank of the river.

As night came on the enemy's searchlights swept the Isonzo. There
in the foreground the Italians could see the barren island, its dust-grey
sand blending with the uniforms of the motionless bodies which lay in
heaps on its surface. They had fallen as they advanced, face downwards,
among them the commander of the second battalion of the advance-
guard. Between them and their only – but now forlorn – hope of safety
stood the few isolated piles of the bridge, standing bare and battered in
the water, like the skeleton of some ship that had been wrecked on a
rock-bound coast. Whispered along the ranks, the news of the destroyed
battalion created among the attacking troops a spirit of despondency
and almost despair.

Having satisfied themselves that the Italian plan had been finally
wrecked, the Austrians switched the current from their searchlights and
withdrew for the night. Then the Italian engineers crept forth once
again. Rescue-parties stealthily crossed the river, punting their craft,
lest the splash of an oar might reach the enemy's ear. The first concern
was for the men on the island. It was possible that all had not been
destroyed, and that some survivors might still be found amid the mass
of prostrate forms. When the rafts arrived many of the 'dead' had
already arisen. Creeping on all fours, they came to meet their rescuers,
not a few straggling survivors, but dense masses of able-bodied men,
fully accoutred and unhurt. When the work of rescue came to an end, it

192

was found that of the five hundred who had been marooned, only fifteen had lost their lives, and fifty had been wounded. They owed their salvation to the alertness and initiative of their officers. Realising the impossibility of moving either onwards or backwards, the officers ordered the men to lie flat and motionless. With bayonets and cutting pincers, and the peaks of their caps for tools, they burrowed in the gravel, half burying themselves, so that to the eye of the onlooker they appeared as so many corpses strewn on the island and intermingled with its gravel through the havoc of the gun-fire.

While rescue-parties thus worked for the safety of their comrades on the island and on the opposite bank, the engineers were once again busy on the bridge. At about two o'clock came the first streaks of dawn. When the Austrians awoke and began to look out over their parapets it was found that the 'dead' had arisen and gone away. Seeing the Italians working as busily as ants, the Austrian commander gave orders for a massed and relentless artillery attack. Guns were rushed to the foremost positions on the Carso, and a wild hurricane of shells hurled on the river. The artillery of the Italians could not reply, because of the danger of injury to the men of the advance-guard, who still remained at the foot of the hill. Under the lee of the spur which juts out into the river at Sagrado the enemy's shells poured harmlessly over them.

When the night came they were brought over in pontoon boats, together with the prisoners whom they had captured at Sagrado. Then a wild holocaust of fire and flame commenced. The Latin blood was up. Both artilleries hurled blind defiance at one another. Throughout the night the storm of shell continued unabated – a terrible night of torrential rain and fog. The Isonzo fumed and steamed. Volumes of vapour, streaked with lurid gashes of flame, arose from the body of the stream. Not a soul was to be seen, but a deafening chorus of hoarse echoes reverberated from hill to hill, as if the spirits of the river were shrieking in pain and torture.

It had now become clear that an isolated crossing was out of the question. Small detachments might reach the opposite bank, but they could not establish a permanent bridgehead unless supported by the troops on the right. These had crossed lower down the river at Pieris, and taken Monfalcone; but the effort to move northwards on the left bank and co-operate with the centre was frustrated by the immense lagoon which the Austrians had created between the foot of the Carso and the lower stretches of the Isonzo. To drain the lagoon was the task to which the Italian centre now set itself.

A little below Sagrado, where the Isonzo bends westwards through the plain of Friuli, leaving a triangle-shaped tongue of lowland between its course and the foot of the Carso, the Austrians had built a dam across the river. This was a permanent structure, serving to divert the water into a canal which ran along the foot of the mountain to Monfalcone. By closing the dam and destroying the mechanism for reopening it, the Austrians succeeded in flooding the Isonzo, already well swollen by the torrential rains. They then opened breaches in the right bank of the canal, and allowed the water to flood the intervening low land. Only by blowing up the dam could the Italians drain the lagoon.

Two cannon of medium calibre were rushed along the right bank and brought into position directly opposite Sagrado. Under open fire from the Austrian gunners they began to pound the great barrier of steel and concrete, but the Italians did not have high explosives of sufficient strength to destroy it. There were hopes that the mechanism might still be repaired, so that the locks could be got to open normally. With this end in view two officers of the engineering corps crept along the left bank of the river from the south, under cover of night. They sprang upon the sentinels, throttled and choked them. Plunging into the stream, they swam to the lock gates, only to find that the joints had been firmly spiked.

Then a private from the ranks of the engineers volunteered to grapple with the difficulty. Placing a sack of dynamite on his back and binding it firmly to shoulders and waist, he plunged into the foaming waters. It was already dawn. A cascade of shells poured upon him, rifle and machine-gun bullets hissed around him. Buffeted by the waves as they broke against the ridge of the dam, and already sorely wounded, he still struggled. Breathlessly he was watched from either bank. It was like an epic struggle of old romance. At length he reached the lock gates. It was the signal for the engineers to turn on the current. Within a few moments the whole structure leaped into the air...

The flooded river began to recede. The right wing moved northwards over what had once been a lagoon. Again the engineers began to build. The troops essayed to cross on rafts. Five times they attempted, five times they were driven back. Night came on. The Italian artillery became silent, and the Austrians believed that the project had been abandoned. At ten o'clock the engineers were busy once again. Hundreds of men rushed to the bank, bearing on their shoulders beams and planks and wire rope and hempen cable. Not a sound reached the ears of the enemy. The officers whispered their commands, the men rushed to and fro on bare feet.

When dawn began to break, the centre of the stream had been reached and the last abutment of the bridge now rested on the island. The farther arm of the river being largely protected by the lee of the Carso, it was decided to use pontoons for the second half of the crossing. The men rushed across the bridge, the boats received them, and rowed them to the shore. Not being strong enough to take a defensive position, the first battalions attacked furiously. They succeeded in reoccupying Sagrado and making some prisoners. At three o'clock the Austrian guns opened fire, and at four the bridge was once again in ruins. But now there could be no turning back. The attack on Sagrado must be supported. Moving a little northwards, the engineers decided to use the remains of an old bridge which the Austrians had destroyed. They commenced to build in open daylight, but this time the Austrian gunners did not find their task of destruction so easy, for Italian bayonets were already pushing them back from their vantage positions on the glacis. The river was quickly becoming 'dead ground', so that the greater number of shells fell wide of the mark, and only fitful gusts of rifle and machine-gun fire obstructed the work of the bridge-builders. Even then the Austrians were able to inflict serious damage on the Italians; so much so that the bridge had to be repaired several times. But the engineers stuck to their work and the troops crossed under fire. Bearing sacks on their shoulders, alternate groups formed a moving parapet for the protection of themselves and their companions. It was a picture which reminded the onlookers of Roman troops storming an ancient citadel. The artillery horses suffered seriously, but their dead bodies were quickly hurled into the stream, and men harnessed themselves to the gun-wagon beside the unhurt animals. In the course of two days several regiments had gained the opposite bank, accompanied by their artillery and supply columns. And the attack on the Carso commenced.

Since that day I have many times stood on the bridge and tried to call up visions of the valour of which it is the symbol. Beneath the limpid waters one can still see human wreckage strewn in the bed of the Isonzo. Let us hope that the structure will be allowed to remain, so that future pilgrims to the spot may be enabled to form a just appraisement of the valour which was shown here.

Battle of Cambrai, 20 November 1917

In late October 1917 plans were agreed for an attack to be based on tanks and led by them, a project dear to the hearts of the General Staff of the Tank Corps, who had long desired to prove that tanks could cross the great trenches of the Hindenburg system, provided that the attack was a surprise, with no preliminary bombardment, and that the supporting infantry displayed enough confidence in their tanks to follow them.

It was an amazing success as the slowly moving mechanical monsters ground their way forward, with the infantry close behind them, on a front of some 13,000 yards, to penetrate more than 10,000 yards in a twelve-hour period. The enemy were dumbfounded, and most fled from the field or surrendered without offering much resistance, so that 8000 prisoners and a hundred guns were captured, the prisoners being nearly double the numbers of casualties sustained by the British III and IV Corps on the first day of the battle.

The Tank Corps personnel involved in the attack consisted of 600 officers and 3500 men, roughly the strength of a strong infantry brigade, economically replacing the normal preliminary bombardment and the usually far-from-successful hope of shells cutting and destroying dense barbed-wire entanglements.

As the bells of London pealed in celebration of their victory, the tank men knew they had introduced a completely new system of tactics and, in so doing, that they had achieved victory in one of the most remarkable battles ever fought. It has never been forgotten by their successors, and to this day each year, on 20 November, the Royal Tank Regiment celebrates Cambrai Day. Their colours of brown, red and green symbolise the achievement of grinding their way through 'the mud and the blood to the green fields beyond'.

A detailed account of a specific action at the bridge of Masnières in the same battle comes from The War History of the Sixth Tank Battalion:

The senior officer present after the capture of the Brown Line was Major C. F. Hawkins, DSO, MC, who detailed twelve tanks to proceed to Masnières. On arrival at the bridgehead it was found to be partially destroyed by the enemy, and the houses on the landing side of the bridge held by snipers and machine guns. A tank was posted close to the bridgehead, and fire kept up on the houses from which the enemy fired. About 12.45 p.m. some infantry of the 29th Division arrived, and the GOC 88th Brigade directed the bridge to be held by a tank, till he could get the infantry over. Major P. Hamond DSO, MC, on his arrival at the bridge, ordered an attempt to be made to cross, but owing to the condition of the bridge the attempt resulted in the tank falling into the canal. The bridgehead was then held by tanks, under the orders of the infantry brigadier, until 22 November, when the infantry took over. The town had been evacuated so suddenly by the enemy that some civilian population still remained. Two cows, belonging to the German town mayor, were presented by the civilian keeper to Major Hamond, as a token of the joy he inhabitants felt at their liberation. The conduct of the mayor of the town is worthy of the highest praise. He went from one side of the canal to the other, under fire from both sides, to warn all of the enemy's preparations to shell the town, and to give every one a chance to take cover. The wooden bridge was not destroyed, and was apparently passable for infantry and cavalry. This bridgehead was also held by tanks.

F7. *Feu de Ciel II*
The first tank to enter Masnières at 11.55 a.m. as the enemy evacuated the village, along the main road to Cambrai. This bridge was reached with a platoon of infantry at 12.30, and fire was opened. After the 6-pounder ammunition had been exhausted F6 relieved this tank, which returned to the rallying point at 11.30 a.m. on 21 November.

F27. *Fighting Mac II*
On arrival was detailed to hold the bridge, and exhausted all the 6-pounder ammunition in so doing, and later was relieved by F26.

F26. *Fearless II*
On arrival relieved F27 on guard, and borrowed 50 rounds 6-pounder ammunition from F22. While on the bridge three men were wounded. The gears were jammed, and F22 towed this tank off, and relieved it on guard.

F22. *Flying Fox II*
Detailed to attempt to cross the bridge; in doing so the girders of the bridge gradually collapsed, and the tank sank into the canal. All the crew escaped without injury, under fire, through the manhole.

F28. *Foggie II*
Arrived at 1.15 p.m. and remained until 9 p.m. on the 21st, when it rallied at the battalion rallying-point.

F30. *Flaming Fire II*
Arrived after F28, and remained until 9 a.m. on the 21st, when it rallied at the battalion rallying-point.

F13. *Falcon II*
Arrived at the bridgehead at 12.30 p.m. and remained until 8.45 a.m. on the following morning, when the tanks rallied at the rallying-point at 11.30 a.m. Windows of houses were swept in places suspected to contain snipers. The officer was slightly wounded from splinters from machine-gun fire.

F1. *Firespite II*
On arrival in the village went straight to the bridge. Later the offlcer and the crew took over F6 from 6 a.m. 21 November to 9.30 a.m., as guard on the bridge. The tank rallied at 11 a.m. 21 November.

F6. *Feu d'Artifice*
Relieved F7 on the bridge, which was short of ammunition. Remained on guard there till the 21st. The officer and crew of F7 relieved the crew

of F6 from 11 p.m. till dawn and the crew of F1 from dawn till 9.30 a.m. on the 21st, when the tank was withdrawn and rallied. While withdrawing from the bridge the officer and the driver were both wounded.

F50. *Fay*
Detailed for the bridge, but having developed mechanical trouble broke down. Rallied on 21st at 12 noon, on being repaired.

F51. *Fortuna*
Arrived at 12.15 p.m. and detailed to hold the wooden bridge to the north of the main bridge. Was relieved by F54 at 3 p.m. After refilling on the 21st this tank was detailed to hold the main (broken) bridge, and remained under heavy machine-gun fire and shell-fire from 8 p.m. to 8.15 a.m. on 22 November, when the tank rallied about 11 a.m. on the 23rd.

F54. *Festine Lente*
Arrived at 12.15 p.m. and opened fire on the far side of the canal, under orders of a staff major, while the wooden bridge was to be stormed (north of the main bridge). Parked up for the night in the main street at 8 a.m. on 21 November. The tanks guarding the main broken bridge were relieved. There was almost continuous shell-fire from 11 to 6.30 on the 21st. At 11 p.m. the tank moved away from the bridge, still having it under observation. At 6.30 a.m. on the 23rd the tank proceeded to the rallying-point, arriving there about noon.

F52. *Foam II*
After being detailed for the bridge, on the way down La Vacquerie valley, a sniper was disposed of at the request of the infantry. Shortly after, a big end ran out, and the tank was unable to proceed further.

During the night of 20–21 November orders were received from the 3rd Brigade to send ten tanks to Marcoing, and any spare tanks to Crêvecoeur, to attack at 11 a.m. on the 21st. Orders were received at the rallying-point, as to the Crêvecoeur operations, and are dealt with under a subsequent paragraph. The actual orders received from the 87th Infantry Brigade at Marcoing were verbal ones, to cut the wire of the Marcoing–Masnières–Beaurevoir line from a point approximately 1,500 yards north-east of Marcoing to Rumilly, and clear the village of the enemy.

Nine tanks of this battalion went into action, one failing to start, having developed mechanical trouble. At Marcoing two tanks of 'A' Battalion were also found to have been told off for the same operation. All tanks crossed over the northern road bridge on the lock east of Marco-ing. The bridge was mined, and the RE engaged in taking out the charge, but owing to the time appointed for the attack the tanks could not wait for this to be finished. Four tanks turned left after crossing the bridge towards Flot Farm, to work south-east along the wire, and five plus the two tanks of 'A' Battalion (seven in all) turned right to work down the wire towards Rumilly. The infantry, with certain exceptions, did not follow the tanks. This appeared to be due to lack of any definite orders issued to them about the intended operations. Very heavy machine-gun fire, with armour piercing bullets, was encountered, and also a certain amount of field-gun fire over open sights.

This story is continued in The Tank Corps by Major Clough Williams-Ellis and A. Williams-Ellis:

At Lateau Wood on the right of the attack heavy fighting took place, including a duel between a tank and a 5.9 in. howitzer. Turning on the tank the howitzer fired, shattering and tearing of most of the right-hand sponson of the approaching machine, but fortunately not injuring its vitals; before the German gunners could reload, the tank was upon them, and in a few seconds the great gun was crushed in a jumbled mass amongst the brushwood surrounding it.

A little to the west of this wood the Tanks of 'F' (6th) Battalion, which had topped the ridge, were speeding down on Masnières. One approached the bridge, the key to the Rumilly Seranvillers ridge, upon the capture of which so much depended. The bridge had, as the tank commander knew, been damaged either by shell-fire or by the German sappers. It was, however, most important that he should cross, and he very pluckily, therefore, went for it. As the tank neared the centre of the bridge, there was a rending of steel girders – the bridge had broken, and as it collapsed the tank disappeared into the waters of the canal. Other tanks arrived and, not being able to cross, assisted the infantry to do so by opening a heavy covering fire.

The tank that had fallen into the canal had been let down quite gradually into the water as the bridge slowly subsided.

There was but one loss. The wig of one of the crew got knocked off as his head emerged from the manhole, and it floated away down the canal and was never seen again. Lost to view, its memory was kept green for many months by its injured owner's claims for compensation.

During the Cambrai battle, British tanks used a bridge crossing the St Quentin Canal in the town of Masnières which, after being mined by the Germans, had not been completely blown. However, when a tank

199

attempted to cross, the much weakened structure gave way under its weight. This incident was to cause a considerable delay to the advancing British forces.

At the time of the battle of Cambrai, and later, much was said and written on the effect broken bridges had on the course of events on 20 November 1917 and after. Despite the Official History stating that the collapse of a vital bridge at Masnières was the reason for failure on the right flank, plus the opportune arrival of a previously unlocated German division, one authority scathingly said that official myth-making had more to do with what happened than did broken bridges. Bad luck and bad planning played their part by concealing from General Byng the knowledge that, a little way to the north, the bridge at Marcoing lay open – the carrier pigeon bearing the news failed to reach the general.

Through this, tragedy was brought to two supporting formations, the 5th Cavalry Division, lacking trench-maps, took an hour to negotiate twenty-two belts of barbed-wire at Masnières, delaying the advance of the Fort Garry Horse of Canada so that they were cut to pieces in the dusk.

Crossing of the River Auja (Palestine), December 1917

This small operation is an almost classic example of a night operation. The situation in Palestine was that Jerusalem had been captured by General Allenby, and he had held it against the Turkish counter-attacks.

The action is described in Major Eady's Historical Illustrations to Field Service Regulations Operations, containing a section entitled An Outline of the Egyptian and Palestine Campaigns by Major-General Sir M. G. E. Bowman-Manifold, from which the following passage is taken:

The presence of the Turks on the high ground near the coast, north of the Auja, and at Bald Hill and Mulebbis south of it, and further east, rendered Jaffa insecure for shipping and threatened the one lateral road Jaffa–Ramleh–Latrun–Jerusalem. The 21st Corps were directed to drive the Turks north and to occupy the line Rantieh-El Jelil.

The River Auja was 40-60 yards wide, averaged 10 feet deep, with few fords, ran at about three miles per hour, and was subject to heavy floods in the winter rains. In winter the river was fordable only at the bar formed just where it enters the sea, and there the depth was about three feet six inches. The Turks had an entrenched post to cover this ford, and also kept it under frequent bursts of machine-gun fire at night.

The Jaffa-Tulkeram road crossed the Auja at Hadrah by a stone bridge, which was also a mill dam; but the Turks had blown this in. East of Stone Bridge, the ground on the south and left bank was marshy. Generally, the banks of the river were low and muddy, but small groves and belts of trees between Stone Bridge and Jerisheh afforded some cover on both banks. The Nahr Burdieh joined the Auja just below Sheikh Muannis. A belt of sand-dunes ran up the coast and from Tel el Rekkit, low cliffs extended northwards.

Inland, north of the Auja, the country consisted of a downland of sandy hills, with a little cultivation west of Sheikh Muannis. South of the river, there were low grassy hills, thin scrub and some orange groves. Besides Mulebbis, on the left bank, the Turks had a strong position at Sheikh Muannis situated on a ridge, about half-a-mile north of the river and one-and-a-half miles inland.

The forcing of a passage was entrusted to the 52nd Lowland Division. The river front was carefully examined... A particularly bold reconnaissance was made by two officers, who swam out to sea, landed on the Turkish side, came back through their lines undetected, and plumbed the ford as they came.

General Hill (52nd Division), proposed to effect the passage by night, and by surprise, without any particular artillery support until after the crossing had been secured. After that, his plan was to proceed covered by a barrage worked to a time-table. But, in order to lull the enemy into a false security, he was to be put under a drill, as regards artillery fire, and to be given a regular dose of night bombardment each evening; so that, when the real attack came, there would be no abnormal artillery action to alarm him.

Broadly, the plan was to take across a small covering force, if possible undetected, then to pass the three brigades over at three points (the ford, below Muannis, and at Stone Bridge), and also to demonstrate further east in order to confuse the Turks. The navy were to cover the left flank and harass the Turks near the coast.

The covering troops were to cross first, at point X, on rafts made up from 2,300 gallon canvas tanks. Each raft carried sixteen men. Then light bridges were to be put across on piers of similar rafts, to take infantry and pack-animals. Subsequently, pontoon and barrel-pier bridges were to be built, and the Stone Bridge repaired. Timber was obtained by pulling down houses and sheds. A pontoon bridge was sent up from the Suez Canal. The rafts were put together under the trees in the German colony of Sarona. The infantry practised embarking and disembarking in a large irrigation tank at night, and also rehearsed cutting through cactus hedges in the dark.

The operation was fixed to begin on the evening of 20 December, at 20.00 hours.

The first troops to cross were to be the 1/7th HLI battalion of the 157th brigade, and its task was to swing left and take the Turkish trenches guarding the ford at the river mouth. It was to be followed by one battalion 156th brigade, which was to move simultaneously on B (Slag Heap Farm), while a company was told off to bomb the stone wall at C. It was hoped that the enemy would be confused, and would wait to clear up the situation before launching a counter-attack, which would then be too late. Two other battalions of 156th brigade were to take Muannis and roll up the trenches at D, respectively. The rest of the 157th brigade were to cross at the ford and move on Tel el Rekkit. The 155th brigade were to demonstrate at G, and later in the night, cross at H and secure Hadrah and the Stone Bridge.

The 19th and 20th of December were very wet days. The Auja rose alarmingly, the valley became waterlogged, and the approaches to the crossing place (at X) were so soft that at the last moment 200 yards of corduroy road had to be laid to enable the rafts to be taken to the river. There was a young quarter moon, the night was uncomfortably light, very cold, and sounds travelled amazingly.

The inter-communication was very complete, and cables from divisional headquarters to brigades and to the artillery were all duplicated.

The operations commenced to time, and in six minutes four rafts were afloat at X; half-an-hour later, half the covering party was also undetected, and the leading raft was at the water's edge by 20.35 hours.

By 22.00 hours, the light bridges were three-quarters completed, the second battalion was crossing, but the bridging parties were experiencing difficulty with the current and soft banks, and in getting the last bay into place. All times were now put back half an-hour. By 22.30 hours, the first bridge was across and in use. By midnight the whole of the 156th brigade was across, and by dawn they had secured ther objectives and were well dug in.

The assault started at 00.25 hours on 21 December. The 7th Highland LI completely surprised the Turks and took the trenches for 1,000 yards north of the ford. The 1/4th Royal Scots took Slag Heap Farm. The 1/7th Royal Scots took Sheikh Muannis by 03.00 hours. The 8th Scottish Rifles cleared the ground at D, south of Muannis. The 1st Scottish Rifles (brigade reserve) put the long wall, C, into a state of defence and had formed a dump of 50,000 rounds of SAA.

Meanwhile at fifty minutes after midnight, the remainder of the 157th brigade began to ford the river-the 1/6th HLI leading.

The ford had not been marked by pickets, owing to the river's swollen state, but the commanding officer found it, and the battalion crossed, the men in fours linked, while the RE put up the pickets as they went. There were thirty casualties from shell-fire. All went according to plan. By 02.00 hours the 157th brigade was across, and they had secured all objectives by 05.48 hours and were dug in.

On the right, the 155th brigade began its demonstration, and its covering party at H got across unobserved by 23.15 hours. The ground was so boggy they could not launch their bridge piers, and so the troops had to ferry over in rafts, and so lost time; and at 02.35 hours, they were thirty minutes late in the programme. But by 03.40 hours two battalions were across, two hours later the 5th Royal Scots Fusiliers had taken Hadrah; and after stubborn fighting Stone Bridge was in our hands at 05.40.

At 06.00 hours, two batteries were ordered to cross the ford, to support 157th brigade, and the navy were informed that all objectives had been taken. It seems that the Turks had expected an attack for some days, but when the artillery fire proved to be normal evening shelling, they regarded the attack as merely local demonstrations. They considered the only feasible crossing to be at Stone Bridge, and that elsewhere was impossible in the existing state of the river.

As a result of this extremely successful night operation, the rest of the force was enabled to move over in daylight next day, and the line of the 1st Corps was advanced so as to give ten miles clear between Jaffa, and our lateral road, and the Turks.

Bridges and engineering in France, 1918

Major Eady comments as follows on bridges and communications in France:

Note the influence of engineers' work on communication, especially in the offensives by material destruction, such as the Somme and 3rd Ypres. It was an impossibility to maintain the roads, which were completely destroyed by shell-fire, weather, and the weight of transport they had to support. Then, in the final advance against the Germans, this advance largely depended on the rapidity with which the road and river bridges, destroyed by the enemy, could be repaired, and the whole system of communications for supplies maintained. When the armistice was signed the allied armies had reached the limits of the possible radius of supply at the time. Until communication, especially over the shattered belt of country, could have been restored, only small portions of the armies could have maintained the pursuit of the German forces.

Many of the bridges over the Somme in the German advance of 1918 were left standing by us, though orders had been issued for their destruction; but the responsibility for preparation and for actual demolition had not been sufficiently definitely laid down.

During the German offensive on the Lys (April 1918), the bridge over the Lys at Sailly was blown up prematurely (though the demolition was not complete), while many British troops were still on the far bank, and their withdrawal was only effected with great difficulty.

In another place, at Nouveau Monde, in the same battle, pontoon equipment was lying on the bank. According to instructions, if a hostile attack were started, this bridge was to be constructed at once, to facilitate communication and withdrawal; but, in the actual attack, nothing was done, as no definite orders had been given nor definite party detailed off to the task.

Crossing the River Jordan (Palestine), 1 May 1918

The following extract from In Araby Orion by Edward Thompson is contained in Vain Glory (ed. Guy Chapman):

When it was too dusk for enemy observation, the battalion fell in. They marched swiftly to the river, and crossed. Here, again, were worlds conducting their existence in entire disconnection. The river, a fiercely purposeful thing, was sweeping up mighty armfuls of dark water and flinging them downward, to disappear into swirling masses beneath the bridge. Again, and infinitely again, the process was repeated, a magnificence of effort which came out of omnipotence and would pass eternally into it. Over all this effort, that was proceeding so far else whither from them, moved the lines of men, their tread sounding dully on the swaying bridge, their equipment sending out a metallic clank. Of these men, how small was the purview and limit within which each was vivid and real! His own mind, inside of which his own being and experience were a flame; the minds of those few, his close companions, where it was a faint and occasional shadow. The battalion outside, where he was a number and presently might be an identity disk, to be sent home when time and other jobs permitted....

It had been a jumpy business, this crossing in semi-darkness. Spasms of machine-gun fire, though their source had been pushed into pockets of the Transjordanic hills that no longer commanded the river, sent strays splashing the lead with a sudden spurt of silver. A few bullets sang over the bridge; several men were hit, and one killed. There was intermittent shelling, due to grow fiercer when night deepened; Martin was glad that the Claphams were after the Brentfords, and not the other way round. Once a shell, aimed at that teasing random which is so hard to endure – it is a tugging at the nerves, when you see shells bursting far apart, and know that your foe is firing without observation, but for that very reason is going to try all possible targets – burst in the river, so little above the bridge that it was almost under it. Jacko had the range all right! It was only luck that he had not caught them. That plane which had spotted them this morning had reported that there would be night crossings; every yard of the road beyond the river would be plastered! Each man felt his heart sink sickeningly as out of night came that swoop and descent. We have lost our fathers' dread of demons; but you who have known a quiet road at night without warning pass into an inferno of shelling know also what Guthlac abroad in a shrieking winter darkness imagined. All the eyes are with your foe; he sees, and strikes out of the blackness. He lets you go forward a while, for no reason but malignant pleasure in your terror, and then he has you. A mighty geyser shot up, the bridge was blinded with spray, a huge muscular beast of water with points of brightness like so many eyes swung over it, serpentine, irresistible. The bridge rocked like a bamboo suspension in a Himalayan storm, the men nearest the shell-burst were tossed against the rail. Two missed it, and when the beast had ebbed again, they had gone with it. Scylla had pounced and taken her prey...

Le Quesnoy: the last attack, November 1918
The final World War One extract, again from Vain Glory, is by Lieutenant-Colonel F. Lushington, entitled La Gambardier.

Ten days before the end, the battery was in action before Le Quesnoy. Merredew had left to command a battery in the north. The guns were in a little field, sloping down to a stream on the other side of which was a large mill. The only road to the front ran over the bridge past the mill. All day long the columns of men, guns and transport passed over this bridge, and all day long they shelled it with a high-velocity gun. In the afternoon when the gunners had ceased firing they lay back on the grass and speculated which of the endless teams of horses and mules, limber and guns would get safely across the bridge. The sappers were working hard at repairs under this steady shell-fire. A gallant party of military police and others were clearing away the dead horses and men that littered the road both sides of the stream. A gun team would come trotting down the hill towards the bridge and a hundred yards from it, break into a gallop. 'Hooray! they are safely across. Here come the next lot! Bang! That's got them. No, it hasn't!' as horses and men, less one driver, emerge from the smoke, and gallop up the road into safety the other side. At dusk the enemy ceased fire, and the mill being the only available billet, the men moved into its vast, underground store-room, whilst Shadbolt and the officers occupied an upstairs room, where there were some beds. Soon after midnight that accursed gun began again. Whee-oo! Whoosh! Bang!

10. WORLD WAR TWO

The assault on Eben Emael, 10 May 1940

In the spring of 1940, eight months after the outbreak of war, Belgium was still hoping to maintain strict neutrality, though conscious that Britain and France would aid if she were attacked. The Belgian command relied on a delaying defensive position protected by a forward line of outposts. At Maastricht, however, where the proximity of the Albert Canal to the Dutch border made outposts impossible, the defenders relied upon the canal's deep cutting, its 100 yards width being spanned by three bridges at Veldzelt, Vroenhofen and Canne. The 7th Infantry Division were responsible for defending the area and had a brigade covering each bridge. The whole position was supported by the powerful artillery fort of Eben Emael.

Well prepared and sited, the bridge defences consisted of four massive concrete pillboxes on the near bank. One, beside the road, mounted an anti-tank gun; the others, one immediately below the bridge, and one on either flank some 500 yards distant, all mounted machine guns. There was also a small post on the far (eastern) bank. The positions were garrisoned by a company positioned on the near bank at each bridge. Canne, the southernmost of the bridges and nearest to Eben Emael, had an anti-tank gun bunker set back into the hillside.

All the bridges had prepared demolition charges in position and could be quickly blown by demolition parties in the anti-tank bunkers. No Belgian forces operated east of the canal because of the closeness of the Dutch frontier, but surprise seemed impossible because the Germans, in the event of their invading the Netherlands, would have to fight their way across the Maastricht 'appendix' of Holland, so that by the time they reached the Belgium border the bridges would be demolished and well-prepared defences confidently awaiting them.

With bitter memories of 1914 when the forts around Liège had been smashed into submission by heavy German siege-guns, during 1933–5 the Belgians had blasted out of natural rock the fortress of Eben Emael, which resembled the great defensive works of the French Maginot Line, with one side rising a sheer 120 feet from the canal. The other faces were protected by concrete pillboxes, 60 mm anti-tank guns, heavy and light machine guns, ditches, a 20-foot wall, minefields and searchlights. The fort's armament consisted of six 120 mm guns in revolving armoured cupolas and eighteen 75 mm guns in cupolas or casemates, mounted in emplacements with walls and roofs of five feet thick reinforced concrete.

In November 1939, a special German combat group under Hauptmann Walter Koch was formed from 1st Parachute Regiment 7th Air Division of Engineers, plus pilots, for the special task of capturing the three bridges intact and neutralising the fort. A parachute unit attacking in DFS 230 assault gliders to ensure a concentration of attackers on the objective, Sturmabteilung Koch trained intensively on full-size mock-ups of the Eben Emael defence system until every man knew his own role and that of his comrades. Towed to the Dutch border, the planes were to be released at 8,000 feet, to glide silently across the Maastricht 'appendix' and onto their objective, undetected by sound location devices of Belgian anti-aircraft defences.

Koch's assault force was in four distinct groups, each with specific duties: 1. Assault group 'Concrete' (Leutnant Schacht) to secure the bridge over the Albert Canal at Vroenhofen and hold it until the arrival of ground forces; 2. Assault Group 'Iron' (Leutnant Schaechter) to secure the bridge at Canne; 3. Assault Group 'Steel' (Oberleutnant Altman) to secure the bridge at Veldvezelt; 4. Assault Group 'Granite' (Oberleutnant Witzig) to land on the flat roof of the fort and cripple the artillery armament, holding on until the arrival of Army Engineer Battalion 51. These trained and experienced engineers were armed with 110 lb hollow-charge explosives capable of punching a hole of 12-in diameter through six feet of concrete.

On 10 May 1940 German forces invaded the Netherlands and Belgium. At 0430 hours that morning thirty-one Junkers, each towing a glider, took off; once airborne, they formed up and wheeled onto course in a steady thirty-minute climb to just over 8,000 feet, moving towards the release point near the Dutch border, indicated by pre-laid ground beacons. One of the gliders, that carrying Leutnant Witzig and part of his Eben Emael Group, broke a tow-rope and landed in a field deep in Germany; another of the same group's gliders cast off too soon and never reached its objective. But the remainder reached the release point and let go the tow-ropes in free flight. The gliders nosed gracefully down towards the Belgium frontier, getting lower and lower until, one by one, their skids touched down, they ran forward twenty yards and stopped.

Even before a wing tip touched ground, the doors were off and soldiers poured out, as each bridge group (consisting of five infantry and four engineer sections) ran swiftly towards the pillboxes and bridges, returning fire opened upon them from the bridge defences. The advance proceeded in leaps and bounds until the engineers were within striking distance of the bunkers, dramatically neutralising them by using hollow charges to blow huge holes in their concrete, and then pouring flame and throwing grenades through the gaps. The two northern bridges at Veldvezelt and Vroenhofen were seized intact and demolition charges removed before they could be blown. The Belgian demolition firing party at Veldvezelt realised that the bridge was going to be captured and radioed to their HQ, three miles north, for permission to blow; but, in disbelief at the story of a glider attack and the presence of German troops on the bridge, permission was refused.

At Canne, surrounding hills delayed the gliders and they put down several hundred yards from their objective, thus forfeiting surprise. The defenders put up a heavy fire that prevented the engineers storming the pillboxes; the bridge was controlled from Fort Eben Emael, itself under attack, so permission for it to be blown was readily given, and it went up in the face of its frustrated attackers.

At Eben Emael, the nine remaining gliders of Witzig's group landed with precision on the roof and disgorged attackers who ran at will all over the exterior of the fort, systematically destroying the twelve emplacements from which fire could be brought to bear on the bridges and the surfaces of the forts. The paratroopers fired and flamed, threw grenades into the embrasures and loopholes, placed charges of TNT on turret-edges and gun barrels, jamming the turrets and destroying the guns, and attacked ventilators and periscopes. Hollow charges detonated on top of the emplacements and turrets blew holes through the armour and concrete, sending a jet of flame and molten metal into the turret structure to wreck internal machinery and kill or stun defenders. Those who survived were assailed by flame-throwers or small charges and grenades dropped through the holes. Blasting open steel doors, the invading paratroopers entered the fort and, once inside, were difficult to eject as the defenders had to attack up 60 feet of spiral staircase.

Crossing the Albert Canal in inflatable boats, pioneers of an engineer battalion brought heavy demolition charges, flame throwers, a Bangalore torpedo for wire cutting, and other materials for prising open the fort.

At 0830 a lone glider flew in from the east, across the Dutch and Belgian frontiers, circled over Eben Emael and touched down in one of the few remaining clear areas: it was Witzig, towed off by a relief aircraft, arriving three hours late to take part in the assault.

At 0610 hours German aircraft, taking casualties from now fully alerted defences, dropped reinforcements and ammunition at each of the bridges. Weak Belgian counter-attacks against the captured bridges were repulsed, and the Canne group, strengthened and reorganised, cleared the last defenders from the demolished structure.

In a few hours, at a cost of six dead and twenty wounded, the seventy paratroopers had neutralised Eben Emael, so that when the main ground forces (who had been delayed outside Maastricht) arrived and attacked the main entrance, the garrison capitulated.

The successful German airborne assault has come to be regarded as a classic example of what can be achieved by a small force against powerful defences, exemplifying the fullest exploitation of all the advantages that lie with the attacker – here they included the virtual beginning of a war rather than a battle. Tactical surprise was achieved by the silent approach of the gliders in an unprecedented landing method against which no defensive tactics had been considered.

Allied airborne assault on Sicily, July 1943

The Allied seaborne assault on Sicily was to be headed by the first large-scale Allied airborne assault, by units of 1st British and 82nd US Airborne divisions. In number and in quality both were quite capable of carrying out their allocated tasks, although air force and glider units lacked the adequate training and experience to carry out such operations in darkness. General Hopkinson, commander 1st British Airborne Division, had persuaded General Montgomery to begin the assault with a massed night glider descent in difficult country by inexperienced crews flying unfamiliar American gliders.

The 1st British Airborne Division was composed of Brigadier Lathbury's experienced 1st Brigade; Brigadier Downs's 2nd Brigade, and the 1st Air Landing Brigade of Brigadier Hicks, consisting of two infantry battalions – the South Staffords and the Border Regiment. The division was brought up to full strength with Brigadier Hackett's 4th Parachute Brigade from the Middle East. General Ridgway's 82nd US Division was formed of Colonel Tucker's 504th and General Gavin's 505th Parachute Infantry Regiments and the 325th Glider Infantry Regiment.

XII US Troop Carrier Command provided 331 C47s, 222 being allocated to the 82nd Division and 109 to the 1st British Division, who also had a squadron of 28 Albemarles and seven Halifaxes, supplied by 38 Wing RAF.

From America 140 Waco gliders arrived in crates, to be assembled by glider-pilots. Lieutenant-Colonel Chatterton, British glider pilot commander, ferried giant Horsa gliders, big enough to carry anti-tank guns and their towing-jeeps, from England to North Africa, nineteen arriving out of the twenty-nine that set out.

Supporting their own countrymen of 1st US Infantry Division, Gavin's 505th Regiment were to drop inland of the invasion beaches and secure Piano Lupo, vital high ground in the Gela area, plus other tasks. Their C47s, in 'V' formations of nine aircraft, were to fly just above sea level and rise to 600 feet during the final approach with pilots identifying DZs from aerial photographs; pathfinders were not used and the zones not marked.

Hicks's Air Landing Brigade were to capture the important Ponte Grande bridge near Syracuse in a three-phase attack – at 2315 hours 9 July, two companies in eight Horsa gliders were to land close to the bridge and seize it. At 0115 hours 10 July, the main body of the brigade in 136 Waco gliders were to come down on a larger LZ some two miles away and then move to the bridge, detaching one company to deal with a coastal defence battery. Finally, the South Staffords were to hold the bridge while the Border Regiment pressed on into Syracuse. Landing from the sea further south, ground troops were to link up by 1000 hours, 10 July.

Flying individually at low level from North Africa, gliders were taken up to 1,900 feet before being released 3,000 yards out to sea, to glide inland while the tug-aircraft returned. It was anticipated that all gliders would land within a twenty-minute period.

Two thousand British troops of the Air Landing Brigade in 137 American Waco and eight British Horsa gliders took off from Tunisian airfields on the evening of D–1 (9 July). Seven gliders did not get as far as the North African coast and about ninety per cent of the tugs entered the second leg of the journey from Malta with their gliders still in tow. The wind had increased to gale proportions, conditions were worsened by flying low to avoid radar detection, and coast landmarks were blotted out by a wall of dust raised by an offshore wind. There was but sparse moonlight.

These factors, perhaps accompanied by timidity on the part of the inexperienced pilots of the tug-aircraft, caused a majority of them to turn too soon for home so that about sixty per cent of the gliders were prematurely parted from their tugs because glider pilots had blindly to slip their tow-ropes. Seventy-five Wacos and three Horsas crash-landed in the sea, a few of their occupants being picked up from the floating wooden wreckage by passing assault-craft; others, including the brigade commander, swam for the shore. At least 252 men were drowned.

Only fifty-two gliders made landfall, a mere twelve landing anywhere near the target, the rest being widely scattered over an area covering twenty-five miles of coast. Of the six Horsas due to land beside the Ponte Grande, three landed two miles distant and their troops reached their objective later. Only two came down in the area; one of them hit the bank of the canal at speed and an explosive device destroyed aircraft and passengers; the other Horsa landed accurately and intact, following the beam of a convenient searchlight right down to the ground. It contained a platoon of fourteen men of the South Staffs under Lieutenant Withers, who sent seven men to swim across the river; then the two small parties attacked from north and south to capture the bridge and remove the explosives. During the night small groups joined them until at first light there was a mixed force of seven officers and eighty other ranks of the South Staffs and Borders; they were armed with their personal weapons, plus one 3-in and a 2-in mortar and four Bren guns. Constantly under shell-fire and attack by Italian infantry, the force held on until only fifteen men remained unwounded. Running out of ammunition, at 1500 hours they were overrun, but the Italians could not destroy the bridge as the explosive charges had been removed. British infantry eventually arrived at 1615 hours (more than six hours late), mounted an attack and secured the bridge. Hicks's Air Landing Brigade suffered 490 casualties, plus 88 casualties among the glider-pilots.

The aircraft carrying the American 505th Regiment lost formation and missed check points in the darkness, losing direction so that pilots approached Sicily from all points of the compass. Eventually, Gavin's Regiment were dropped some thirty miles from their correct dropping zone, scattered between Gela and Modica, some up to sixty-five miles off-course. Although numerous groups and individual paratroopers fought courageous and successful actions against the enemy wherever they encountered them, less than 200 men out of the 3,400 dropped were on the important high ground of Piano Lupo.

On the second night of the invasion, the 504th US Parachute Regiment were flown in as reinforcements to jump over the American-held Gela–Farella airstrip. All naval and army commanders and formations were given strict orders that anti-aircraft gunners were to hold their fire while the C47s were overhead. All was quiet when the first troop carrier formation arrived and their drop went smoothly. As following formations approached the dropping-zone, however, a single nervous machine-gunner set off a contagious outburst of anti-aircraft fire and within seconds every army and naval anti-aircraft gun for miles around was blasting away. Twenty-three of 144 aircraft that left Tunisia were destroyed, thirty-seven were badly damaged and eight returned with their passengers; 229 of the 2,000 paratroopers became casualties during the night – some were shot after landing when ground units convinced themselves they were facing a German airborne attack. Subsequently, the troop carriers dropped their men as inaccurately as on the previous night and by late afternoon on 12 July, only 558 of the 504th remained, although they had hardly been involved in ground-combat and had flown over no enemy-held territory.

To secure 8th Army's line of advance to Catania, 1st Battalion Parachute Brigade set out on 13 July to attack Primasole bridge spanning the River Simeto a few miles south of Catania. They emplaned in 105 C47s and eleven Albemarles with Halifaxes and Stirlings towing eight Waco gliders, and eleven Horsas carrying twelve medium anti-tank guns and crews, engineers and a medical section. Lathbury's Brigade (1st, 2nd and 3rd Bns – 1,900 men) were to land on four DZs and two glider LZs, west of the main road within two and a half miles of the bridge. The 1st Battalion were to approach the bridge from both sides and secure it; the 2nd and 3rd were to take the high ground south of the Gornalunga Canal and north of the Simeto. It was to be the first occasion when 21st Independent Parachute Company acted as pathfinders to light the glider LZs. The 50th Division and an armoured brigade were expected to link up with the paratroops during the following morning.

1st Airborne's RAF Adviser prevailed upon the American C47 pilots to abandon their usual formation tactics and fly as a 'bomber stream' (pairs of aircraft separated by one-and-a-half minute intervals) without appreciating that these aircrews, inexperienced in night navigation, relied on following-their-leader. Then Allied naval anti-aircraft gunners brought down two aircraft and damaged nine that had to turn back. This caused even greater dispersal and loss of course, accentuated by Axis anti-aircraft fire that shot down another thirty-seven aircraft and forced ten more to drop out and return home. Taking violent evasive action, pilots haphazardly dropped paratroopers and cast off gliders; thus thirty-nine aircraft dropped their troops within half-mile of DZs but the remaining forty-eight pilots ditched them many miles distant. Four out of the eight gliders that landed intact were in the right place, nine others crashed on landing or were lost at sea.

At dawn, of the 1,900 men who had taken off from North Africa, only 250 from 1st and 3rd Battalions with three anti-tank guns were on or around the bridge. The bridge demolition-charges removed, Lieutenant-Colonel Pearson (1st Battalion), in command of bridge defences, ordered his troops to dig in on the north side of the river; three anti-tank guns, two 3-in mortars, light machine guns and a Vickers were sited and the road mined.

On the previous day German General Heidrich's 1st Parachute Division had dropped south of Catania to reinforce the defenders – excellently demonstrating the value of airborne reserves during defensive operations. These experienced high-class troops were now sent against the British position at the bridge. Throughout the day Pearson's force resisted strongly against increasingly heavy German attacks by paratroopers, then infantry supported by tanks and self-propelled guns; fighter aircraft strafed incessantly. By early evening the survivors were forced to withdraw to south of the river but still denying the bridge to the enemy; then, under cover of darkness, they moved south to link up with Frost's 2nd Battalion operating in the hills south of the river. Next day contact was made with 50 Division infantry and tanks who had fought their way to a hill a mile short of 2nd Parachute Battalion's position, but it was not until the 15th that the infantry and armour were able to attack the bridge in what was a costly and unsuccessful assault. Several forceful attacks by British tanks, paratroopers and infantry were held by the Axis troops until, during the night of the 16th, Pearson led an attack by an indirect route and recaptured the intact Primasole bridge before dawn.

In Sicily, the 1st Airborne Division lost 454 dead, including 57 glider pilots, 240 wounded and 102 missing.

The Allied High Command were well aware that the airborne operations in Sicily (described by General Gavin as 'a self-adjusting foul-up') had been so technically inadequate that they put in doubt the whole future of airborne warfare. A painful Pyrrhic victory through inadequate crew training, errors in airborne methods and tactics, shortage of air transport and adverse weather conditions, nevertheless it is doubtful if without that experience faults would have been righted in time for D-Day.

Commando attack on the Ponte dei Malati Bridge, 13 July 1943

Shortly before the airborne assault by British 1st Parachute Brigade, No. 3 Commando were to land 10 miles ahead of 50 Division, at Angone with the objective of taking the Ponte dei Malati bridge which, like the Primasole Bridge, lay on the road running north to Catania. The distance separating these air and amphibious operations was sufficient for each to be quite independent of the other. The plan was for Nos. 1 and 3 Troops to push quickly inland to the bridge, while No. 2 Troop and Headquarters held the beach; No. 4 Troop was to send patrols north to contact 1st Parachute Brigade and south to 50 Division. Coming inshore in the moonlight, the assault craft came under enfilading fire from steep cliffs dominating the landing area. Commando leader Peter Young came ashore on the extreme right as his men swept towards wire obstacles, jostling to find a gap to a background hubbub of Troop commanders' whistles and No. 1 Troop's hunting horn, Young led a ragged column of commandos inland, moving along a railway track, one file on each side.

After marching over three miles of rough ground carpeted with cactus and orange groves, with occasional steep-sided ravines, Peter Young's commandos reached the bridge and took the defences on its northern aspect, attacking the pillboxes by dropping hand grenades through the gun-slits. About 300 commandos were on the spot and consolidated their position, having been reinforced by troops from the second beach landing. After a short period of quiet, a German half-track ammunition carrier appeared, to be destroyed by a section officer with a close-range Piat ambush, losing his life in doing so. Then they were shelled by a German tank, which left the area shortly, but was quickly replaced by strong enemy forces with more tanks. After removing charges from under the bridge and taking casualties while seeking to take the south end of the bridge, the commandos were forced to leave the area with the bridge still in enemy hands, breaking up into small parties and lying up under cover. The bridge was eventually taken some hours later when reached by 50 Division, who found it intact and unguarded.

Attack on Primasole Bridge, 13 July 1943

The first three days of the Sicilian invasion had gone well for the British and their next objective on the advance to Messina was Catania, twenty miles north. Seven miles north of that town the River Simeto wound its way towards the sea, being crossed by a road over the Primasole Bridge. As it was a natural defensive position, the Germans blocked the narrow coastal belt between the mountains and the sea with the Schmaltz Battle Group of the Hermann Göring Division and the Italian Napoli Division. Thus, they covered the Primasole Bridge, centrepiece of the vital area which was to be attacked by British 1st Parachute Brigade on 13 July, dropping some 20 miles north of the British 50th Division positions. Commanding the Brigade, Brigadier Lathbury planned to land on four dropping zones and two glider-landing zones, within a radius of 2½ miles of the bridge and all west of the main road – the 1st Para Battalion were to secure the bridge itself while the 2nd and 3rd respectively held the approaches from the south and north. In the event, the dropping routine became chaotic with forty-eight of the air-craft dropping their loads from half a mile to more than ten miles distant, thirty-nine dropped their troops within half a mile, the remainder were shot down or failed to drop troops; four out of the eight gliders that landed intact were in the right place and nine others crash-landed or were lost at sea. At dawn there were less than 300 men with 3 anti-tank guns on or around the objective, but they held the bridge and demolition charges were removed; rapid reinforcement was essential.

Throughout the day the British airborne troops, a force that numbered less than one-sixth of their intended numbers, defended the bridge against recently dropped German airborne forces, later reinforced by artillery and supported by fighter aircraft. Directed by parachute artillery observers, fire from an offshore British cruiser's 6-in guns broke up a German attack on the high ground south of the river, held by the 2nd Battalion of the brigade. But the under-strength force holding the area came under pressure that forced the remnants of the 1st and 3rd Battalions, still denying the bridge to the Germans, to move south under cover of darkness and join the 2nd Battalion.

Slowly advancing towards the beleaguered airborne troops, the infantry and supporting tanks of the 50th Division were within a mile of the 2nd Parachute Battalion's position by nightfall on the 14th. On the morning of the 15th the infantry made a costly, unsuccessful attack on the bridge, but an indirect approach during the night captured the Primasole Bridge by dawn on the 15th. As in the case of the Ponte Grande, although airborne troops had been forced off their objectives, they had managed to remove explosive charges on the bridge so that it was eventually captured intact.

D-Day landings in Normandy, 6 June 1944

The British airborne brigades were given diverse tasks. Poett's 5th were to capture the bridges over the Caen Canal, and the River Orne at Benouville and Ranville. A party was to land in gliders five hours before dawn, then paratroops were to drop in brigade strength to take over the bridges, and establish defensive positions in the surrounding villages, orchards and farmland. At the same time, Hill's 3rd Brigade were to neutralise the heavy-calibre guns in the concrete-emplaced coastal battery at Merville, before daylight exposed the invasion fleet. Then, the bridges at Varaville, Robehomme, Bures and Troarn were to be destroyed to prevent enemy rein-forcements passing south; the ridge Le-Plein–Le Mesnil–Troarn dominating the Dives river-line and the east-west lines of communications had to be seized, before the brigade concentrated in the woods and orchards of the Bois de Bavent. On the afternoon of D-Day, Kindersley's 6th Air Landing Brigade were to be brought in near Ranville to help secure the canal and river crossings.

At 2303 hours 5 June 1944, six Albemarles carrying sixty pathfinders of 22nd Independent Parachute Company took off as the spearhead of the invasion of Europe. Immediately following were six gliders bearing the Oxford and Bucks Light and Royal Engineers, bound for the Caen Canal and Orne bridges; then the two Parachute Brigades were airborne, followed by an assault party from 9th Parachute Battalion in the three gliders that were to make a pin-point crash-landing on the Merville battery.

The night sky pulsated with the throb of more than a thousand aircraft engines as the Allied airborne troops began the invasion of France on a night of grey cloud that screened the moon, as light rain misted the cockpit windows.

When 82nd and 101st US Airborne Divisions began dropping their leading units at 0130 hours on D-Day it became immediately apparent that their pathfinders had landed wide of the mark, frequently failing to locate the exact DZs. This caused 101st Division to be scattered over a 15-25-mile area, with 1,500 paratroopers either killed or captured immediately after landing, and about sixty per cent of their equipment lost when bundles were dropped into swamps and woods. Enraged paratroopers reported that the pilots, hedge-hopping to avoid flak, were flying too low for parachutes to open. Most of the American difficulties were caused by deficiencies in aircrew training and performance, and poor weather; the night glider landings were made at a high cost to life and stores – only a small proportion of anti-tank guns and equipment reached the paratroopers who badly needed them. Daylight reinforcement landings were much more successful.

In spite of concentration difficulties, 101st quickly seized objectives behind Utah Beach and when the glider regiment was flown in later, the western ends of the causeway leading inland and the bridges over the Douvre River were quickly taken.

Hindered by dense clouds, the 82nd Division drop was widely dispersed and they were forced to fight isolated battles, failing to occupy the river's banks, or to destroy its bridges. Rendezvousing on the village of St Mère-Eglise as instructed was almost the only part of their plans that went right. But by courage and determination they overcame all difficulties. By dawn they were holding a firm divisional perimeter around the area, and west of the Merderet River were fiercely engaged in preventing the German 91st Division from moving eastwards. Although handicapped by the death of their commander, throughout the day this division made determined but unsuccessful efforts to dislodge the American paratroopers and link up with their isolated beach defences.

Despite their scattered delivery, both American airborne divisions succeeded in most essentials without the predicted fearful casualties from anti-
aircraft fire and enemy fighters. At D-Day plus one, both divisions had
linked up to form a six-mile bridgehead.

The airborne sector presented an incongruous and colourful scene at
daybreak with hundreds of coloured silken canopies strewn in the fields and

On DZ 'N' near Ranville, as some 2,000 men of 5th Parachute Brigade
disentangled themselves from their parachutes, they encountered some
opposition from German defences alerted by the pathfinders. Men lost their
bearings in the waist-high Normandy corn, and by 0300 hours Lieutenant-
Colonel Pine-Coffin was accompanied by only about forty per cent of his 7th
Parachute Battalion as he moved off to link with Howard's men on the river
and canal bridges. Behind them, airborne engineers worked hard clearing the
area of obstacles for the glider landings that were to come later in the day.
draped across hedgerows; parachute harnesses hung limply by rigging-
lines from the branches of trees, and empty containers were scattered
across the dropping-zones; some lay unopened in lanes and ditches.

Johnston's 12th Battalion of the brigade captured the village of Le Bas
de Ranville and dug themselves in, as Luard's 13th Battalion occupied
Ranville le Mariquet. Both were taken in face of fierce resistance and held
against counter-attacks supported by tanks and self-propelled guns. In
spite of the Rommelspargel, some cargo gliders had been included in this
force and the anti-tank guns and crews were invaluable, destroying at least
one tank and three self-propelled guns.

By dawn, B Company 7th Parachute Battalion had reached the Caen
Canal bridge and came under heavy counter-attack; the battalion, occupying Benouville, withstood eight counter-attacks and many attempts to infil-
trate its defensive positions. At 1000 hours General Gale and his staff,
wearing red berets, arrived on the scene; at 1300 hours, five hours before
other seaborne units, Lord Lovat and a lustily blowing bagpiper marched in
at the head of No.1 Commando, to link with the paratroopers in holding their
objective.

Six gliders released their tow-ropes 5,000 feet above the mouth of the
Orne and divided, to aim for the canal bridge LZ 'X' and the river-bridge LZ
'Y'. It was planned for three Horsa gliders to land between each bridge,
their six platoons to take out enemy guards, remove demolition charges
and hold off counter-attacks for an estimated two hours until reinforced by
7th Battalion, who at 0050 hours were to jump a mile east of the river. Spot-
ting the bridges 3,000 feet below, the leading Horsa made for them
descending on half-flap until, at a thousand feet, an arrester-parachute was
released and the glider touched down less than 100 yards short of the
bridge, breaking through the perimeter wire of the German defences. The
other two gliders followed in and landed a few yards away.

216

Major Howard led the assault party of the Oxford and Bucks Light Infantry in a race for the bridge under a hail of Schmeisser machine-gun fire; one platoon overran the defenders on the far side of the bridge while the others cleared a pillbox and a network of trenches on the near bank. Of the three gliders heading for the Orne bridge, two landed within a few hundred yards of their objective which they secured without opposition. The demolition charges on both bridges were swiftly removed and linked bridge-heads formed astride the canal and river. The third glider touched down fifteen miles to the east in the Dives valley.

At 0020 Hours, British pathfinders dropped on DZ 'N' north-east of Ranville; 'K' west of Troarn, and 'V' between the Merville battery and Varaville. Elsewhere sticks of pathfinders had not always been dropped accurately, although good enough to avoid the chaos that occurred with 82nd US Division.

Dropped from C47s, 3rd Parachute Brigade were the victims of inaccurate delivery through failure to locate DZs, or the inadequacy of Eureka pathfinder beacons. Several sticks of 1st Canadian and 9th Parachute Battalion dropped near the River Dives intending to use the marshes as a natural flank barrier, but the Germans had flooded the area and many parachutists went straight into the water.

Landing before 0100 hours on DZ 'V' near Varaville, an area of orchards and fields divided by bocage, only about fifty per cent of the widely scattered Canadians arrived at their rendezvous and moved off to capture and destroy the bridges over the river, before moving to the northern end of the Bois de Bavent.

Landing on DZ 'K' west of the Bures and Troarn bridges and well south of the other battalions, Pearson's 8th Battalion, only 180 strong, utilised engineer's jeeps to drive through the confused enemy to reach and destroy the two Dives bridges; then they occupied the southern part of the Bois de Bavent. Here Colonel Pearson, a courageous and militant commander, used his battalion in an offensive patrolling role as though an outpost of a formidable defence that deterred the enemy from attacking.

The most wondrous and splendid spectacle of D-Day came late in the warm, sunny evening.

Men who that morning had felt the exhilaration of the first victory on the beaches were tiring, yet mentally they were tensed, waiting for the expected counter-attack from the 12th SS Hitler Youth and 21st Panzer Divisions.

Suddenly someone gasped: 'Cor blimey – look!' As they gazed up over their shoulders the men's eyes brightened, their hearts throbbed warm. The sky seemed filled with aircraft as gracefully, majestically, 250 gliders sailed in. Over the coast the aircraft cast off and turned back towards England: for a second each glider seemed to pause then, swiftly and silently, dived down into the bridgehead. The 6th Air Landing Brigade had come in to reinforce the hard-pressed 6th Airborne Division on the left flank.

No Luftwaffe aircraft had attempted to intercept; the RAF tug-planes seemed to disdain the flak that burst around them. It was simply a superb manifestation of the complete Allied domination in the air over the front.

In a few minutes it was all over. The gliders were down, the aircraft back over the horizon; yet every man in the bridgehead felt a warm glow of pride mingled with reassurance. But it was east of the Orne where they touched down that the gliders were most welcome. There the paratroops and advance gliders had already been in action for some twenty hours, fighting desperately against increasing odds to hold the vital bridges over the Orne and the Caen Canal.

They were the spearhead of the invasion. Of them there are no pictures: they came in darkness. There is only the story, a story of courage and heroism that was unsurpassed in this day when bravery was commonplace.

The battle for the bridges began just after midnight.

Still far out in the Channel, the invasion armada was steaming steadily towards Normandy when the first six gliders slipped their tow-ropes and sped down towards their objectives, the only sound being the sigh of the wind whistling past their wings. At the canal three gliders crash-landed almost on the bridge itself. The men leapt out frantically into bedlam as the enemy opened up with Spandaus and rifles. Scorning the fire, the 'Red Devils' hurled themselves on the enemy positions and, in a matter of minutes, the first small, vital battle of the invasion was fought and won.

Near by the men bound for the Orne bridge touched down some way from their objective. Crashing out of their wrecked gliders, they moved forward without a pause ready for action: but there was none – the enemy had fled.

Both bridges had been taken intact.

In the meantime the pathfinders had marked out the dropping zones and over 2,000 paratroops came in. It was a difficult drop, many having to jump from weaving aircraft with a 60lb kit-bag tied to one leg.

In the wilderness of the night men were slow to rally. Due to launch a battalion attack against the strongly held Merville battery, which could threaten the seaborne assault, the commanding officer of the 9th Parachute Battalion found he had only 150 men – but the attack went in and after a desperate bloody battle lasting over an hour the position was taken, a success signal fired, and a carrier pigeon despatched with the news.

Before the dawn of D-Day General Gale's 6th Airborne Division were in position and holding the enemy. Meanwhile to the west the 82nd and 101st US Airborne Divisions had landed on the neck of the Cotentin peninsula. Running into flak, the pilots of the aircraft flew too fast and too high, making the jumping exceedingly difficult, men being scattered over a wide area. The 101st Division were particularly badly scattered and of over 6,000 parachutists, only 1,000 had reached their rendezvous by dawn.

The 82nd Division took Ste Mère Eglise to block the Carentan–Cherbourg road, but elsewhere in the dropping zone the paratroops were so heavily engaged fighting for their lives they had no chance of performing their operational tasks of blowing the bridges over the River Douve, or forming a compact bridgehead over the Merderet.

Never was night so long as, fighting valiantly, the Allied airborne forces held off all attacks and waited for the seaborne troops to land with the dawn. Only then could they expect reinforcements.

Operation 'Market Garden', 17–26 September 1944

Devised by General Montgomery commanding the Allied 21st Army Group, Operation 'Market Garden' planned for airborne forces to seize bridges in advance of British 2nd Army as it struck north-east from the Meuse-Escaut Canal towards the Zuider Zee. Its aim was to cut off the German forces in Western Holland, outflank the Siegfried Line defences to the north, cross the River Rhine and sweep down in the heart of Germany – to end the war in 1944. The essence of this daring and ambitious plan was speed, to throw the enemy off-balance long enough to allow the Allies to complete their decisive stroke before being halted through lack of supplies. Two-pronged, the 'Garden' part of the operation was the ground advance of General Horrocks's British XXX Corps, with XII and XIII Corps advancing more slowly on the western and eastern flanks respectively. As the countryside was largely waterlogged, movement was virtually restricted to a single road, only wide enough for one tank.

The 'Market' part of the operation required airborne troops to hold open the canal and river crossings on the Eindhoven–Arnhem road and defend them until relieved by ground forces, thus providing a sixty-mile airborne carpet for the ground troops to advance over. This meant that five major bridges had to be taken and held. It was estimated that the northern-most bridge at Arnhem could not be reached until between forty-eight and seventy-two hours after the start of the operation. General Browning, the British Corps Commander, expressed a note of caution when he said, 'We can hold the Arnhem bridge for four days, but I think we might be going a bridge too far.'

The operation was to be carried out by all available troops and aircraft of US General Brereton's 1st Allied Airborne Army, under British General Browning's corps command. There was the US XVIII Airborne Corps (US 82nd and 101st Airborne Divisions); British 1st Airborne Corps (1st and 6th Airborne Divisions, 1st Special Air Service and 1st Polish Independent Parachute Brigades); the British 52nd Lowland Division – the Airborne

Army's air-landing formation; the Delivery Group, Engineers and an anti-air-craft unit – lifted by the IX United States troop carrier command and the RAF's 38th and 46th Groups. The entire airborne force for the 'Market' operation consisted of more than 25,000 troops, 511 vehicles, 330 artillery pieces and 590 tons of equipment. General Browning planned to bring about two-thirds of his Airborne Division in on Lift One on 17 September and to fly the balance of these divisions, with supplies, in on the 18th and 19th; 52nd (Lowland) Division to stand by for flying into an airfield north of Arnhem after it had been taken by ground forces. The Delivery Group, with engineers and anti-aircraft artillery, were to be held in readiness to glider-land in any of the divisional areas, to improvise and operate an airstrip, if necessary. From south to north, divisional tasks were as follows.

US 101st Airborne Division were to drop north of Eindhoven to seize and hold the bridges on XXX Corps line of advance – at Eindhoven, over the Wilhelmina Canal at Zon, the Zuit Willensvaart Canal at Veghel and the River Aa, plus two other smaller bridges.

US 82nd Division were to drop and take the Groesbeek, the sole domi-nating land feature. They were also to take and hold bridges over the Maas at Grave, over the Maas–Waal Canal just west of Nijmegen and over the Waal on the northern outskirts of the town. This involved defending a perimeter much larger than could normally be held by a single division. Subsequently Browning told General Gavin, the divisional commander, to first secure the high ground, leaving the Waal bridge until circumstances permitted dispersion of his forces. Lifts Two and Three were planned to arrive on the Groesbeek feature as reinforcements.

Of 1st British Airborne Division, Lathbury's 1st Parachute Brigade were to drop on DZ 'X' north of the river some six miles west of Arnhem bridge which they were to seize, with the pontoon bridge 1200 yards away and to hold north and south banks east of Arnhem. Simultaneously, Hicks's 1st Air-Landing Brigade in 345 Horsa and 13 Hamilcar gliders would land on LZ 'Z', just north of DZ 'X', secure the landing areas for the lifts on the follow-ing day and then occupy an area on both banks of the river extending west-wards from Arnhem about a mile beyond Oosterbeek. Gough's Reconnaissance Squadron (in armoured jeeps) were to make the initial assault on the Arnhem bridge. On the following day, Hackett's 4th Para-chute Brigade were to drop from 127 C47s on DZ 'Y' 2,000 yards north-west of 'X' and 'Z'. LZ 'S' to the east of DZ 'Y' was to receive 286 Horsas and 15 Hamilcars carrying the remainder of 1st Air Landing Brigade and the Royal Artillery, who were to seize the high ground north of Arnhem. On the third day, Sosabowski's 1st Polish Independent Parachute Brigade Group were on-call to drop from 114 C47s on DZ 'K', one mile south of the Arn-hem bridge, to assist in the capture of the bridge if necessary and pass through 1st Parachute Brigade to hold ground north-east of the town. More

Polish troops and engineers were to come in gliders on LZ 'L', used on the previous day as a re-supply area.

The main tactical flaw in the British plan was the location of the dropping and landing zones for General Urquhart's 1st Airborne Division which ought to be dropped as close as possible to the Arnhem bridge, accepting some landing casualties to prevent the bridge being destroyed before capture. With 1st Parachute Bde. dropped close to the bridge and 4th Bde. on high ground north of Arnhem, supported and supplied from the air, the Division could have held out for a long period. But regarded as air operations, airborne activities were under RAF control until the troops actually landed and concern over possible heavy casualties from AA fire caused the RAF to disagree to the proposed landing sites. Subsequently Generals Browning and Urquhart, led to believe by intelligence reports that their men could march to the objectives with little danger, agreed to dropping zones some five miles from their objectives in Arnhem.

The 82nd and 101st US Divisions devoted more than three-quarters of their first-day lift to foot-soldiers, whereas the British decided to allot only half their first-day capacity to infantry, instead transporting all their vehicles and heavy gear on the first day rather than delivering all three parachute brigades supported by anti-tank weapons, or two parachute brigades and a glider brigade, keeping a parachute brigade in reserve. The 1st Air Landing Brigade had to remain out of the battle to guard the landing areas so that the 4th Parachute Brigade and the balance of the gliders could come in safely on the following day. Thus of four brigades, only one (the 1st) was to attempt to seize the division's objectives during the first twenty-four hours. In general, Browning's corps plan possessed inflexible aspects that totally disregarded the enemy's reaction – a time-table laid down when and where each unit was to be delivered during the three days of the air lift, instead of the uncommitted troops being held in reserve to be employed as the situation demanded. Optimistic appraisals of the operation arose from hopelessly incorrect Intelligence assessments of German strength in the area, and a disregard of Dutch Resistance reports of local concentrations of German armour (including 'twenty to thirty Tiger tanks'). In fact, General Bittrich's élite although battered veteran II SS Panzer Corps had reached rest areas in the vicinity of Arnhem a few days earlier. Extricated from battle and sent to the area for refitting and rehabilitation, Harzer's 9th 'Hohenstaufen' Division of 6,000 men, twenty Mk V tanks, some self-propelled guns, armoured cars and forty armoured personnel carriers with heavy machineguns plus artillery were hidden in the densely wooded National Park north and north-west of Arnhem. And Harmel's 10th 'Frundsberg' Division, desperately short of armoured vehicles but with formidable artillery, mortar and anti-aircraft units, was encamped in a semi-circle to the north-east, east and south-east of the Dutch town. One of Germany's most competent, experienced senior officers, General-Feldmarschall Model, had set up his headquarters in Oosterbeek, three miles from the broad expanse of heathland where the 1st British Airborne Division were scheduled to land on 17 September. To make room for Model's headquarters, Krafft's understrength SS Panzer Grenadier Training and Reserve Battalion's three companies (another 1,000 SS recruits were due to arrive at any moment for training) bivouacked in the woods and farms north-west of Oosterbeek, not far from the village of Wolfheze – directly between the zones where the British 1st Airborne Division were to land, blocking the route into Arnhem.

Moreover, within the week preceding the attack, the experienced General Student had moved to an HQ at Vught, between Nijmegen and Eindhoven, to recreate his 1st Parachute Army and establish a defence line in-depth behind the Albert Canal covering the front from Antwerp to Maastricht. One of Student's units, von der Heydte's 6th Parachute Regiment had provided stiff opposition to a Guard's Armoured Division attack on 10 September to secure a bridgehead across the Maas–Scheldt Canal twelve miles south of Eindhoven, as a preliminary to Operation 'Garden'.

General Model was an experienced soldier whose rapid reactions could well lead to improvised but flexible defences, and General Student, one of the most experienced airborne leaders in the world, could possibly outguess the Allied commanders and frustrate their intentions.

During the night of 16/17 September, the RAF attacked airfields in Holland; in the morning two waves of 139 Lancasters and 20 Mosquitos attacked German anti-aircraft positions, followed by 816 Flying Fortresses escorted by 161 Mustangs and 212 P47s, who bombed coastal anti-aircraft and inland batteries.

Sunday 17 September 1944 was bright and clear as Lift One took off from seven British and seventeen United States airfields scattered from Dorset to Lincolnshire – an armada formed of two great streams of 2,023 carrier-planes, tugs and gliders. The smaller stream of 494 C47s and 70 Waco gliders carrying 101st US Division flew a southerly course, crossing the English Channel at the North Foreland, proceeding almost due east to Gheel, wheeling left to dropping-and-landing-zones north of Eindhoven. A larger column, the US 82nd Airborne and paratroop elements of the 1st British Airborne Division took off in 625 troop carrier planes and 50 gliders towed by C47s from air bases in the Grantham area. At five- to twenty-second intervals the IXth Troop Carrier Command's planes left the ground to rendezvous in wave after wave before setting out in three parallel streams to cross the coast near Aldeburgh. From eight bases in Gloucestershire and Oxfordshire huge sky 'serials' raised gliders and tugs at an unparalleled launch rate of one combination per minute. Their very numbers made forming-up intricate and dangerous as they climbed slowly to altitude and headed west over the Bristol Channel; then, with their speeds synchronised, the tugs and gliders echeloned to the right in pairs, and made for the marshalling point above Hatfield, north of London. Innumerable Sky-trains of British bombers – Halifaxes, Stirlings and Albemarles, tugged equipment-and-troop-carrying gliders, bounding behind them at the end of 300-foot-long ropes with massive Hamilcars ploughing along among the smaller Horsa and Waco gliders.

Landing furthest north at Arnhem, the British required artillery and anti-tank guns in the first lift to capture and hold their objectives until land forces could link up. This meant that gliders carried the bulk of General Urquhart's Division. The 135 troop-carrying planes bearing Brigadier Lathbury's 1st Parachute Brigade did not take off until half an hour later because the paratroop-carrier planes were capable of 140 miles an hour against the 120 miles an hour of the unwieldy gliders and tugs.

Immaculate General 'Boy' Browning was in a glider piloted by Brigadier Chatterton, Commanding Officer of the Glider Pilot Regiment. His Corps Headquarters bound for Nijmegen, travelled in a special series of thirty-eight gliders, with the 82nd Airborne and 1st British Divisions along the northern track.

Air-Sea Rescue launches were positioned in a chain across the North Sea to pick up survivors on the few occasions when an aircraft put down with engine trouble, or a glider tow-rope snapped. Technical and other difficulties caused twelve gliders to ditch in the sea or force-land well short of their objective. Lift One was remarkably successful: enemy anti-aircraft fire destroyed 35 C47s and 16 Waco gliders carrying the American Divisions but not a single troop-carrier on the Arnhem lift was lost through enemy action. The extensive preliminary air operations were the reason for the slight losses in carrier aircraft during the outward journey, and the two carrier fleets were also protected by 371 Tempests, Spitfires and Mosquitos, 548 Thunderbolts, Mustangs and Lightnings.

Precisely at midday, in the face of light small-arms fire, pathfinders of the 21st Independent Parachute Company dropped from twelve Stirlings to capture a German platoon position. On landing they set up their beacons to mark the LZs and DZs and waited for the deep throb of the glider-tugs and carrier aircraft. Occurring between 1315 and 1400 hours, the glider landings were the most successful of the war as the pilots skilfully brought in their flimsy craft on to the pathfinders' smoke signals and orange-and-crimson nylon markers. Two Hamilcars nosed into the soft soil and overturned, disabling two valuable heavy anti-tank guns, and thirty-five more gliders failed to make the landing zone, including those carrying the Reconnaissance Squadron's armoured jeeps. The glider-borne troops moved away as the C47s arrived and the blue sky blossomed with more than 2,000 varied coloured parachutes of the 1st Parachute Brigade floating gently down to earth, dropping accurately and safely onto their zone, with negligible landing casualties, and everyone in his right place at the right time.

Back in Belgium General Horrocks, standing on a slag heap by the Meuse–Escaut Canal, had his field glasses pointed northwards seeking the airborne armada. The Guards Armoured Division headed some 20,000 vehicles awaiting orders that would send them clattering down the road to Eindhoven. At 1330 hours, the tanks of the Irish Guards led off XXX Corps attack, behind a moving barrage fired by 350 guns; overhead 200 RAF Typhoon fighter bombers screamed down to silence the German anti-tank batteries who, from well-sited positions, were already inflicting losses on British armour. Immediately it became clear that the 'Garden' part of the operation was going to be a desperate and urgent business if the essential speed of advance was to be attained so that the airborne divisions were not sacrificed. Major Gough's Reconnaissance Squadron, without their jeeps, could make only a greatly reduced attempt through woods and villages to capture the Arnhem bridge by coup-de-main – none got through. Lieutenant-Colonel John Frost's 2nd Parachute Battalion marched in single lines on either side of the road that ran close to the north bank of the River Rhine, advanced into Heelsum and through the Doorwertsch wood. Fitch's 3rd Battalion north of them, set off on a more direct route along the main Utrecht–Arnhem road; Dobie's 1st Battalion moved off to approach Arnhem on the high ground via Wolfheze on the Ede–Arnhem road. The peaceful atmosphere of the dropping zones prevailed for the firs two miles of the advance, and well-dressed Dutch civilians poured out to greet their deliverers as they marched past red-tiled cottages and palatial villas.

The Air Landing Brigade took up defensive positions to protect the Landing Zone for the Second Lift's arrival on the following day. Forty officers and 700 other ranks of the 7th Battalion King's Own Scottish Borderers marched off to positions surrounding Dropping Zone 'Y' at Ginkel Heath, with pipers at their head playing 'Blue Bonnets'. It was to be the 7th KOSB's first and last action of the Second World War and at its end only four officers and 72 men remained. McCardie's 2nd South Staffords dug-in around the perimeter of LZ 'S' near Reyerscamp, to the east of the Scots; Hadden's 1st Battalion Border Regiment occupied their allotted area south of the railway line at Renkum Heath.

The Germans acted swiftly to the landings. Field Marshal Model abandoned his headquarters at Oosterbeek and drove to Arnhem where he gave orders to General Kussim, commander of the town garrison; then east to Doetinchem to Bittrich's II Panzer Corps HQ, who had already issued orders to his two SS panzer divisions. General Horzer's 9th SS Panzer Division 'Hohenstaufen' were rapidly to occupy the Arnhem area and destroy the enemy forces who had landed to the west of the town, denying them the bridge at Arnhem. The 9th SS Panzer Division split into two groups on arriving in Arnhem on the evening of the 17th. Brinkmanns's group patrolled the town with armoured infantry to clear British parachutists from houses, while Spindler's Sperrgruppe (blocking-group) formed a barrier of armour and infantry on the outskirts of the town and patrolled forward along the three approach routes. The 10th SS Panzer 'Frunsberg' Division moved quickly to Nijmegen and occupied the main bridge area in strength.

A set of Allied operation orders found on the body of an American officer killed when one of the 82nd US Division's Waco gliders was brought down by AA fire had come into General Student's hands, and after the war, the German Airborne Commander wrote: 'The importance of this capture was immense, for we learnt at once of the enemy's strength and intentions and the speed and comparative success of our counter-action was to no small extent due to early knowledge of this hostile move.' At the time of the drops, the only Germans between the landing areas and Arnhem were the SS Training and Depot Battalion under Krafft who witnessed the landings and positioned his force in a screen running north to south, about halfway between Oosterbeek and the British assembly areas. Acting as a delaying group between the DZs and the bridge, Krafft's force won time for the 9th SS Panzer Division to get into position, and played an important role in the battle that had just begun. As the day drew on, in the centre Lippert's and Krafft's battalions were in position with machine-guns, mortars and riflemen; von Tettau's units were moving in from the north and west; and Brinkmann's men were edging along the north bank of the river.

Through the mist of the autumn evening, the British 1st Airborne Division and the German 9th SS Panzer Division were both moving towards the Arnhem bridge, with the Germans possessing the great advantage of being aware of their opponents' general position and intention, whereas the airborne force were not even aware of the existence of the German armoured formation! Meanwhile, the 1st Battalion on the river road had advanced through Heelsum, ambushing German vehicles and taking prisoners despite opposition in the Doorwertch wood. B Company attacked enemy machine-gun positions on the Den Brink high ground and then moved to capture the brigade's second bridge target, the pontoon bridge that was still undamaged although the Germans had removed some of the barges and towed them to a nearby dock.

Throughout, the 1st could raise nobody on their radios and inter-unit communication was non-existent. By dusk, A Company, 2nd Battalion, were near the road bridge in Arnhem and Lieutenant Grayburn's platoon attempted to rush the bridge from the north but were turned back by two quick-firing 20mm flak-guns and the machine guns of an armoured car. Although wounded, Grayburn organised his force in a house near the approaches to the bridge. Frost led his determined party towards their objective; taking advantage of the darkness which hampered German fire

and hindered their armour, the paratroopers brushed aside minor opposition at the northern end of the road bridge which they reached at 2000
hours. Frost established his headquarters in a house in De Kraan street
north-west of the bridge, which was intact but under mortar fire, and sent a
runner to B Company ordering them to cross the river in boats to secure the
southern end of the bridge. But this group was still engaged in a sharp fight
at Den Brink and there was no sign of C Company who were fighting hard
at the railway bridge near Den Brink. Fortifying the houses controlling the
northern approaches to the bridge, Frost's party launched several attacks
against the Germans holding the southern end of the objective, but all were
beaten back.

During the night elements of Fitch's 3rd Battalion, 1st Brigade Headquarters, some Engineers, and the HQ of the Reconnaissance Squadron,
with a platoon of service troops, slipped through on the same southern river
road to reinforce Frost's party, so that by daylight he commanded some
600-700 men. This small party represented the net strength on the main
objective from a tactical plan based on more than 10,000 men, 92 guns,
500 jeeps, 400 trailers and 300 motor-cycles.

Their approach route remained open for so long that better reconnaissance could have redirected the whole of the 1st Parachute Brigade to the
bridge by that route. Had not the 1st Air Landing Brigade been ordered to
protect DZs and LZs for Lift Two's arrival on the following day they could
have been pushed through hard on the heels of Frost's party. Nevertheless
this small force on the bridge had completely disrupted German defensive
plans as only one company of Panzer Grenadier Infantry had crossed the
bridge to reinforce the Nijmegen garrison before Frost's party had isolated
the main body of 10th Panzer Division on the wrong side of the Rhine.
Model must have been well aware that if the airborne attack at Nijmegen
were to be held and the XXX Corps relief force halted, then the small party
of British paratroopers on the northern edge of the Arnhem bridge had to
be rapidly removed.

On the central approach route, the 3rd Parachute Battalion had been
slowed by mortar fire from Krafft's defensive screen and then halted completely by armoured vehicles of 9th SS Division. In an early encounter General Kussin, commander of the Arnhem garrison, drove headlong into the
battalion and was immediately killed.

The 1st Battalion on the northern approach route were warned by Major
Gough that tanks were blocking the road and Panzer Grenadiers in position
along the railway line from Wolfheze to Arnhem; subsequently the battalion
entrenched themselves on the edge of the line of woods east of Wolfheze
station.

General Urquhart, badly handicapped by lack of communication through
inefficient radios whose effectiveness was limited by the heavily wooded

terrain, had personally to acquaint himself with the situation, so he and Brigadier Lathbury set off in a jeep and eventually spent the night of the 17th with the 3rd Battalion halted on the Utrecht–Arnhem road.

Throughout the night the struggle for Arnhem bridge swung in the balance and substantial reinforcements might have enabled Frost's party to affect the battle decisively. By daylight they were securely lodged at the northern end of the bridge in groups in houses and warehouses, repulsing with grenades, anti-tank guns and Piats, attacks by armoured cars and Panzer Grenadiers in half-tracks. German counter-attacks were prevented from forming up on the southern approaches by continuous machine-gun fire directed across the bridge. Soon the northern end, under fire by guns and mortars, was a blazing inferno strewn with the wreckage of vehicles and the debris of war.

Gradually, British 1st Airborne Division were relinquishing the initiative, being unable to hold off assaults by mobile armoured forces because of lack of offensive air-support fire-power denied them through confusion in responsibility. In a house outside the main defensive perimeter, exposed and difficult to defend, Lieutenant Grayburn and the survivors of his platoon held out against ceaseless enemy attacks for two days, until German tanks and self-propelled guns firing at under 100 yards range forced them from their positions. Grayburn led repeated fighting patrols to prevent the enemy laying demolition charges, consistently exposing himself to point-blank enemy fire until he was killed by a flame-thrower. Lieutenant Grayburn, 2nd Parachute Battalion, was posthumously awarded the Victoria Cross.

Lack of communications now played a vital part in the battle. On the morning of the 18th, 1st Parachute Brigade plus divisional troops were to be dropped on the western DZs, held by the Air Landing Brigade. But the Germans had successfully halted the advance from these DZs, and to use them again was to reinforce failure. Had 4th Brigade's DZ been switched to the subsequently unused DZ 'J' south of the approaches to Arnhem bridge, then they could have linked-up with Frost's force and the three battalions of the Air Landing Brigade would have been freed from their unproductive task to take a more constructive part in the battle. With General Urquhart missing, no one on the spot could alter arrangements and General Browning, on the Groesbeek, could have no idea of the situation.

Fog delayed landings until 1500 hrs, when Hackett's 4th Parachute Brigade were dropped and decimated four miles west of their objective, being flown in at 500 feet through AA shell bursts and the smoke from blazing woodland around the zones, dropping into heavy small-arms fire. The Air Landing Brigade were fighting hard to keep the enemy off the DZ. Payton Reid's 7th KSOB fixed bayonets and desperately charged to clear the woods, fields and ditches of Germans firing at the descending parachutists. On landing, Brigadier Hackett learned that General Urquhart was missing and that Brigadier Hicks of the Air Landing Brigade was acting in his place (as the General had earlier specified). Being senior to Hicks, Hackett drove to Divisional Headquarters where the two brigadiers had an argument as to who was in command!

The strongest efforts were being made to reach Frost. Before nightfall on the 17th, Fitch's 3rd Battalion, enfiladed from high ground on both sides by machine-guns and mortars, and by artillery firing from the south of the river, desperately tried to press forward into the town. Eventually the regiment were split in half and fell back under cover of darkness to the Rhine Pavilion on the embankment. At daylight on the 18th, the 3rd Battalion, with the 1st and 11th Battalions and the South Staffs, doggedly fought their way yard-by-yard into the town, trying to force a passage through a network of streets lying between the railway line and the river. The 1st Battalion moved along the lower road on the embankment, swinging left for the bridge, as the other two battalions advanced along the main road from the St Elizabeth hospital. The South Staffs battalion front was only the width of the street, and from the upstairs rooms of the houses Germans fired machine-guns and dropped grenades onto their heads, causing them to take shelter in a museum until forced out by mortars, 20mm guns and self-propelled artillery. Then tanks swept down the road to the hospital, wiping out the South Staffs and the 11th Battalion until only a group of survivors escaped to the outskirts of the town. By 0700 hours, Dobie's 1st Battalion with only 49 men left standing, had virtually ceased to exist. Dobie was wounded and taken prisoner, Firth was killed by a mortar bomb.

Hackett's 4th Brigade, led by the 156th Para Battalion, moved along the line of the railway past the Reyerscamp LZ, where the gliders had brought in the 4th Brigade's transport and equipment towards the high ground north of Arnhem, but were repulsed with heavy losses, and dug in alongside the main road under devastating fire from anti-aircraft guns, self-propelled guns, tanks and mortars. Their task on Ginkel Heath concluded, 7th KSOB were moving on the left flank to secure LZ 'L' for the Polish gliders landing on the following day, while the 1st Borderers, who had taken heavy casualties at Renkum Heath, were advancing south of the railway line towards their allotted position in the Arnhem perimeter. These battalions were supported by glider pilots and other divisional units acting as infantry, and three 75 mm batteries of Johnson's 1st Light Regiment RA. But by evening, 4th Parachute Brigade was beginning to share the fate of the 1st, as the new arrivals vainly but bravely attempted to pierce the German armoured screen that stood between them and 2nd Parachute Battalion, still grimly holding on to their end of the bridge, hoping that reinforcements would soon arrive.

Attempting to return over the Arnhem bridge early in the morning of the 18th, the SS Reconnaissance Unit were engaged by every weapon, including anti-tank guns, Piats and grenades, until they turned back, leaving eleven blazing armoured cars and half-tracks on the embankment.

Frost's original force, A and C Companies of the 2nd Battalion, C Company of the 3rd Battalion, 1st Parachute Brigade HQ and elements of the Recce squadron led by Major Gough and a few anti-tank gunners, engineers and RASC (personnel), were now reduced too heavily to make any further attacks on the southern end of the bridge and were garrisoning some 40 houses and a school. The area was blazing fiercely, and Tiger tanks rumbled through the streets blasting buildings at point-blank range and forcing the defenders to evacuate them one by one. Frost was wounded and Major Gough assumed command of the rapidly diminishing force who continued to offer resistance, securing minor successes against tanks with their anti-tank guns and Piats.

Both British and Germans were discovering that street fighting absorbs soldiers in the same way as blotting paper absorbs ink, and a battalion spread over a map-square (a kilometre by a kilometre) are hard put to man a cohesive defensive line whereas the same force in open country could occupy and hold the area. It is even more marked in the attack because the objectives have to be cleared at every level which multiplies as much as tenfold in the manpower requirements. Street fighting also absorbs time as each action has to be repeated at several levels.

On the following day the 19th, the Polish Brigade were due to be flown in on Lift Three landing south of Arnhem bridge. Adverse weather conditions forced their flight to be postponed for twenty-four hours; their zone was changed and their gliders were scheduled to come in on an LZ north of Oosterbeek. But this area was not securely held by British troops, nor was the Supply-Drop Point 'V' north of Warnsborn, where 38th and 46th Groups RAF were scheduled to make a supply drop on the afternoon of the 19th. A signal sent requesting a change of dropping zones was not received, causing both drops to be tragically wasteful.

The 163 supply aircraft came in at 1500 feet into murderous anti-aircraft fire that flayed them for eight minutes as they slowly crossed and recrossed the dropping zone while despatchers desperately pushed out 190 tons of food and ammunition – mostly to the waiting Germans. Those British paratroopers who could see the drop were wild with anger and frustration, leaping from slit-trenches as they tried desperately but unavailingly to attract the pilots' attention. Fourteen aircraft were shot down and 97 damaged in this courageous but futile action. The tug-planes and gliders carrying the Poles located the landing zone and the 31 gliders remaining out of the original 46 met an inferno of fire as a squadron of Messerschmitt Me 109s descended on the helpless gliders, riddling their thin canvas and plywood. Some broke up in the air or caught fire as the petrol in the punctured tanks of the jeeps they carried set them alight. Then the aircraft were gone and torrents of AA fire hit them. Gliders, some on fire and others badly damaged, crash-landed, ploughing into fields and trees, landing directly in the middle of a battle. In the confusion the Poles took fire from both friend and foe – and returned it. Then, under heavy fire, they blew off the glider tails with explosive charges and unloaded their equipment. Trailers and 6-pdr anti-tank guns were hitched up to jeeps and running a gauntlet of fire, three of the eight guns reached British lines. Many of the Poles, bewildered and shocked, were taken prisoner.

On the 19th General Urquhart managed to rejoin his force at Oosterbeek, having been trapped with Brigadier Lathbury in a house in Arnhem surrounded by Germans. Realising that the link-up with Frost's bridge defenders was out of the question, he now had to plan to survive while maintaining a bridgehead reception zone for Second Army when they arrived on the north bank of the river. He proposed to defend a four-mile-square perimeter based on Oosterbeek with its southern edge resting along the bank of the Rhine for about a mile; his divisional headquarters were near its centre at the Hartenstein Hotel. At the extreme south-western corner of the perimeter, weakly defended and vulnerable to German attack, was the Heveadorp ferry which, firmly held on the northern bank, could provide Horrocks with a reasonable alternative to the intact Arnhem road bridge. This might also have occurred to General Browning who switched the long delayed drop of the Polish Parachute Brigade to a DZ at Driel south of the ferry.

Resembling the thumb of the right hand jutting northwards from the river bank, the perimeter was garrisoned by the 21st Independent Parachute Company in the north-west corner; on the left were about 250 men of the 7th KOSB defending the White House Hotel, reduced to rubble and the scene of fierce hand-to-hand fighting; behind were Mackenzie's Airborne Light Artillery Regiment of 75 mm howitzers; the north-eastern corner of the perimeter was defended by the 156th and 10th Battalions of 4th Parachute Brigade; the western half manned by three skeleton companies of the 1st Borderers, the Polish glider troops and some engineers; in the south-east near Oosterbeek Church were a mixed force of about 400 survivors of the 1st, 3rd and 11th Battalions of the Parachute Regiment and the South Staffords under Major Lonsdale; the Glider Pilot Regiment held two positions, one at the artillery site and one in a wood further north.

Organised resistance at the Arnhem bridge ended on the morning of Thursday 21 September, after Frost's small force had achieved the whole division's objective by holding the bridge against overwhelming strength for three and a half days. Conditions had steadily deteriorated until the only means of moving under cover was by blowing holes in the dividing walls of houses. Such vital defence buildings as the school were in ruins, walls so perforated as to be no longer bullet-proof, and rubble piled high on all sides. The defenders, mostly wounded, huddled in twos and threes manning positions that really required twice their numbers but, believing themselves superior to the enemy of whom they had killed four times their own number, their morale was still high. At dusk on the 20th and throughout the night the last remaining strongholds were being assaulted by tanks, self-propelled guns and flame-throwers. Many attacks were repulsed but it had become hopeless and by morning when half Frost's force were casualties, 200 wounded, including Frost himself, surrendered to the Germans; most of the rest of his force were captured trying to make a fighting withdrawal.

Whilst all this had been occurring in the British area of operations, the two US Airborne Divisions had been resolutely fighting and achieving their objectives to the south of the Rhine. On the 17th, 101 US Division's pathfinders had quickly marked the DZs and LZ near St Oedenrode and Veghel, so that the division made a well-patterned drop according to plan, supported by fighters and dive-bombers, attacking anti-aircraft emplacements and engaging eight German tanks near the main dropping zone, destroying two and driving off the remainder. Otherwise no significant opposition was encountered on the ground and the units were able to assemble quickly and move out to secure their objectives. Reaching the bridge on the southern edge of Zon, 506th Parachute Regiment found it had been blown. Engineers rapidly set up a replacement and by midnight the regiment was south of the Wilhelmina Canal. On the following morning they encountered fierce resistance on the northern outskirts of Eindhoven, but by midday had outflanked the German positions, entered the town and made contact with the leading reconnaissance elements of the Guards Armoured Division.

Farther north, the main body of 502 Parachute Regiment secured the divisional bridgehead while part of the formation captured St Oedenrode and its bridge intact before dark. Another detachment, after first being repulsed, seized the bridge over the Wilhelmina Canal at Best, some miles west of Zon. By dusk on the following day, the Guards tanks had crossed this canal and an engineer-erected bridge and were through St Oedenrode and on their way to Veghel, which had been the objective of 501 Parachute Regiment, dropped on both sides of water obstacles to attack and seize two roads and two rail bridges. By 1500 hours on the first day the regiment had taken its objective and were well dug in and ready to resist counter-attacks but encountered little opposition, and were at full strength and fresh when British armour passed through Veghel at 0645 hours on 19 September. The 101st Airborne Division had successfully accomplished their part in the 'Market' part of the operation.

Gavin's 82nd US Airborne Division, dropping only ten minutes after their Pathfinders, encountered considerable anti-aircraft fire around their dropping-zones and lost a number of C47s. However, in some areas para-troopers dropped right onto anti-aircraft batteries and immediately put them out of action.

Tucker's 504th Parachute Regiment set off in four directions to secure bridges over the Maas–Waal Canal and the vital Maas bridge north of Grave, where a company had dropped in a direct attack. One platoon fell close to the bridge and moved towards the canal under enemy fire from buildings and flak-tower on the southern approach to the bridge. The American paratroopers knocked it out with bazooka fire and turned its 40 mm gun against the enemy. The platoon was joined at the bridge by the 2nd Battalion and by dusk 504 regiment were holding the Grave bridge and the southernmost of the four bridges over the canal. General Gavin himself described how it was captured:

'By keeping the bridge under fire and slowly walking in, the leading unit finally managed to drive out the German defenders into a house, on a small island on the locks of the canal. Then by keeping them pinned down by firing into the house, the troopers managed to get onto the bridge and cut the wires and remove the charges.'

Two central bridges over the canal were blown before paratroopers could reach them and the northern one, at Honinghutie, was the objective of another regiment. Ekman's 505 Parachute Regiment captured Groesbeek and organised it for defence and, although enemy probing attacks were seen building up, they had not been attacked by nightfall.

The most easterly DZ just south of Wyler was to be used as LZ for Second Lift gliders on the following day, so it had to be defended by Lindquist's 508th Parachute regiment, who had jumped onto it. Also they had to defend the northern approaches to the Groesbeek Heights and assist in capturing Honinghutie road bridge on the main XXX Corps axis. Finally, they were to capture the Nijmegen bridge, but only if it did not seriously weaken the division's hold on the heights. In the hope of securing the bridge intact, General Gavin ordered Lindquist to send a battalion under cover of darkness to achieve the objective. The chosen battalion, Warren's 1st, penetrated about halfway through the town of Nijmegen before being forced to take cover in houses – in the post office they destroyed the electrical controls for blowing the bridge.

The first night of the battle found the 82nd US Airborne Division more or less intact and in full control of the dominating ground; they had captured the Grave bridge, a bridge over the canal (although not the one on the main axis) and had prevented the Germans destroying Nijmegen bridge. 18 September was a day of hard fighting for Gavin's 82nd US Airborne Division. Battling desperately for the Honinghutie Bridge, the 508 Regiment asked the 504th Regiment to try to attack the German defenders in the rear. With the Germans fully occupied fighting to the east, a 504th patrol crept across the bridge and fired into their rear, causing their resistance to collapse and, although damaged, the bridge was secured.

The 1st Battalion 508th Regiment had to disengage from Nijmegen to join the main body of their regiment in a fierce battle to eject Germans who had overrun the landing zones on which the 82nd's gliders were due to arrive. Fortuitously, they had been delayed two hours; even so, the gliders landed under fire, but the delay destroyed any chance of capturing Nijmegen bridge on that day. This lift consisted of 450 Wacos carrying three light field artillery battalions, the balance of the anti-tank battalion and some additional divisional troops – all were in action by mid-afternoon.

At 0830 hours on 19 September, reconnaissance elements of XXX Corps contacted the 82nd US Division's road block south of Grave and the main body of the Guards Armoured Division started coming on the scene at noon. General Gavin committed Vandervoort's 2nd Battalion 505th Regiment, assisted by the Grenadier Guards Tank Battalion, to capture the Nijmegen bridge and by nightfall their forces were within sight of the southern end of the bridge. Then the attack ground to a halt short of the objective, largely because of lack of sufficient infantry to press it home – the same weather conditions that had held up the Polish brigade had also grounded Gavin's Glider Regiment, nor could he send reinforcements because everyone was involved in repulsing German attacks against the Groesbeek.

On this day the Germans, unable to reinforce their defensive positions holding the Waal rail line while Frost still blocked the Arnhem bridge, crossed the Rhine well to the east. The 10th SS Panzer Division ferried tanks and vehicles across the river in what was a slow business, although apparently undetected by the 2,000 Allied fighters and bombers supporting the 'Market' operation.

Meanwhile, on the evening of 20 September, Generals Gavin and Adair, commander Guards Armoured Division, made a plan for an attack on the following morning, when an American parachute regiment were to cross the Waal by boat, followed by a simultaneous assault against both ends of the bridge. Assault boats were to be brought up on XXX Corps transport, but the attack, although supported by fire from tanks and artillery and with smoke concealing the crossing, would still be exceedingly hazardous in the face of a determined German defence.

First, Nijmegen had to be cleared of German forces to allow the assault troops to gain access to the south bank of the Waal, a mopping-up process that took the whole of Wednesday morning. It was not until 1500 hours that the 504th were in position to launch their assault boat into the 400-yard-wide fast-flowing river. The smoke cover was not very effective and only half the first wave of boats reached the north bank, many being destroyed by enemy fire and swept away by the strong current. However, some 200 determined men scrambled ashore and established a shallow bridgehead, being gradually reinforced by further waves of boats crossing the bullet-swept swirling water in broad daylight. By 1830 hours the Americans had routed enemy opposition to the bridgehead and were moving towards the road bridge. It is said that they signalled success by raising the Stars and Stripes on the northern end of the railway bridge.

On the southern side of the bridge, the Guards Armoured Division had been fighting their way through, supported by Vandervoort's 2nd Battalion 505th Regiment, whose mortars and artillery pounded the German defences while men advanced from house to house. The Guards tanks, including Sherman Fireflies with 17-pdrs, forced their way to the southern approaches as the enemy defence ring of anti-tank guns were knocked out one by one. Finally there were only four self-propelled guns dug into the centre of a traffic circle; at 1600 hours they were overrun by American para-troopers with bayonets and grenades. Then British tanks, lined up four abreast, charged through the little park that led to the open approaches to the apparently intact great Waal bridge. It was later revealed that the Ger-mans attempted to blow the bridge while attacking tanks were crossing but the explosives failed to detonate. A troop of four Guards tanks in line ahead charged across the bridge, coming under fire from an 88mm anti-tank gun sited on the other side of the river – 100 yards from the north end of the bridge in a sandbag emplacement by the side of the road. One of the four tanks and the 88 exchanged four rounds apiece, as the tanks' machine-guns chattered away; suddenly the big German gun blew up. Clinging to the girders of the bridge, Germans with grenades, rifles and machine-guns fought courageously, being knocked off like nine pins by the machine-guns of the passing tanks. One by one the tanks negotiated a road block of con-crete cubes, then knocked out another 88 mm gun 400 yards away on the right by the roadside, then a self-propelled gun that opened fire on them. Suddenly, the tank men saw Americans huddled in the ditch by the road-side and realised they had made contact with the 504th Parachute Regi-ment. The huge multi-span Nijmegen bridge and its half-mile-long approaches, last but one of the 'Market Garden' bridges, fell intact into Allied hands at 7.15 p.m. on 20 September. Arnhem was only eleven miles away.

It is reported that on meeting General Gavin after this success, General Dempsey, commanding Second Army, said: 'I am proud to meet the com-mander of the greatest division in the world today.'

Farther south, greatly strengthened German forces, including Meindl's Parachute Corps, were strongly counter-attacking out of the Reichswald; the Americans were holding them but badly needed their Glider Infantry Regiment due on Lift Three. They arrived, together with the remaining Pol-ish Parachute Battalion, into the 82nd Division's area just east of Grave late on the afternoon of 23 September. Rather than reinforcing Urquhart or drawing German opposition away from him, or strengthening XXX Corps' advance, Browning showed that he was more concerned with holding what he had, conscious that the 1st British Airborne Division would have to be evacuated as soon as possible.

At Arnhem, after Frost's resistance ended on the bridge, German General Harzer began flat-out attacks on Urquhart's defences, turning Oosterbeek into blazing rubble as HE, phosphorus and mortar shells poured into the area at a rate of more than fifty a minute. Launched simultaneously from two sides of the perimeter, frequent German attacks by tanks and groups of 20–30 infantry were repulsed by Vickers and Bren machine-guns, mortars, rifles, Piats and grenades, while parachutist sharp-shooters often brought German snipers down out of the trees. British anti-tank guns were being knocked out one by one, but Piats fired at point-blank range destroyed numerous German tanks.

The South Staffs withdrawing from Arnhem were rallied by Major Cain and successfully attacked Den Brink, the wooded hill position commanding the Oosterbeek–Arnhem road and then took up positions in front of the white church in Oosterbeek. Almost at once tanks and self-propelled guns began to edge towards their position and 22-year-old Lance-Sergeant Baskeyfield won a posthumous Victoria Cross when he destroyed two Tigers and at least one self-propelled gun at 100 yards with his 6-pdr anti-tank gun, loading and firing single-handed when his crew were cut down by intense close-range fire. The gun was put out of action and the wounded NCO crawled to a nearby abandoned 6-pdr and knocked out another self-propelled gun, before being killed by a tank shell.

On the 21st, the Germans made their first really determined effort to break into the perimeter, being ejected at bayonet point by the 1st Borderers. The woods were full of tanks and armoured cars prowling about, and enemy snipers and machine-gunners fired from the trees. The White House Hotel changed hands several times during the day before being finally recaptured at the bayonet point by the KSOB. Casualties were heavy and by the 22nd, 156 Battalion Parachute Regiment was down to 100 men and the 10th Battalion was 30 men strong with no officers remaining. Also on the 22nd, Major Lonsdale's force began fortifying the church, and their commander preached them a sermon from the pulpit: 'You know as well as I do that there a lot of bloody Germans coming at us. Well, all we can do is stay here and hang on in the hope that somebody catches us up. We must fight for our lives and stick together. We have fought them in North Africa, Sicily, Italy, at times against odds. They were not good enough for us then and they are not bloody well good enough for us now. An hour from now you will take up defensive positions to the north of the road outside. On these positions we must stand or fall and shoot to the last round. Make certain you dig in well and that your weapons and ammo are in good order. We are getting short of ammo so when you shoot, you shoot to kill. Good luck to you all.' (This was scrawled on the church door and can now be seen in the Airborne Forces Museum at Doorwertsch, near Arnhem.)

On the afternoon of 21 September, their dropping-zone switched to the south side of the river at the Heveadorp Ferry, the unfortunate Polish Para-chute Brigade were again affected by bad weather which caused nearly half their C47s to turn back without dropping their men. General Sos-abowski, after landing against light opposition, found himself on the south bank of the river with only 750 men. Assembling his force and moving to the bank, he discovered that the British had been driven off the small hill that dominated the area and had lost the ferry. So, with no boats or rafts to ferry them across, the Poles established a defensive area at Driel. Now the Ger-mans were able to push forces across the Arnhem road bridge to reinforce the 10th SS Panzer Division who had been ferried across the river earlier. These increased armour and anti-tank forces held up the Guards Armoured Division and Horrocks replaced them with the 43rd (Wessex) Infantry Divi-sion; but their training and experience caused the infantry to remain on the roads and to expect tank and artillery fire support so that they advanced slowly, and it was nearly dark before their leading battalion reached Driel and contacted Sosabowski's Poles. Early on the following day, 22 Septem-ber, reconnaissance elements of the Guards Armoured Division, advancing out of the Nijmegen bridgehead, contacted the Poles. Subsequently Gen-eral Horrocks conferred with Sosabowski, Browning and General Thomas of the 43rd Wessex Division, when it was decided to send the Poles across the river, although all hopes of establishing a northern bridgehead were abandoned.

Each day, when weather permitted, RAF Transport aircraft coura-geously flew in and dropped supplies to Urquhart's force, suffering 20 per cent losses in aircraft from AA fire and German fighters. Tragically, only 7 per cent of these supplies landed within reach of the garrison, because the perimeter was continually shortening and it was impossible to redirect the pilots.

The 23rd saw the heaviest German onslaughts fall on Lonsdale's sec-tor, where Major Cain of the South Staffs won the Victoria Cross and lived to tell the tale. First he immobilised a Tiger tank with a Piat fired from the Red House at 20 yards range; then, although wounded by machine-gun fire and collapsing brickwork, he crept out and brought up a 75 mm gun that completely destroyed the Tiger. Later he drove off three tanks with a Piat, and on the 25th manned a 2 inch mortar and repelled an attack by SPs and infantry with flame-throwers.

The beleaguered airborne troops were now receiving fire support from Spitfires and Typhoons, escorting supply aircraft and strafing German gun positions. A 4.5 inch artillery battery south of the river, directed by Airborne OPs in the perimeter, started directing a steady stream of shells at enemy targets; then the gunners erected a 25-foot wireless aerial that gave better reception to the radio messages coming from the perimeter, and increased their fire with two batteries of 5.5-inch and 155mm guns.

But the impetus of XXX Corps' attack had petered out and heavy flank attacks had cut their slender supply line in several places. By now, even if the Arnhem road bridge had been secured, it is unlikely that British 2nd Army would have been able to exploit the situation.

On the night of the 22nd, General Urquhart had sent officers across the lower Rhine in inflatable dinghies to report the worsening situation to General Horrocks. They returned on the following night and confirmed that the 2nd Army were remaining on the south bank, but that General Dempsey wished the perimeter to be reinforced before attempting a withdrawal. A small group of the 3rd Polish Parachute Battalion had already managed to cross the river in boats and on rafts and, at midnight on the 23rd, some more Poles and 5th Battalion Dorset Regiment attempted to cross near the Heveadorp ferry. Detecting them, the Germans raked the boats with machine-gun fire so that only 250 Poles and 350 Dorsets managed to get across. By this time, 1st Airborne Division was down to about 2,500 men, short of ammunition and supplies – and very tired.

Urquhart began planning to evacuate the perimeter, but the actual decision to withdraw was taken on 25 September by General Browning on General Dempsey's authority. Considerable fighting continued throughout the 24th and well into the 25th when at 1830 hours Urquhart's officers were told to prepare to move out. The northern positions, some two miles from the river, were to be evacuated first, gradually progressing southwards so that the last to leave would be the men nearest the river banks. All the doctors volunteered to stay with the wounded, who had to be left behind.

At 2200 hours the withdrawal began along the designated escape corridor, with glider pilots posted as guides. Faces were blackened, boots muffled and loose equipment tied tightly as the first men left their posts. In pitch-blackness and pouring rain men moved in single file, each man grasping the smock of the man in front, shuffling along through the muddy Dutch polder-land down to the river banks, to lie in wet slime waiting their turn, with mortar bombs, shells and machine-gun fire raining down upon them. Earlier, there had been only desultory German shelling and mortar fire, and British gunners on the south bank fired on enemy positions flanking the perimeter to keep them quiet.

Inevitably, there were not enough boats, and some were sunk as they plied back and forth, so that when dawn came several hundred men remained unevacuated; some attempted to swim the river and were drowned. Realising what had happened, Germans swarmed into the abandoned perimeter and the early morning air resounded to the crash of tank guns and small-arms fire as isolated parties of trapped defenders made their last stands. Then it petered out and for the first time in eight days, Arnhem was quiet.

Why had such an adventurous and promising enterprise failed? There are many reasons that singly were serious and collectively fatal. The advance of XXX Corps, acknowledgedly difficult, was not as rapid as it could have been, particularly as 82nd and 101 US Airborne Divisions had provided a continuous carpet almost as far as Nijmegen. If Horrocks's force had advanced as rapidly as predicted, then Frost's small force on the bridge might have held long enough to complete the link up. Or, if all 1st Airborne Division had reached the bridge as planned, there is little doubt that they would have held out until XXX Corps arrived, even though the delay at Nijmegen caused them to take seven days to reach the Rhine.

The operation was gravely handicapped by decisions over Lifts Two and Three having to be taken without proper knowledge of the tactical requirements on the ground.

The airborne technique in 'Market Garden' was good, units and formations being dropped or landed with unparalleled precision and concentration, indicating that there was excellent cooperation between airborne units and troop-carrier squadrons. But it can be claimed that the airborne forces had some cause to complain that offensive air support – their 'sword and shield' – was poorly provided.

The operation involved many notable ground actions that will go down in military history, with that on the 82nd US Airborne Division being almost classical. In the south, the airborne operations were a complete success; in the centre they did not fully succeed but were still first-class; in the north, in the strict sense of the plan, they just about succeeded through the courageous efforts of Frost's 2nd Parachute Battalion. Operation 'Market Garden' was a failure in a number of tactical respects but, rather than battlefield errors, its strategic failure can be blamed more on its timing, and the energetic recovery of an underestimated enemy.

The Bridge at Remagen, 7 March 1945

The bridge at Remagen was built during the First World War at the urging of the German generals, so that more troops and war materials could be brought to the Western Front. Designed by Karl Wiener, an architect from Mannheim, it was 325 metres long, with a clearance of 14.80m above the normal water level of the Rhine, and at its highest point measured 29.25m. The bridge carried two rail lines and a pedestrian walk-way. It was considered one of the finest bridges over the Rhine. In 1925, a devastating fire took place on the bridge. Damage was, however, minimised largely due to the efforts of the Remagen fire department.

On 7 March 1945 an advance element of the 9th US Armored Division, led by Lieutenant K. H. Timmermann, an American of German descent, reached the last intact Rhine bridge, just after the German defenders twice failed in their demolition attempts.

The capture of the bridge is known in the annals of war as the 'Miracle of Remagen'. General Eisenhower stated that 'the bridge is worth its weight in gold'. In the days immediately following, the German High Command made desperate attempt to destroy the bridge by bombing from the air, and even employed frogmen. Hitler irately convened a summary court, which condemned five officers to death, four of whom were actually executed in the Westerwald Forest.

On 17 March 1945 the bridge collapsed due to overloading, 28 American soldiers losing their lives.

Crossing of the River Senio, 9 April 1945

Major Peter Jeffery was awarded a Military Cross in Italy during the passage of the River Senio in northern Italy in April 1945.

On 9 April, Jeffery's company, the 13th Frontier Force Rifles, was assigned the role of crossing the river and securing a bridgehead on the far bank, where the enemy was strongly entrenched with machine guns sighted to fire in enfilade down the river. The assault led by Jeffery depended for its success on speed and dash. Disregarding the dangers of fierce Spandau fire and minefields, Jeffery hastily planned and then successfully carried out the establishment and rapid widening of the bridgehead, through which the remainder of the battalion could then pass. During the mopping-up of pockets of enemy on the banks, he again directed his company with fearless skill.

In the night operation which followed, he led his company forward to secure a position by the Luga Canal, 2,000 yards ahead. Consolidating round a small bridge over the canal, he drove off four enemy counterattacks, and by the end of the battle the company had captured two German officers and sixty-six soldiers.

Jeffery's determination in leading and directing his company was critical in maintaining the momentum of their attack – a factor which accounted to a great extent for the number of prisoners taken.

EPILOGUE

A bridge may be defined as anything that provides a connection between different things. In their way, these pages serve as a bridge to link the many structures built over rivers which, throughout history, have been fought over by soldiers of all ages, armies and nations.

The omission may be noticed of one of the most famous of all bridges – the bridge over the River Kwai. Although not an 'operational' bridge in the military sense of those mentioned in this book, hundreds of soldiers, prisoners of the Japanese in World War Two, died at the bridge – the difference being that they were virtually murdered, rather than dying in battle.

The very nature and role of bridges confers upon them in wartime an inevitable and deadly channeling that time cannot change. Nor can passing years lessen the dogged courage demanded of soldiers throughout military history who have had to fight on or near a bridge. It is hoped that this book will be considered a eulogy to all soldiers throughout military history who have fought and given their lives in battles for bridges, whether in attack or defence, over a period of two thousand years – from that legendary Roman of 508BC to the men at Arnhem in World War Two.

BIBLIOGRAPHY

Ambrose, Stephen E., *Pegasus Bridge*, London, 1980

Becke, A. F., *Napoleon and Waterloo*, London, 1936

Boatner, Mark M., *Biographical Dictionary of the American Revolution*, London, 1919

— *Biographical Dictionary of the American Civil War*, London, 1959

Burne, Alfred. H., *The Art of War,* London, 1944

— *The Crécy War*, Westport, Conn., 1955

Cammidge, John, *The Black Prince*, London, 1943

Chandler, David, *A Guide to the Battlefields of Europe*, Wellingborough, 1965

— *Dictionary of the Napoleonic Wars*, London, 1979

Chapman, Guy, *Vain Glory*, London, 1937

Clery, C., *Minor Tactics*, London, 1880

Clough, W. E and A., *The Tank Corps*, London, 1919

Coles, Harry L., *The War of 1812*, Chicago, 1965

Commager, Henry Steele, *The Blue and the Grey*, New York, 1952

Cullen, Joseph P., *A Concise Illustrated History of the American Revolution*, Harrisburg, PA, 1977

Dupuy, R. Ernest and Trevor N. *The Encyclopaedia of Military History*, London, 1970

Eady, H. G., *Historical Illustrations to Field Service Regulations 'Operations'*, London, 1933

Edwardes, Michael, *Red Year*, London, 1975

Eggenberger, David, *A Dictionary of Battles*, London, 1967

Featherstone, Donald, *Wargames Through the Ages, 3000BC–AD1599*, London, 1972; *1420–1783*, London, 1974; *1792–1859*, London, 1975; *1861–1945*, London, 1976

— *Colonial Small Wars, 1837–1901*, London, 1973

— *Wargaming Airborne Operations*, London, 1977

— *Victorian Military Campaigns in Africa*, London, 1992

— *Victorian Military Campaigns in India*, London, 1992

— *The Battlefield Walker's Handbook*, London, 1998

Fleming, Peter, *Bayonets to Llasa*, London, 1962

Flower, Desmond and Reeves, James, London, ed., *The War 1939–1945*, London, 1960

Forrest, G. W., *A History of the Indian Mutiny*, Edinburgh, 1904

Fortescue, J. W., *History of the British Army*, London, 1912

Fuller, J. F. C., *Tanks in the Great War*, London, 1920

Fussell, Paul, *The Bloody Game*, New York, 1990

Glover, Michael, *The Peninsular War 1807-1814*, Newton Abbot, 1974

Grant, James, *British Battles on Land and Sea*, London, 1885

— *British Battles on Land and Sea*, London, 1897

Green, Howard, *Guide to Battlefields of Britain and Ireland*, London, 1973

Gregory, Barry, *British Airborne Troops*, London, 1974

Griess, Thomas E.,, London, ed., *The American Civil War*, London, *West Point Historical Series*, Wayne, NJ, 1987

Hamley, Sir Edward, *Operations of War*, Aldershot, 1885

Harvey, John, *The Black Prince and His Age*, London, 1976

Hastings, Max, *Overlord*, London, 1984

Hibbert, Christopher, *The Great Mutiny*, Harmondsworth, 1978

Hitsman, J. Mackay, *The Incredible War of 1812*, Toronto, 1965

Howard, David, *Dawn of D-Day*, London, 1959

Johnson, Curt, *Battles of the American Revolution*, London, 1975

Johnson, Robert Underwood and Buell, Clarence Croft, *Battles and Leaders of the Civil War*, New York, 1883

Johnstone, Iain, *The Arnhem Report*, London, 1977

Kennedy, Francis H., *American Civil War Battlefield Guide*, Boston, Mass., 1950

Kinross, John, *Walking and Exploring the Battlefields of Britain*, Newton Abbot, 1983

Kruger, Rayne, *Goodbye Dolly Gray*, London, 1959

Ladd, James, *Commandos and Rangers of World War Two*, London, 1978

Lancaster, Bruce and Plumb, J. H., *The American Heritage Book of the American Revolution*, New York, 1958

Lord, Walter, *The Dawn's Early Light*, Baltimore, 1974

Marzials, Frank, London, ed., *Passages from Froissart*, London, nd

Mitchell, Joseph. B., *Decisive Battles of the American Revolution*, New York, 1962

Morgan, H. F., *A Summary of Tactics*, London, 1883

Murphy, Dr James, 'Building the Bridge' – *Masterpiece Library of War Short Stories*, London, 1918

Napier, William, *Battles and Sieges in the Peninsula*, London, 1910

Oman, Sir Charles, *A History of the Art of War in the Sixteenth Century*, London, 1937

Pemberton, W. Barry, *Battles of the Boer War*, London, 1964

Ryan, Cornelius, *The Longest Day*, London and New York, 1958

— *A Bridge Too Far*, London and New York, 1974

Sandes, E. C. W., *The Military Engineer in India*, Chatham, 1937

— *The Royal Engineers in Egypt and the Sudan*, Chatham, 1937

Schear, George F. and Rankin, Hugh F., *Rebels and Redcoats*, New York, 1957

Sears, Stephen W., *Landscape Turned Red (Antietam)*, New York, 1982

Seymour, William, *Battles in Britain*, London, 1975

Smurthwaite, David, *Complete Guide to the Battlefields of Britain*, London, Ordnance Survey, Exeter, 1984

Somers, Lord, *The War History of the Sixth Tank Battalion*, London, 1919

Stafford, William Cooke, *England's Battles on Land and Sea - The Indian Mutiny*, London, 1865

Symonds, Craig L., *Battlefield Atlas of the American Revolution*, Baltimore, 1986

Terraine, John, *Mons*, London, 1960

Tugwell, Maurice, *Airborne to Battle*, London, 1971

Urquart, Fred, *Men at War*, London, 1957

Warner, Philip, *British Battlefields*, Reading, 1975

Weller, J. A. C., *Wellington in the Peninsula*, London and New York, 1962

— *Wellington at Waterloo*, London, 1967

Wilson, H. W., *With the Flag to Pretoria*, London, 1900

— *After Pretoria - the Guerrilla War*, London, 1902

Wood, Sir Evelyn (ed.), *British Battles on Land and Sea*, London, 1915

Young, Peter and Holmes, Richard, *Commando*, London, 1969

— *The English Civil War*, London, 1974

Chambers History of the Revolt in India, London, 1859

Official Account HMSO *By Air to Battle*, London, 1945

Ministry of Information *Combined Operations*, London, 1943

INDEX